9/19/12

Exploring the Spirit of Maine

A Seeker's Guide

D0366409

by
Karen Wentworth Batignani

Dedication

This book is dedicated to those committed individuals who are working to create a spiritual/religious environment in Maine that is vibrant, compassionate, tolerant, and visionary.

Copyright © 2005 by Karen Wentworth Batignani

All rights reserved

Printed at Versa Press, Inc., East Peoria, Illinois

5   4   3   2   1

Down East Books

Camden, Maine

A division of Down East Enterprise, Inc.

Book orders: 800-685-7962

www.downeastbooks.com

Batignani, Karen Wentworth.

Exploring the spirit of Maine : a seeker's guide / by Karen Wentworth
Batignani.-- 1st ed.

p. cm.

ISBN 0-89272-692-X (trade pbk. : alk. paper)

1. Maine--Religion. 2. Religious institutions--Maine--Directories. I.
Title.

BL2527.M2B38 2005

200'.25'741--dc22

2005016184

Acknowledgments

I extend my heartfelt thanks to the many people who shared their time and knowledge in formal interviews and followed through by checking my drafts for accuracy. It is due to your efforts that I can feel confident that the material presented is accurate. I wish to thank the dozens of people that conversed with me about their personal experiences, beliefs, and practices. The insights I gained from those conversations are invaluable. I am deeply moved by the openness with which people invited me to partake in their practices and prayers. Thank you.

I love you, Michael. Thank you for your support and patience.

Table of Contents

Introduction   ix

Inspired Alternatives: Religions

Bahá'í   2

Paganism   9

Spiritualism   16

Swedenborgian Church   25

Unity Church of Greater Portland   33

By the Way: Northern Lights: A Metropolitan

  Community Church   41

Practicing Mindfulness: East Meets West

Hridaya Hermitage   44

Meetingbrook Dogen and Francis Hermitage   50

Morgan Bay Zendo   54

Shambhala Center   58

Sufi Order International   63

By the Way: The Dances of Universal Peace   69

Coming Together: Communities

Amish 71

The Shakers at Sabbathday Lake 74

St. Anthony's Monastery and Shrines 84

Wabanaki Confederacy 89

By the Way: Seeds of Peace 98

Pursuing Higher Wisdom:
Degrees, Certificates, and Programs

Bangor Theological Seminary 101

Chaplaincy Institute of Maine 106

Iseum Musicum and the Temple of the
Feminine Divine 111

Rudolf Steiner Institute 117

Spirit Passages 123

The Standing Bear Center for Shamanic Studies 128

By the Way: The Turtle Mountain Drummers 135

Reflection and Renewal: Retreats and Camps

Green Acre Bahá'í School 137

Greenfire 145

Living Water Spiritual Center 150

Marie Joseph Spiritual Center 156

Notre Dame Spiritual Retreat Center 160

Sewall House Retreat   166

Temple Heights Spiritual Camp   171

Two Roads   177

By the Way: Chatauqua-by-the-Sea   182

Transforming Vision to Action:
Organizations and Councils

Feminist Spiritual Community   185

Interfaith Maine   189

Kairos   193

Maine Council of Churches   197

Maine Gnosis Center   201

Spiral Arts Inc.   205

By the Way: The Institute of Noetic Sciences   210

Sacred Architecture: Churches

Cathedral of the Immaculate Conception   213

The Cathedral Church of St. Luke   216

Saint Ann Indian Island Church   219

Saints Peter and Paul Basilica   222

Saint Savior's Church   225

Inspirational Teachers: Recommended Reading   228

Introduction

An ashram in Industry, a yoga retreat in Island Falls, Franciscan friars in Kennebunk, two schools for shamanism and one that ordains high priestesses—these are just a few of the surprises I found while mapping the spiritual landscape of Maine. In my travels, I located nonmainstream religions, Eastern traditions, communities, schools, retreats, organizations, and sacred architecture. The result is a selection of interesting and unique offerings that are covered in enough depth to satisfy the spiritually curious and enable those who are seeking spiritual community to find the right fit.

In a sense, by writing Exploring the Spirit of Maine, I created my own theological education program and designed it for the experiential learner that I am. My education called for considerable amounts of research, interviews, and location visits. The abundance of my findings far exceeded my initial expectations. I have researched Swedenborg, Spiritualism, New Thought, Unity, Bahá'í, Shakers, Anabaptism, Native American religion, Paganism, Shamanism, Buddhism, Sufism, Gnosticism, Ayurvedic healing, yoga, Rudolf Steiner, interfaith ministry, Metropolitan Church, Franciscans, and numerous other spiritually focused organizations. I have meditated with Sufis, Tibetan Buddhists, Zen Buddhists, Spiritualists, Gnostics, and Roman Catholics. I have participated in a sweat lodge, journeyed with shaman, performed ritual with Pagans, recited devotions with Bahá'ís, and prayed in community on countless occasions. Best of all were the conversations with over one hundred incredibly helpful people willing to share their time, knowledge, and beliefs. This compilation is by no means complete; there are churches, communities, schools, and organizations that I never found the time or energy to investigate.

It is not surprising that during this process there were times when my thoughts spun with doctrines, deities, beliefs, theories, paths, prescriptions, and philosophies. Fortunately, those chaotic and sometimes exasperating moments were balanced with a supreme optimism arising from my contact with people who are deeply committed to their path and to being of service to humanity. Each of the forty-five churches, communities, and organizations in this book is possible because of the hard work of committed people, and their efforts should not be overlooked. I am in awe of their generosity, hope, vision, and dedication.

Discovering Maine's rich religious history was an unanticipated piece of my education. When I began researching religions, I was amazed by the deep roots the largely unrecognized religions of Shakerism, Swedenborgian, Unity, Spiritualism, and Bahá'í have in Maine. I have attempted to bring their heritage to light throughout those entries. In order to put that historical information in context, the following is a brief overview of Maine's religious history in a very, very small nutshell.

Though much has been made about Puritans in early New England, they never made much headway in Maine. Congregationalism, the faith of the Pilgrims, was the dominant religion. Its focus on individual responsibility and the autonomy of local congregations fit well with Maine's rural geography and independent residents. This tradition lives on today at Bangor Theological Seminary, which was founded in 1814 as a Congregationalist seminary.

Following the American Revolution, there was a proliferation of evangelistic religions that swept through Maine. The newcomers held revivals and camps where personal, direct contact with God was preached by ministers whose only qualifications were their desire to serve God and spread the word. Quakers, Shakers, Free Will Baptists, Methodists, and other Millennialists gained converts in Maine's rural areas where they set up camps. The Shakers established two settlements in Maine, one of which is still with us as the only active Shaker community in the world. Meanwhile, at the other end of the spectrum, Unitarians, who discarded the Trinity and applied reason to religion, put down roots in Maine's larger cities.

The 19th century was a time of spiritual exploration and exchange of philosophies, beliefs, and visions. Maine's history is ripe with activity from this period when it played a leading role in the development of new religious movements. Swedenborgians, Transcendentalists, Spiritualists, and people involved in the New Thought movement were influenced by each other and were active in Maine. Swedenborgian discussion groups developed into churches whose parishioners were often the wealthy and educated members of Maine's communities. New Thought, a little known spiritual movement that spawned Unity and Christian Science, is thought by many to have originated with Portland's Phineas Quimby. Three out of the four oldest Spiritualist camps are in Maine, and all three are still operating. The Transcendentalists were a major influence upon Sarah Farmer, who brought the Bahá'í faith to Maine in the early 1900s when she began a school/retreat that is currently growing and recognized by Bahá'ís the world over.

The largest change in Maine's religious landscape that needs mentioning, but is not covered in this book, is the huge influx of Roman Catholic immigrants that flooded into the state starting in the 1840s with the Irish escaping the potato famine, and of particular significance to Maine, the arrival of French-Canadians from the 1860s through the 1890s. Their history in the state is well documented, and delving into it was beyond the scope and subject matter of this book.

Once again, Maine is experiencing an exciting time of religious change and exploration. Many of Maine's residents have found Buddhist, Hindu, and Sufi paths that suit them and are pursuing those practices with commitment. Paganism and shamanism are ancient belief systems that have resurfaced as serious spiritual paths. Maine's oldest people, the Wabanaki Confederacy, who have been here for more than 10,000 years, are continuing a renewal and reclaiming of their traditional beliefs that began in the 1960s. Recent years have brought new immigrant populations from the Near East, southeast Asia, Africa, and eastern Europe. Though some of the newcomers are Christian, they are largely Buddhist and Muslim.

There is a movement toward honoring the wisdom found in traditions not usually associated with American religion. Meetingbrook is both a Zen Dogen and a Christian Hermitage. At Unity Church, parishioners use the traditional Hindu greeting gesture Namaste during their services, and nearly half of the membership at the Swedenborgian Church in Portland identify themselves as Sufis. The teachings at the Maine Gnosis Center draw from all of the world's great religions, while many retreat centers insure through their diverse programs that everyone feels welcome.

Denominations are less segregated as they come together to work for common goals and toward greater mutual understanding. Maine Council of Churches is an ecumenical organization that plays a leading role in the state by uniting congregations around the issues of environment, poverty, and restorative justice. All faiths are invited to Interfaith Maine's events and dialogues that broaden perspectives and break down stereotypes. Interfaith chaplains are ordained at the Chaplaincy Institute of Maine, and the student body at Bangor Theological Seminary is no longer exclusively Christian as learners come from a wide variety of traditions.

It is an inspiring time to be a spiritual seeker. Wisdom from the world's faiths is easily available; there is a multitude of opportunities to deepen one's faith; and from what I have witnessed in my travels, there is a path for everyone who is sincerely looking. Though intolerance of religious differences seems to be on the rise in many places, the people I met were open-minded and curious about the beliefs of others. Nearly everyone expressed a deep, and sometimes urgent, concern for the state of our world, and they are committed to its healing through a vision of unity and the practice of compassion, prayer, and above all, service.

Having graduated from my own educational program, I will take the opportunity to present a small lecture on money and time. There is not a single church, community, or organization in this book that is flush with money. Most exist on a shoestring budget and the commitment of their stewards. I found in my everyday conversations that many people are reluctant to spend money on spiritual pursuits and believe that things pertaining to religion should be free, on a donation basis, or offered for a minimal charge. Many of the organizations also believe this and offer programs well below costs to make them affordable to everyone. While that policy is commendable, it creates an energy-draining, ongoing need to find funding. There is a rich spiritual life in Maine that offers a wide range of options for community, education, reflection, and service; but its existence is dependent upon people willing to make a meaningful commitment of money and time. This can entail a painful evaluation of priorities, but if every spiritual/religious person who is able would pledge to make a whole-hearted commitment to one group or cause, the short-term result would be to insure the vitality of our spiritual communities and organizations, and in the long term, result in a deep social, political, and religious transformation.

Writing Exploring the Spirit of Maine was a wonderful education for me, and it is my hope that readers will use it as an invitation to grow. It provides the resources needed to:

- expand one's worldview by exploring unfamiliar religions, belief systems, communities, practices, ceremonies, and celebrations
- rejuvenate the spirit and rethink old concepts by returning to school
- reflect in retreat and in places of sacred beauty
- transform spiritual drive into service and community.

Thank you and enjoy!

Karen Batignani
Summer, 2005

Inspired Alternatives: Religions

Bahá'í

Paganism

Spiritualism

Swedenborgian Church

Unity Church of Greater Portland

Bahá'í

"The religion of God is for love and unity; make it not the cause of enmity and dissension."

"Close one eye and open the other. Close one to the world and all that is therein, and open the other to the hallowed beauty of the Beloved."

"Ye are the fruits of one tree and the leaves of one branch."

—Bahá'u'lláh

Years ago religious scholars debated if the Bahá'í faith was a cult, an Islamic sect, a religious movement, or the newest world religion. Presently, the Bahá'ís claim a membership of five million members in 233 countries, encompassing more than 2,100 ethnic groups and tribes, and it can no longer be considered anything but a world religion. Born in 1844, during the Millenarian movement that proliferated among Shi'ite Muslims, the Bahá'í faith swept through Persia and has continued to attract followers throughout the world with its visionary prophecy of promised peace in a world unified by one God, one race, and a universal culture.

The prophecy is from the teachings of Bahá'u'lláh, who Bahá'ís believe is the most recent incarnation in a series of divine messengers, or manifestations of God. Their doctrine of "progressive revelation" is the most distinctive aspect of the Bahá'í faith. It states that humanity is guided through spiritual evolution by Divine Educators who arrive in each age to lead them to the next stage of development by addressing their collective level of maturity. Bahá'u'lláh taught that the messengers are perfect reflections of God, and though they appear in different times and places, they are all of the same essence. Abraham, Krishna, Zoroaster, Moses, Buddha, Jesus, and Mohammed were all divine messengers who arrived when the world was in a period of darkness and stagnation to address social issues and point the way to the next stage of spiritual growth. Bahá'ís believe their religion is the next evolutionary phase of the world's major religions of Hinduism, Judaism, Zoroastrianism, Buddhism, Christianity, and Islam. As a divine manifestation, Bahá'u'lláh came to usher in a period when spiritual adolescence would give way to adulthood, and to establish the path to world unity under one God.

Bahá'u'lláh made clear that a unified world would not come without considerable pain. He wrote, "The signs of impending convulsions can now be discerned, inasmuch as the prevailing Order appeareth to be lamentably defective. Soon will the present-day order be rolled up and a new one spread out in its stead." His prophecies warned of political, social, and religious catastrophes that would signify the failure of the old world order and be requisite for a new world order. Momentous destruction would signify the rolling up and away of a failed world, which in turn would create dynamic growth as a new world unfurls.

The new world order of Bahá'u'lláh's vision is utopian in its scope and quite radical considering that he was writing from the mid-1860s through the 1890s while imprisoned. He stressed women's rights, universal education, representative government, religious freedom, racial equality, and harmony between science and religion. The adoption of Bahá'í principles would lead to a federation of states of the world. Borders and national identities, while existing and valid, would be subordinate to a global identity. Unity would be reinforced through a universal language and standardized currency, weights, and measures. Free trade would be genuine and wages equitable based on a worldwide scale. Mass travel and global shrinking would bring people a new awareness and respect for cultural differences. In this new world, everyone would be employed in meaningful work. Income disparities would be moderate, relieving the rich of their idleness and the poor of their dependence. Agriculture would serve as the backbone of the world's economy, creating environmental sustainability. Consultation and cooperation would replace competitive modes of management.

Most Bahá'ís believe the prophecy will take hundreds, if not thousands, of years to be fulfilled. (Bahá'u'lláh foretold that another divine manifestation would appear, but not before one thousand years.) Grand ambitions for a better world take efficient planning, and Bahá'u'lláh left a detailed roadmap for the Bahá'ís to follow. It is a formula for social action that combines selfless service, socially progressive ideas, high moral standards, and prescribed administrative principles. The faith stresses the need to put greater emphasis on collective responsibility rather than individual responsibility while maintaining self-love and releasing self-interest. They consider collective social action imperative for the survival of humankind. It is not an easy road to follow.

The call to collective action can be advanced only by disciplined individuals, and the Bahá'ís are expected to adhere to a demanding moral code. They follow the ethical standards found throughout the major religions as they believe in one God, one religion. In addition, intoxicating drugs, alcohol, gambling, gossip, and backbiting are prohibited. Unmarried people and homosexuals are expected to remain celibate. The primary purpose of marriage is to have children, and parents must approve of the union in order to support and strengthen the family unit. Divorce is allowed after a "year of patience" during which institutions of the faith offer support to the troubled couple. Partisan politics are not allowed as it creates divisions, and all are required to respect and obey their governments.

Bahá'ís take their moral code seriously, and offenders are subject to sanctions that lead to banishment from community activities and administrative rights such as voting. The sanctions are enforced only after a period during which members offer guidance and when the person remains noncompliant. Several examples of infractions worthy of sanctions are drug and alcohol use, marriage without the parents' consent, and living together outside of marriage.

Bahá'í doctrines complement the major world religions. The soul can grow only through a relationship with God, which is nurtured by prayer, meditation, and scripture reading, as well as by practicing morality, self-discipline, and service to others in daily life. There is no concept of original sin, as people are understood to be primarily good, with peace being a natural and normal state for humanity. The Holy Trinity is conceived as God, the primal will of God, and the divine manifestations of God. God is transcendent and unknowable. Souls continue to exist after the demise of the physical body and guide the living from beyond. Heaven is closeness to God, and hell is separation from God. They do not believe in reincarnation, though there are hints that other dimensions exist.

The Bahá'í faith originated in Iran out of the Babi movement which was founded by the Bab, meaning "the Gate." On March 23, 1844, the date that Bahá'ís mark as their inception, the Bab proclaimed that he was a Messenger of God appointed to announce the arrival of another Divine Messenger. Playing a role similar to that of John the Baptist, the Bab foretold of someone greater than himself who would lead the world to a new era of peace. The Babi movement spread quickly and, by some estimates, had as many as 100,000 adherents within the first five years.

The movement's rapid growth is attributed to the societal upheavals that were rocking nineteenth-century Iran, but more so to age-old Shi'ite Muslim beliefs. The majority of Iranian Muslims were, and are, Shi'ites or Twelvers. Twelvers believe the rightful succession of Mohammed's authority derives from the descendents of his daughter Fatima and his son-in-law and first cousin Ali. This line of succession halted abruptly with the mysterious disappearance of the Twelfth Imam (successor). Shi'ite teachings state that he exists in a supernatural state until his return as the Mahdi, or messiah, to affirm Mohammed's message and bring an era of justice, peace, and harmony. The year 1844 marked one thousand years since the disappearance of the Twelfth Imam, and some Shi'ites were anticipating his return.

In this period of millenarian fever, the Bab not only announced the coming of a new divine prophet, but also proclaimed himself to be the Mahdi, igniting the wrath of the established Shi'ite clergy. The Shi'ite clergy were the powerful caretakers of the office of Imam until his return as Mahdi and had much to lose if the Babis were not contained. They convinced the government authorities that the Bab was a dangerous rebel, and in 1850 he was executed. During this brief period, twenty thousand Babis were put to death.

Upon the Bab's death, Bahá'u'lláh, who had been an early follower, took a leadership role in the Babi faith. His activities led to his imprisonment in the "Black Pit," an infamous prison in Tehran. He wrote:

> "Upon Our arrival We were first conducted along a pitch-black corridor, from whence We descended three steep flights of stairs to the place of confinement assigned to Us. The dungeon was wrapped in thick darkness, and Our fellow prisoners numbered nearly one hundred and fifty souls: thieves, assassins and highwaymen. Though crowded it had no other outlet than the passage by which We entered. No pen can depict that place, nor any tongue describe its loathsome smell. Most of these men had neither clothes nor bedding to lie on. God alone knoweth what befell Us in that most foul smelling and gloomy place."

He was slated for execution, but family connections and fear of further upheavals freed him, and in 1853, he was forced out of Iran, living the next forty years in exile, imprisonment, and persecution.

Bahá'u'lláh was exiled as a prisoner throughout the Middle East while continuing in his role as a Babi leader. After ten years of exile, Bahá'u'lláh gathered his followers on the banks of the Tigris River from April 21 to May 2, 1863, and proclaimed himself to be the Divine Messenger of God of the Bab's prophecy. Some Shi'ite sects believed that the arrival of the Mahdi would herald the return of Christ, and thus as the Bab's, or the Mahdi's successor, Bahá'u'lláh was declaring that he was the return of Christ. The spot became known as the Garden of Ridvan, which means paradise, and the twelve days are celebrated each year by the Bahá'ís as the Ridvan Festival.

Bahá'u'lláh's religious teachings called for social and political reform, and though he had no political ambitions, he was a continuous source of agitation to authorities. He sharply criticized war, colonialism, taxing the poor for military purposes, theocracies, and proscribed roles for women, and dismissed as backward the division between science and religion, all of which were threats to the prevailing powers of the time. To rid themselves of his irksome presence and out of fear of his ever-growing number of followers, Bahá'u'lláh and his family were sent to the penal city of Acre in the Ottoman Empire in 1868, where they remained for twenty-four years until Bahá'u'lláh's death in 1892. During this period he wrote prolifically, producing thousands of letters, tablets, and books that are the foundation of the Bahá'í faith and have been interpreted by his son 'Abdu'l-Bahá and great-grandson Shogi Effendi.

If persecution is a hallmark of powerful religious movements, then certainly the Bahá'ís and Bahá'u'lláh qualify. He survived torture, assassination attempts, forced travel through frigid weather, and years of imprisonment. The Bahá'ís have endured government and clerical persecution, including pogroms, since their inception as Babis. Thousands have been killed and imprisoned as apostates from Islam. The Iranian Revolution in 1979 led to outright state-sanctioned persecution and discrimination that denied Bahá'ís legal, property, and employment rights. Two hundred Bahá'ís were killed and hundreds imprisoned in the years following the revolution. Due to pressure from the international community, persecution has abated, though the civil rights of Bahá'ís are still largely ignored, and prejudice and discrimination are commonplace as their progressive social ideas are viewed as subversive. The approximately 350,000 Iranian Bahá'ís are not allowed to worship freely or organize, cannot pursue higher education, and are denied employment on the basis of their faith. Presently, Iranian Bahá'ís can apply for religious refugee status, allowing some of them to immigrate to the United States.

People interested in the Bahá'í faith will find it unlike any other, starting with the lack of clergy. Bahá'u'lláh taught that the time for religious clergy had passed, and he laid out a careful blueprint of how the Bahá'í faith should be administered. The administration occurs through local and national governing bodies called Spiritual Assemblies with the Universal House of Justice serving at the international level. Nine members are elected to hold one-year positions in the governing bodies, and all laity are potential candidates. Ballots are cast in secret, and the people who receive the most votes are elected.

The radical aspect of this process is that no one is allowed to campaign for office and there are no nominations; people receive votes based on their wisdom, integrity, and experience.

The Universal House of Justice sits at the head of Bahá'í governance. It was designed by Bahá'u'lláh to be the major decision-making body after the deaths of his son and great-grandson, who were the guardians of the faith. The Universal House of Justice, which is located on Mount Carmel in Israel, is composed of nine men who are elected from National Spiritual Assemblies and serve five-year terms. In all other governing assemblies, women are fully represented, but it was proscribed that only men may serve on the Universal House of Justice. The followers have faith that the reason for this incongruity has yet to be revealed. The Universal House of Justice interprets Bahá'u'lláh's writings in terms of issues that arise but were not foreseen and so are not specified in the Sacred Texts. Their decisions are unerringly guided, though their legislation can be repealed or amended to keep flexibility.

In Portland, Bahá'ís gather as a community for weekly devotions. Each week a different member plans the gathering, which generally consists of recorded music or singing, and the reading of verses and the Bahá'í Tablets. The formal reading is followed by individuals' offering their own prayers or thoughts. Social time or study groups follow devotions. Every nineteen days area communities meet for the Nineteen Day Feast, which consists of administrative duties, worship, and socializing. There are nine holy days that require the suspension of work and other obligations. Seven of these holidays are joyful and are celebrated in community with food, music, and prayer. The Martyrdom of Bab and the Ascension of Bahá'u'lláh are solemn occasions that call for quiet prayer and reflection. Rituals are not part of the Bahá'í faith so holidays generally call for gathering, sometimes gift-giving, eating, and music.

There are currently seven beautiful Bahá'í Temples that are dedicated to "the unity of God, the unity of all his prophets, and the unity of humankind." The temples are in Australia, Uganda, Germany, Panama, India (outstanding architecture!), Samoa, and in Wilmette, Illinois. The spiritual headquarters for the faith is at the Shrine of Bab in Haifa, Israel, often referred to as the "city of tolerance" as it is one of the few places in the Middle East where Christians, Jews, Muslims, and Bahá'ís live together in peace.

The first Maine Bahá'ís settled in Eliot around Green Acre in the first decade of the twentieth century. In 1900, Sarah Jane Farmer, one of the founders of Green Acre, studied with 'Abdu'l-Bahá in Egypt and came back to share the news of the "Persian Revolution." (For more information, see Green Acre on page 137.) Though there is no written history for Maine, it is assumed that some Bahá'ís moved from Eliot to other parts of the state. When the Bahá'ís in the Portland area declined and aged in the 1960s, families were sent as "home front pioneers" to reinvigorate the community. Currently, according to the Bahá'í National Office for Public Information, Maine has 773 declared Bahá'ís and seven active Local Spiritual Assemblies in the following areas: Auburn, Eliot, Lewiston, Portland, South Berwick, South Portland, and York. Study circles and intensives are offered in a variety of towns and cities and may include a service project depending on the needs of the area.

Bahá'ís are true to their teachings about embracing all races and ethnicities, and devotional gatherings offer rare opportunities to meet with diverse people in a state known for its uniformity. At the community gathering in Portland, expect to hear Persian, Russian, and Korean spoken and to meet with up to forty-five Iranians who are new arrivals in the United States or have been here for twenty years.

Bahá'ís offer a unique religion with a beautiful and hopeful vision of humanity's future. They are a thoughtful group who take their faith seriously and express an optimism that is contagious.

Contact Information:

The easiest way to find a Bahá'í community is to call the national headquarters. Within a week you will receive a packet of Bahá'í information and local contacts.
Telephone: 1-800-22-unite (1-800-228-6483)
Web site: *www.us.bahai.org*

Information on study groups and intensives:

Martha Martinez
Northeast Regional Coordinator for the Training Institute
NC@RBCNorthEast.org

Paganism

"And you who seek to know Me, know that your seeking and yearning will avail you not, unless you know the Mystery: For if that which you seek, you find not within yourself, you will never find it without. For behold, I have been with you since the beginning, and I am that which is attained at the end of desire."

—Starhawk
Excerpt from her adaptation of
"Charge of the Star Goddess"

Maine Pagans fit well in a state known for its independent thinking and living. They are a diverse, self-reliant, and self-governing community that is found throughout the state practicing their religion in solitude, covens, groves, or loosely formed groups of the like-minded.

The word pagan originally referred to "country dweller." The term was used in a derogatory manner by sophisticated Romans and directed at rural people whom they considered to be backwards. In general, the original Pagans practiced a nature-based, polytheistic religion that recognized the sacredness of the Earth. Contemporary Paganism is based on the "Old Religion" with modern adaptations including Wicca, Druid, Alexandrian, Garderian, Reclaiming, and many revisionist traditions such as Celtic, Norse, Greek, and Egyptian. All of these religions fall under the umbrella of Paganism. In Maine, many practitioners use the beliefs and methods of witchcraft, or the craft, as the center of their religious activity. It should be understood that not all Pagans are witches, but most witches are Pagans.

Paganism is possibly the most misunderstood religion in America today due to silly media representations, as well as persistent and false stereotypes that depict witches as Satan worshippers who cast harmful spells on others. People are often surprised to learn that it is a legal religion with ordained clergy. Priests and priestesses perform legal ceremonies and act as spiritual guides, but because the religion is radically non-hierarchical, they cannot and will not dictate beliefs to others. There is no singular doctrine, and believers are highly autonomous with most in solitary practice. Each Pagan speaks only for him- or herself. That said, everything that follows is a generalization that does not define all Pagans or their beliefs.

The gods and goddesses of Paganism may be seen to embody archetypal energies. Some Pagans believe that all deities are aspects of one divine energy. Imagine a mirrored disco ball that is a single globe comprised of multiple deities, each with an individual name and purpose. Others reject the concept of oneness, arguing that it leads to detrimental thinking based on one god, one truth, and one way. For them, each deity is a distinct sacred energy. Depending on the practitioner, deities are benign forces until the witch imbues them with energy, or they embody powerful energies that must be carefully controlled and respected.

Many Pagans are pantheistic, believing that divinity is found in all of creation. A helpful clarification is that Christians believe God is the creator and transcendent, while Pagans believe God/dess is creation and immanent.

Male and female deities are worshipped equally, keeping with the balance found in nature. Due to the large number of women in the religion, goddesses tend to receive more attention for reasons of personal healing or as compensation for the patriarchal overload of masculine energy.

There are no sacred texts, though independent reading is essential to forming beliefs and experimenting with the craft. Elders are respected for their experience and skill and often offer classes or apprenticeships. Each person is responsible for his or her own spiritual development; therefore, practice, experience, and education are the only possible avenues to calling oneself a Pagan.

"If it harms none, do what ye will," is one of the two rules that many Pagans follow. It is fine to indulge in the comforts of life and to seek one's own happiness as long as no one is hurt in the process, including oneself. The rule encourages conscious behavior based on self-knowledge and the will to follow the best course of action. The second rule is the Rule of Three, which dictates that whatever is sent out is returned multiple times, be it good or bad.

Ever mind the Rule of Three
Three times what thou givest returns to thee
This lesson well thou must learn,
Thou only gets what thou doest earn!

Over the centuries, Christian institutions have persecuted and misrepresented Pagans with such intense fervor that many people still associate Paganism with evil. Ill-informed extremists persist in accusing them of Satanism even as it has become common knowledge that thousands of innocent people, mostly women, were tortured and executed during the Burning Times that lasted from approximately 1400 through 1700. The witch-hunts gained ferocity with the circulation of the *Malleus Maleficarum,* or "Hammer of the Witches." It was written in 1486 by two Dominican monks who captured in writing the intense fear of women that was propagated by the Christian Church. This guidebook to witch extermination told of women's insatiable sex drive, their desire to emasculate men, and, incredibly, tales of women literally stealing men's penises. Women, who were often herbalists or midwives, were accused of casting spells affecting all aspects of life ranging from a crop failure to the Black Death. In those highly superstitious times, ordinary people turned against one another for petty reasons, while local leaders and the Church profited from executions by seizing the deceased's property.

It is a tragic irony that Paganism has no relationship whatsoever with evil or Satanism. Satan is a Judeo-Christian concept and has no place in Paganism. Pagans do not need salvation because they do not believe they were born sinful. Christianity often presents evil as an external force, which Pagans believe allows people to escape responsibility for their actions, as in the late Flip Wilson's adage, "The devil made me do it." They see danger in viewing evil as external in that it encourages the repression of the shadowy side of human nature, leading to destructive and ill-informed psychological projections.

Many Pagans attempt to look clearly at their shadowy side recognizing that humans have the capacity to either help or harm. They are responsible for themselves and assume they have the wisdom to monitor their own behavior. The Rule of Three reinforces the concept that ill will expressed toward another is returned multiple times. That said, another myth can be dispelled—Pagans do not harm people or animals in their rituals. In fact, some pets are revered as "familiars" who enjoy a spiritual bond with their human caretaker.

Pagans enjoy an open-minded approach to sexuality. All aspects of material life are celebrated, including sexuality and sex. Doreen Valiente wrote a statement of faith that has been adopted by many Pagans called the "Charge of the Star Goddess." One of its verses expresses this philosophy perfectly: "For behold all acts of love and pleasure are my ritual." Pagans honor sexual diversity by affirming and accepting differences in people's sexual orientation. The open attitude toward sexuality reflects a non-dualistic approach that does not separate the body, mind, and spirit into distinct categories; therefore, there is no guilt associated with pleasure.

Mainstream religions are based on linear time where there is progression towards salvation or enlightenment, while Paganism is based on the present, and time is attuned to the cycles of the seasons, moon, and stars. Self-development is a spiraling and organic process best represented by the cycles of birth, death, and rebirth that are inseparable from nature and guide Pagans to flow with change. "Be here now," is a phrase used as an invocation to deities, and "Blessed be," closes rituals and prayers, with both indicating a preference for the present moment.

There are eight solar holidays, called Sabbats, that are aligned with the agricultural calendar: the two solstices and equinoxes called quarter days, plus four cross quarter days, each of which is between the quarter days. The seasonal quarters and cross quarters are marked as times for celebration, ritual, and magic. Rituals and magic are attuned to the waxing and waning of the moon. For example, the new moon is an excellent time to perform magic that intends to bring something to fruition because the energy of the spell will increase as the moon waxes to fullness.

Though magic is most often done in harmony with seasonal and lunar cycles, it can be performed anytime and anywhere. Magic may take a few moments or a few hours depending upon its purpose. There are many different definitions of magic, though all express the use of natural energy to bring about change through acts involving imagination, concentration, emotions, and consciousness. It is performed for purposes of prayer, healing, self-development, conflict resolution, love, prosperity, career, selling or buying a house, and energetically shielding oneself from disagreeable people. There are no restrictions on what is asked for, though careful consideration is given to all craft workings to insure there will not be harmful repercussions. Gray magic refers to magic done for other people and is not allowed unless the witch has the permission of the involved person.

Although tools are not necessary, almost all Pagans use them to support the energy of magic. Standard tools are an athame (a double-edged knife), a wand, broom, cauldron, chalice, pentacle, crystal sphere, and bell. The craft may entail working with a collection of candles, incense, herbs, crystals, craft goods, and divination tools. An altar is at the center of craft practices, and each is individually designed according to the season and intent of the magic and/or ritual. Generally, an altar will have magic tools, candles, incense, chalices, salt and water for clearing energy, and representations of the elements and the deities.

Celebratory rituals are performed to honor the gods and goddesses, to recognize the seasonal holidays, or as rites of passage, such as hand-fastings (weddings), blessings, namings, and honoring the dead. Rituals are also designed to induce altered states of consciousness or for purposes of self-exploration. In general, a ritual includes casting a circle, invoking the deities, stating a purpose, raising energy, sending the energy, and closing the circle. Imagination, concentration, and tools are used to intensify the connections with inner energy, which is matched with the external power of the deities.

Much of the ritual and magic that is done today stems from the 19th century when Western occult, Gothic Romanticism, Kabbalah, and such esoteric groups as the Order of the Golden Dawn, Rosicrucians, and Freemasons grabbed the attention of many. In 1921, Dr. Margaret Murray, an anthropologist and Egyptologist, wrote The Witch Cult. Murray claimed to have found an ancient, pre-Christian religion in western Europe that worshipped the Goddess Diana. Though her work was later discredited, she brought covens, the eight holidays, fertility rites, and goddess worship to the forefront. Gerald Gardner (1884–1964) blended Western esoteric rituals, Kabbalah, magic, and folklore in his book *Witchcraft Today*, published in 1954, and again in *The Meaning of Witchcraft* in 1959. Gardner's beliefs about the Mother Goddess, reincarnation, and magic are largely considered to be the foundation of Wicca.

Since the 1960s, Paganism has grown and evolved rapidly with major influences derived from the increase in anthropological knowledge of past and present cultures, indigenous religions, and Eastern practices. Then as now, feminism, ecology, and social justice, coupled with disillusionment with mainstream religions and politics, inspire many to choose Paganism as a viable spiritual alternative. Today, Paganism is far from monolithic. Formalists study Gerald Gardner or Alex Saunders, while social activists look to Starhawk, and feminists to Z Budapest. Free spirits, by far the largest segment, absorb multiple influences and create an individualized, eclectic belief system and practice. Paganism may integrate hands-on healing, aromatherapy, herbalism, astrology, divination, channeling, chakras, chanting, and drumming.

It is commonly said that organizing Pagans is like herding cats. In Maine, it can be particularly difficult because they are geographically distant from one another, and the majority are solitary practitioners. There is no accurate count of Maine Pagans available, though a very rough estimate is from four to seven thousand. For those who are interested in networking, there are many opportunities.

EarthTides Pagan Network (EPN) began in 1989 to help connect Pagans and non-Pagans alike. In 1994, EPN became a state-recognized non-profit organization intent on outreach, networking, and education. Eight times a year, around the Sabbats, they publish EarthTides Pagan Network News, which features networking information, a calendar of events, opinion pieces, and literary and artistic contributions from the Pagan community. EPN disseminates basic information about Paganism to Maine school administrators and has written the "Guide for Teen Pagans" pamphlet, which educates parents and teens and offers advice on how to avoid negative situations. The network sponsors Sabbat gatherings, coffee houses in various state locations, and booths at the Full Circle and Common Ground fairs. Since 1982, EPN has sponsored the Beltane celebration in early May. It is the state's most significant and longstanding Pagan celebration. Up to two hundred people gather at Popham Beach to picnic, dance around the maypoles, and participate in the torch race dedicated to Pan.

The Internet has had an immeasurable impact upon the ability of Pagans to connect across the state. Jane Raeburn, an author and a member of the Maine State Clergy Association, has taken a leadership role in establishing and maintaining several cyberspace options. (For more on the Maine State Clergy Association, see the Temple of the Feminine Divine on page 111.) The "Maine Pagan Resource Page" lists events, covens, groves, homepages, organizations, and Pagan-friendly businesses. The "Maine Pagan Mailing List" offers E-mail conversations on a wide range of topics, and "Maine Pagan Politics" is limited to political issues of interest to the Pagan community.

Various covens and groves offer open rituals, meaning that anyone with a sincere interest is welcome, though there are strict guidelines requiring that those who are under the age of eighteen must have parental permission. Many of these events are potluck meals that allow time for conversation, friendship, and networking.

The Circle of the Silver Cauldron Coven conducts Vacation Pagan School entailing thirteen monthly classes that guide novices through craft basics. Cynthia Jane Collins is one of the coven's High Priestesses and is also an author and a member of the Maine State Clergy Association. Collins is a board member for Interfaith Maine and dedicated to educating Pagans and non-Pagans. (For more on Interfaith Maine, see page 189.)

If access to the Internet is not possible, finding Pagans can be a challenge, as many of them prefer a low profile. The best places to inquire about activities are in holistic stores that sell Pagan books and supplies.

Surrendering stereotypes that are both destructive and foolish will bring non-Pagans a long way toward understanding a religion that reveres the Earth, embraces equality, and embodies a love for life in the present. Direct contact with the Divine, however defined, is experienced through nature, deity worship, ritual, and magic. This beautiful and ancient religion will continue well into the future and offers valuable guidance for living in harmony with nature.

Contact Information:

EarthTides Pagan Network
P.O. Box 161
East Winthrop, ME 04343
Web site: *www.earthtides.org*
E-mail: epn@maine.rr.com

Maine Pagan Resource Page
Web site: *www.janeraeburn.com/maine/*

Circle of the Silver Cauldron Coven
Vacation Pagan School
Cynthia Jane Collins
Telephone: (207) 282-1491
E-mail: Oldewtch@maine.rr.com

Witchvox
Web site: *www.witchvox.com/wotw/home/maine.html*

Spiritualism

Churches in Portland, Westbrook, Augusta, Bangor, Hartford, Madison, Waterville, and Northport
Summer Camps in Etna, Madison, Hartford, and Northport

"I ask the great unseen healing force to remove all obstructions from my mind and body and to restore me to perfect health. I ask this in all sincerity and honesty, and I will do my part. I ask this great unseen healing force to help both present and absent ones who are in need of help and to restore them to perfect health. I put my trust in the love and power of God."
—Spiritualist Healing Prayer

Spiritualist worship services are in many ways indistinguishable from those that occur across the land every Sunday. Services take place in churches, often Universalist, and include the usual elements of worship: announcements, hymns, prayers, greetings, and sermons. The remarkable difference is that when most congregations are heading for the door, Spiritualists stay to witness their minister or a visiting medium or bring communications from the spirits of family and friends who have crossed over. Most often, the messages are personal and poignant, though at times they are comical but useful, such as advice on how to fix a leaky toilet.

The definition of modern Spiritualism is "The Science, Philosophy, and Religion of a continuous life, based upon the demonstrated fact of communication, by means of Mediumship, with those who live in the Spirit World." When looking at Spiritualist history, one can see how science and philosophy found their way into the definition. Spiritualism was not officially incorporated as a religion until 1893, and in the fifty years prior to becoming a religion, it was a philosophy that was one piece of a large cultural movement of social and religious reform. It may be thought of as scientific because from its beginnings scientists investigated the paranormal phenomena associated with Spiritualism.

16

As a religion Spiritualism is relatively young. However, Spiritualists trace their beginnings back through the ages. Shamans spoke to animal guides, Greeks went to oracles, and the Bible tells of prophetic dreams, visions, voices, and spiritual healings. New knowledge about the early Christians indicates that they viewed clairvoyance, prophecy, divination, and healing as gifts from the Holy Spirit.

It was in the 4th century that the Catholic Church first repressed metaphysical activity. At the Council of Nicea, it was determined that priests must be the intermediary between divine guidance from the Holy Spirit and recipients. The infamous Inquisition manual *Malleus Maleficarum,* or "Hammer of the Witches," was written in 1486 and gravely endangered those who practiced herbal and hands-on healing or exhibited psychic abilities. The persecution continued throughout the 16th and 17th centuries as Protestants and Catholics alike condemned any practices not sanctified by their churches, as the work of the Devil.

Conservative Protestant sects joined Catholics in their persecutions but, ironically, their more liberal branches may have contributed to the rise of Spiritualism. By claiming that priests were not necessary to access God, Protestants paved the way for everyone to have direct experiences with God. Many early Protestant sects were spirited and energetic where anyone and everyone could hear the voice of God. Shakers, Baptists, Anabaptists, Seventh Day Adventists, and evangelicals felt at home speaking directly to God. Though their religions did not practice mediumship, and certainly most would have condemned it, they transformed how people viewed their religious relationship with God.

Three 18th-century contemporaries who were unknown to each other played a role in preparing the conceptual groundwork of Spiritualism. In the United States, Mother Ann Lee, founder of the Shakers, had visions and spoke to the deceased. (For more on the Shakers, see page 74.) Anton Mesmer of Vienna healed people with a technique he called "animal magnetism," which he attributed to the action of mysterious body fluids. (Spiritualist healers still refer to fluids and use magnetic healing.) His experiments led to putting people into trance states, which was called mesmerism and eventually became known as hypnotism. Mesmer was the forerunner of Phineas Quimby, an energy healer from Portland, Maine. Emmanuel Swedenborg, the Swedish scientist, wielded the most influence upon the development of Spiritualism. He spoke with spirits and angels during his deep meditations, and though he cautioned against mediumship, some Spiritualists see him as the father of their religion. A later but important figure was Andrew Jackson Davis who wrote *The Principles of Nature: Her Divine*

Revelations and a Voice to Mankind in 1847. He claimed the book was channeled from the spirits of Galen and Swedenborg. News of clairvoyance, mesmerism, healings, visions, and channeling permeated enough of the culture to set the stage for Spiritualism to become a cultural phenomenon. (For more on Swedenborg and Quimby, see page 25.)

The movement began in 1848 when three Fox sisters heard unexplainable noises and rappings at their home in Hydesville, New York. The sisters worked out a code with the spirit, and it was established that he had been a traveling peddler who was murdered at the house and buried in the basement. A hubbub ensued, causing the girls' parents to send them to Rochester only to find that the paranormal activity followed them.

The fame of the sisters spread. Catherine and Margaret were the mediums, and Leah managed their activities. Hundreds of sittings and séances were conducted, often with people in the highest echelons of society. Harriet Beecher Stowe had a private sitting, and Mary Todd Lincoln attended a séance. Despite the widespread interest in their mediumship, their activities were overshadowed by harassment, death threats, and demonstrations. They were continuously the subject of ridicule and damnation from both the press and the pulpit.

The criticisms seemed only to fuel the public's fascination with mediums, while the publicity inspired many to develop their own medium, psychic, and healing skills. From the 1850s through the 1860s, Spiritualism grew wildly as people, mostly from the North, attended Spiritualist activities, meetings, and organizations. The *Spiritualist Register,* 1857, claimed to have 780,000 registered Spiritualists, with 10,000 in Maine. *(www.spirithistory.com)*

The image of gullible victims taken in by crafty con artists is not an accurate representation of Spiritualism. In its first decades, it involved scientists, physicians, intellectuals, writers, religious leaders, and artists who were fascinated by what appeared to be proof of life after death. Paranormal activities were viewed as science, not superstition. Spiritualists were part of a broad social and religious reform movement that advocated for women's rights, abolition, better treatment of prisoners, and social justice. As a group, they were politically liberal, anti-authority, and socially progressive. Women had a strong role in the movement and enjoyed equal footing with men. Many of the mediums were women who channeled guides that spoke of peace, abstinence from tobacco and alcohol, and suffrage. In this framework, Spiritualism was a movement attempting to liberate humanity from death, religious authority, slavery, inequality, war, and injustice.

Unfortunately, the success of the movement provided incentive for fraudulent mediums to set up shop. Throughout the 1870s, there was a constant stream of people exposed as fakes. Harry Houdini offered a reward to any medium that he could not prove to be using trickery. Traveling shows demonstrated techniques for fooling the public and how popping double-jointed knees could create "rappings."

A devastating blow came when Catherine and Margaret Fox denounced Spiritualism. Margaret, who had converted to Catholicism, referred to Spiritualism as a cult, and Catherine claimed she used her double-jointed big toe to fool her clients. By this time, both Margaret and Catherine were alcoholics and estranged from Leah. The press was jubilant at the confessions, yet made little note when one year later the sisters retracted their statements. Catherine claimed to have been paid $1,500 by a reporter to confess and give him exclusive rights. To this day, Spiritualists support the Fox sisters and claim their denouncements were the result of years of public abuse, alcoholism, and constant stress. They abide by the statements made when the women recanted their renunciations and by the integrity of their readings. As one example of proof, they point to a November 23, 1904, *Boston Journal* article citing that a skeleton of a man was found in the walls of the house occupied by the sisters—the murdered peddler from the first rappings.

As the century drew to a close, the glory days of Spiritualism faded, and those who had originally been supportive, such as Swedenborgians, Charles Filmore from Unity, and some from the New Thought movement, dropped away in the face of endless controversy. Despite their damaged reputation, many Spiritualists remained undiscouraged. True believers were determined to see Spiritualism continue. The decision to become a religion was made in order to give like-minded people a unified community and to provide legal protection from persecution. By the early 1890s, the first Spiritualist churches were established, and in 1893, the National Spiritual Association of Churches (NSAC) was founded to serve as a parent organization and provide support to churches and camps. At the end of the century, guiding principles were established for all churches falling under the NSAC umbrella.

The principles are still in place, though they have been amended over the years:

1. We believe in Infinite Intelligence. (This is a supreme impersonal power that is present everywhere.)

2. We believe that the phenomena of Nature, both physical and spiritual, are the expression of Infinite Intelligence. (Included in this is the belief that the Infinite Intelligence is immanent.)

3. We affirm that a correct understanding of such expression and living in accordance therewith constitute true religion.

4. We affirm that the existence and personal identity of the individual continue after the change called death.

5. We affirm that communication with the so-called dead is a fact, scientifically proven by the phenomena of Spiritualism.

6. We believe that the highest morality is contained in the Golden Rule: "Whatsoever ye would that others should do unto you, do ye also unto them."

7. We affirm the moral responsibility of individuals, and that we make our own happiness or unhappiness as we obey or disobey Nature's physical and spiritual laws.

8. We affirm that the doorway to reformation is never closed against any soul here or hereafter.

9. We affirm that the precepts of Prophecy and Healing are Divine attributes proven through Mediumship.

All of Maine's Spiritualist churches are members of the NSAC and adhere to their "Religious Foundation Facts." The foundation facts are based on teachings from progressed souls in the Etheric Planes. These spirit guides teach that physical life is preparation for continued work and evolution in the spirit world, and they assist humanity in both worlds. In the physical world, the support consists of allowing communication between physical and nonphysical worlds, bringing helpful guidance for life's decisions, and proving that there is life after death. In the Etheric Plane, the teachers provide guidance for continued evolution by helping souls reach their highest attributes. Evolution is a natural law that applies to all souls and to the entire manifested universe.

Circumstances in the spirit world are considerably more agreeable if, while on earth, one is responsible for the soul's growth and does not yield to temptations that come from within. Therefore, it is essential to practice self-reliance, self-discipline, and pay attention to spirit guidance. Everyone is capable of finding contentment and joy on earth by living by the Golden Rule and Jesus' counsel to "Love thy neighbor as thyself." Like all religions, Spiritualism stresses the need for perfect faith.

The Spiritualist theology concerning heaven and hell closely follows Swedenborg's teaching. Heaven is a state of contentment gained through a life of service and love; hell is ignorance and choices that bring harm to the self and others. Each soul determines its own heaven or hell. Spiritualists differ from Christians in that they believe Jesus was a teacher, healer, and medium, but not a savior.

Spiritual healing plays a large role in Spiritualism. The Spiritualist healer is "one who, either through his or her own inherent power or through mediumship, is able to impart vital curative forces to pathological conditions." The healing energy that passes through the healer gives relief and has the potential to cure mental and physical illnesses. Spiritualist healers are required to complete coursework, pass an exam, and provide six affidavits from people validating their ability before being commissioned by the NSAC. The primary method of healing is the laying on of hands, though absentee healing is also done. All healings are from God, and the healer prepares for the task by praying and practicing love and compassion throughout the session. They do not give a diagnosis, provide counseling, recommend treatment, or sell any products.

Spiritualism, Christian Science, Swedenborgianism, Seventh Day Adventistism, Unity, and New Thought developed in the same general time period, and they all recognized the connection between illness and the mind, body, and spirit. From these roots, Spiritualism has fully integrated healing into its services. The first thirty minutes of every church service are dedicated to healing. "Healing chairs" at the front of the church are open to any person in attendance. Commissioned healers or students pass healing energy to the recipient by placing hands on their shoulders or above their head. People are also welcome to sit on behalf of someone else. There is a healing book available to place names on a healing list. Self-healing is encouraged through a healthful lifestyle, prayer, meditation, positive thoughts, and self-love. Many ministers are also healers, as are many of the members. Classes that teach healing are regularly offered at the churches.

Education for spiritual growth is paramount and emphasized throughout all Spiritualist organizations. The NSAC has a Bureau of Missionaries whose function is to provide auxiliaries with teachers who travel the country conducting workshops on spiritual development and/or managing auxiliaries. The bureau has a board and a Superintendent of Education whose duties include insuring that the appointed missionaries are qualified and nominating them to the NSAC board for appointment.

Spiritualists who want to pursue higher education enroll with the Morris Pratt Institute where they are prepared for examinations by the NSAC. The NSAC is responsible for official documentation for

Ordained Ministers, Nationalist Spiritualist Teachers, Certified Mediums, Licensed Ministers, and Commissioned Healers. Before receiving certification, mediums must provide six affidavits stating that they provided accurate and valid proof by providing specific descriptions, names, and dates of the continuity of life. The education for all three areas stresses that character and conduct must be held in accordance with the highest teaching. The Center of Spiritual Studies is seeking accreditation from the state of New York and will offer degrees in Ministry and Religious Studies.

The Spiritualist churches in Maine are very active in providing people with the opportunity to experience or learn mediumship. Each affiliate church creates its own schedule, and several sponsor biannual "Medium's Day" fairs that provide readings, healings, angel readings, auric readings, and raffles. Augusta, Bangor, Hartford, and Westbrook offer Development Classes three times a month. Examples of classes are *Numerology, Meditation and Mediumship,* and *Healing.* Some churches conduct a monthly Gallery Night where the medium gives readings to the audience.

Spiritualism enjoys a rich history in Maine. By the mid-1860s, there were regular Sunday meetings in several communities, including Old Town, Dover-Foxcroft, Portland, Rockland, and there was an abundance of Spiritualist activities throughout the state. Three of the four oldest camps in the country are in Maine, and all three are still operating. Of these, Camp Etna is the oldest, dating back to 1877. The railroad tracks that brought people from Boston are still there and witness to the thousands in attendance on any given day. Temple Heights Spiritual Camp in Northport is thriving, with thousands passing through its doors each summer. (For more on Temple Heights, see page 171.)

Augusta Spiritualist Church is the state's oldest church recognized by the NSAC. In 1905, a group of Spiritualists formed the Sunflower Club, paying tribute to the religion's symbol. Three years later the name changed to the Progressive Spiritual Society, and in 1911, the active and motivated group was issued a church charter from the NSAC. They enjoyed their first service in their own church in 1924 and are still holding services in the same building.

The oldest church dates to 1911, and the newest, Inner Light Spiritualist Church in Portland, received its NSAC charter in 2003, demonstrating that Spiritualism is still strong. In Maine, the membership is approximately two hundred, but many more attend services without officially joining. There are 150 Spiritualist churches in the United States, with approximately 2,500 members in all.

It appears that modern Spiritualists share with their forerunners a progressive stance on issues of the day. Though speakers are discouraged from advocating for specific issues while on the platform, the NSAC "Social Policy Statements" depicts a liberal organization that advocates for women's rights, demands freedom of religious thought and expression, abhors war, works to free those who are oppressed by a political system that is unjust, stands against capital punishment, affirms the right to death with dignity, and supports planned parenthood including informed choice for terminating pregnancies.

Unbeknownst to many, Spiritualism's dynamic history and religious practices have shaped current New Age beliefs. Channeling, angels, spirit guides, energy healing, and spiritual evolution through education defined the Spiritualist movement more than one hundred and fifty years ago. It still has detractors, but the independent-minded Spiritualists are used to standing up for what they believe. They guarantee that Spiritualism will continue to comfort, heal, educate, and offer proof of the continuity of life for generations to come. The Spiritualist sunflower motto will hold them in good stead: "As the sunflower turns its face to the Sun, so too does Spiritualism turn the face of mankind to the face of truth."

Contact Information:

Maine State Spiritualist Association of Churches
President Graham Connolly
Telephone: (207) 655-6673
Web site: *mssac.tripod.com*
         mainespiritualism.org

Augusta Spiritualist Church
Corner of Perham and Court Streets, Augusta
Co-Pastor Earl Wallace
Telephone: (207) 582-6745
Co-Pastor Vaiko Allen
Telephone: (207) 622-2799
Web site: *augusta_spiritualist.tripod.com*

Harrison D. Barrett Memorial Church
114–118 Harlow Street, Bangor
Betty Simpson
Telephone: (207) 848-2273
Web site: *www.hdbspiritualistchurch.org*
E-mail: Hdb@mainespiritualism.org

Pinpoint Spiritualist Center
Location: Camp Road, Hartford
Address: R-1, Box 91, Canton, ME 04221
Rev. Rupert Sigurdsson
Telephone: (207) 597-2600
E-mail: rupert@megalink.net

Portland Spiritualist Church
719 Main Street, Westbrook
President Graham Connolly
Telephone: (207) 655-6673
Web site: *portlandspiritualistchurch.org*
E-mail: pschurch@maine.rr.com

Inner Light Spiritualist Center
Gov. William King Lodge
No. 219 at 649 Rte 1, Scarborough
Reverend Gloria Nye
Telephone: (207) 786-4401
E-mail: spiritspeaks2you@adelphia.net
President Mary Bruce
Telephone: (207) 510-1147
E-mail: mibruce@maine.rr.com

Swedenborgian Church

Churches in Portland, Bath, and Fryeburg

"It seems to me the New Church has a great mission in the world. The people are in need of just the message that Swedenborg gave for humankind. Instead of merely listening to that message, we should go out and teach it."
—Helen Keller

"The Second Coming of the Lord is not a Coming in Person, but in the Word, which is from Him, and is Himself. We read in many places that the Lord will come in the clouds of heaven. The "clouds of heaven" mean the Word in its natural sense, and "glory" the Word in its spiritual sense, and "power" the Lord's power by means of the Word. So the Lord is now to appear in the Word . . . ."
—Emanuel Swedenborg

Emanuel Swedenborg was a major influence on writers, artists, and philosophers of the 18th through the 20th centuries, yet few people today have heard of him or of the churches that are rooted in his teachings. Helen Keller was an ardent advocate of Swedenborg's writings and wrote *My Religion* about her faith. Ralph Waldo Emerson wrote *Swedenborg the Mystic,* and George Inness painted gorgeous landscapes inspired by Swedenborg's teachings. Others who refer to him in their works are William Blake, Edgar Allen Poe, Honoré de Balzac, Robert and Elizabeth Browning, and W. B. Yeats. It is thought that Bill Wilson, the founder of Alcoholics Anonymous, was influenced by his writings. The most famous Swedenborgian is the American nurseryman John Chapman, known as Johnny Appleseed, who spread Swedenborg's books along with apple seeds.

Emanuel Swedenborg was born in Sweden and lived from 1688 to 1772. He was a well-educated scientist, researcher, and writer who enjoyed a prestigious reputation throughout Europe and

England. Gifted with an extraordinary intellect, he spoke nine languages, constructed telescopes and microscopes, wrote a number of well-respected scientific works, and was a member of the Swedish Parliament.

In the 1740s, Swedenborg was at the pinnacle of his life with prestige, wealth, and a successful career as the official assessor of mines; yet he found himself yearning for a relationship with God. Years of focus on the intellect left his emotional and spiritual attributes neglected. This deep conflict arose through powerful dreams that he studied for symbolism and meaning. Shortly after Easter, in 1744, he had a blissful vision of God, followed by a visitation from Christ. Afterwards, he dedicated his life to understanding the spiritual realms through meditation and Bible study with the goal of explaining them to others.

Without any previous knowledge, he developed a form of meditation that mirrors yoga nidra, which is the practice of self-awareness while the brain and nervous system sleep. He found that, as in yoga, breathing corresponds directly to thought and breath manipulations lead to deeper meditations. During his inner journeys, he learned to track his rational mind and saw with clarity his egotism. He held combat with unintegrated aspects of himself, and like Padre Pia years later, fought interior battles that lasted for hours. Slowly, he came to realize that it is the emotions, not the intellect, that are the guide to consciousness.

As his meditation skills grew, he would remain in altered states for days where he experienced visions of heaven and hell and had extended conversations with angels and spirits. In a mystical vision, Swedenborg saw that the Second Coming was not the physical return of Jesus, but was Christ Consciousness making itself known on the material and spiritual planes of existence. He believed the Second Coming came in 1757 and would continue to occur, bringing new knowledge to humanity. This new age would result in the increasing obsolescence of the Christian Church as an institution because individuals would come to understand that the church was in their own hearts. As part of this transition, people would see that science and religion do not disprove each other and that all of creation is one. Swedenborg referred to the Second Coming as the New Church or the New Jerusalem, names later used for churches established in his name.

Swedenborg's conversations with angels led him to believe that he had been given the true meaning of the Bible's wisdom and that these lessons would enable Christians to gain deeper meaning from their religion. As a result, he reinterpreted many Christian principles. For example, Protestantism teaches that salvation is found in the acceptance of Jesus as a personal savior through the crucifixion and resurrection, but Swedenborg believed that "salvation" came to all those who led a good life regardless of their beliefs about Jesus. In a break from conventional theology, he claimed Jesus did not die for our sins but as the ultimate act of letting go of God, thereby reaching mystical union with God. Nor did he believe in original sin or that God is divided into a trinity. He emphasized that to be closer to God one must walk a spiritual path of love, wisdom, and service—the true trinity. More specifically, he wrote that the three steps to spiritual growth were repentance, reformation, and regeneration. Repentance is achieved through confession, reformation through faith and charity, and regeneration through a daily inventory, prayer, and usefulness.

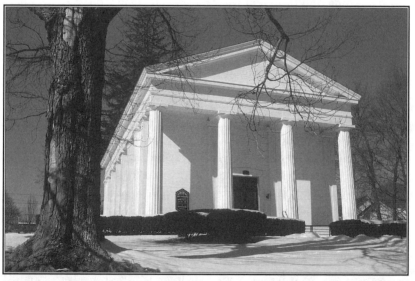

The New Jerusalem Swedenborgian Church is one of Maine's most unusual churches and the oldest continually running church in Bath.

He published his beliefs anonymously and at his own expense. The most well known is the *Arcana Coetestia* or *Heavenly Secrets* in which he wrote of the wisdom he found in the Bible during his meditations. He published anonymously, but people came to know that he was the source. As his books reached larger audiences, the Christian Church took note and firmly denounced his work, and like many mystics before him, he was accused of heresy.

Regardless of the Church's denunciation, Swedenborg's interpretations touched many people. According to Swedenborg, good intentions without action are sterile, as it is essential to do good, pursue good, and be of service. One of his most profound teachings is that love, wisdom, and use (service) cannot be separated, as love and

27

wisdom are ideals that do not become real until they are in use.

His theology on the afterlife also breaks from conventional Christianity. He claimed that heaven or hell are states that are created by the choices people make during life. Hell is separation from others, lack of sincere communication, exploiting others, and being dominated by the demands of the ego. At death, the true self is met in a life review process that reveals all the good and bad of a lifetime. God does not judge people; they judge themselves. Those hoping to get a rest in the afterlife will be disappointed to learn that work, activities, and spiritual evolution continue.

Ultimately, love is his major message: it is within us at birth; it is the unifier that moves humanity past dualism; it is inseparable from truth; and it is heaven, the world, and the self.

Swedenborg never intended his teachings to become a religion, rather he envisioned their being integrated into Christian churches, and it is the Protestants that were the most drawn to his work, though often their parishes were not receptive to new ideas. Frequently, discussion groups originated in Protestant churches, then became controversial and participants found themselves unwelcome in their congregation, which resulted in Swedenborgian churches. Fifteen years after his death, in 1787, a Methodist minister established the first Church of the New Jerusalem in England. The first church chartered in the United States was started in the early 1800s.

Swedenborg's prediction of the coming of new religious perspectives appeared true in the 19th century with its groundswell of new ideas on spirituality: Utopian communes, Transcendentalism, New Thought, Theosophy, Spiritualism, Christian Science, and of course, the New Church. Swedenborg influenced, either directly or indirectly, many of the new religions. The Spiritualists, who channel the spirits of the deceased, consider Swedenborg to be a forerunner of their religion because he channeled and described the afterlife. (For more on Spiritualism, see page 16.)

Swedenborg appealed to wildly divergent groups. During the same period that the Spiritualists were making claims to Swedenborg, his books were influencing a small group of radical thinkers and writers who were known as the New England Transcendentalists: Ralph Waldo Emerson, Henry David Thoreau, George Ripley, and Margaret Fuller, among others. From the 1830s through the 1850s, they rebelled against the dryness and rationalism of Unitarianism and offered Americans an idealistic view of humans as intuitive, mystical, and at one with nature and God. Emerson was particularly inspired by Swedenborg's emphasis on ethical behavior, mysticism, and the correspondence between physical and spiritual worlds.

In turn, the New Thought movement was influenced by Transcendentalism, and Emerson in particular. Emerson and Swedenborg were voices in New Thought, but the movement began in the mid-1800s with the Portland healer Phineas Quimby. Quimby healed by energetically replacing people's negative thought patterns, which were linked to their illnesses, with positive patterns, thereby making a connection between the mind, body, and spirit. He is said to have healed thousands, many of whom were influential people who expanded on his ideas. It is commonly believed that Quimby's healings evolved into New Thought, which in turn splintered into many factions, including Christian Science and Unity. (For more on Quimby, Unity, and New Thought, see page 33)

Charles Braden in *Spirits in Rebellions*, writes that New Thought spread primarily through the writings of Walter Felt Evans and Horatio Dresser. Of interest here is that both men were Swedenborgians and active in Maine. Evans, a Methodist minister, was healed by Quimby in 1863, and began healing using Quimby's technique. In this same period, he became Swedenborgian and conducted services at the New Church in Portland. He opened a healing practice in Boston in 1867. In his prolific writings, he applied Swedenborg's beliefs and psychology to Quimby's findings and was especially receptive to Quimby's doctrine of a direct correspondence between the physical and spiritual worlds, which Evans felt addressed healings that had no rational explanation.

Horatio Dresser was the son of Julius Dresser, who was born in Portland and was an editor of a Portland newspaper for a time. In 1860, Julius was healed by Quimby and was so impressed with him that he and his wife later moved to Boston where they taught Quimby's techniques using his manuscripts. In 1921, Horatio edited and published Quimby's manuscripts, which had been embroiled in a controversy surrounding Mary Baker Eddy, the founder of Christian Science. Eddy had been Quimby's student in the 1860s and claimed at the time to have been healed by him. She later denounced him as a mesmerist (hypnotist), but some believed she used his manuscripts as a basis for Christian Science, a claim she vehemently denied. By publishing Quimby's manuscripts, Dresser made it possible for people to decide for themselves.

As a pioneer in New Thought, Horatio Dresser wrote extensively and, like Evans, integrated Swedenborg into his work. In 1919, Dresser served for one year as a minister at the New Church in Portland. Unfortunately, he was more of a lecturer than a minister and lacked the skills to both manage a church and spiritually engage parishioners.

Portland has the oldest congregation in Maine, incorporated on August 31, 1836. Like many Swedenborgian churches, it stemmed from a discussion group that met monthly and longed for a place to worship. In general, Swedenborg churches experienced their highest membership from the 1850s through the 1920s. In Portland, the peak years were from 1851 through 1876, when the charismatic Reverend William Hayden led the church. The official membership peaked at one hundred and eighty-three, but hundreds turned out for Sunday worship to listen to his dynamic sermons. The parish was gentrified and influential, with James Phinney Baxter being a member. After losing their church to a fire, a large and expensive replacement was built in 1867. When Reverend Hayden retired, membership steadily declined, and the church proved to be a financial drain. In 1903, the small congregation sold the church and made plans for a less costly place to worship. The present Portland Swedenborgian Church was built in 1910 and is undeniably charming.

Though Portland has the oldest congregation, Swedenborg's teachings arrived in Maine via a Baptist missionary to Bath in 1793. The Bath Society formed in 1829 to study Swedenborg, and in 1844, they established the New Church. The early membership was large and included freethinkers who questioned the doctrines of mainstream religions. Many were wealthy shipbuilders and respected community members, such as the first president of Bath Iron Works, Thomas Hyde.

They used their wealth to build a stunning Greek Revival church that is one of Maine's most unusual churches. It is the oldest continually operating church in Bath, and the oldest New Church building still used by Swedenborgians. In 1920, Reverend Paul Dresser, the brother of Horatio, awoke to find that a heavy snowfall had brought down the roof and two sides of the church. The front pillars remained as did the chancel with its inscription, "Search for Scriptures, for in them ye have eternal life and they are they that testify of me." The sides were rebuilt to give the roof a steeper slant, thereby avoiding future catastrophes and maintaining its architectural appeal.

In Fryeburg, the Congregationalist minister Bamon Nelson Stone used his pulpit to preach some interesting doctrines. He did this for three years before a visiting Methodist minister recognized his sermons as originating with Swedenborg. After some of the congregation were informed, Reverend Stone confessed and resigned. Not surprisingly, many people found wisdom in Swedenborg and approached Reverend Stone about starting a church. In 1877, the New Church opened with one hundred and fifty people in attendance.

Unfortunately, its opening caused much disruption among family and friends in the small town, as traditionalists resisted new translations of Christianity. It withstood the controversy and is still an active congregation, worshiping for more than one hundred years in the same warm, inviting sanctuary.

Visitors to Maine's three Swedenborgian churches will have three very different experiences. Services in Bath are indistinguishable from mainstream Christian services except that Swedenborg's teachings are woven into the sermons. Portland developed a very open approach, with frequent nods to other traditions. It is interesting that approximately half of the membership identify themselves as Sufis, as well as Swedenborgians. Fryeburg is a small town congregation that runs from conservative to liberal and has a strong sense of shared history and community.

The defining characteristics of the Portland and Fryeburg churches are their congregations' love of music and their skill at providing it. In Portland, the songbooks are loose-leaf notebooks containing a compilation of everyone's favorite spiritual songs, which are divided into categories such as Gathering and Invocation, Prayer, Devotion, Chants and Rounds, Peace and Justice, Celebration and Affirmation, and Blessing and Benediction. At the beginning of services, the parishioners call out the numbers of the songs they would like to hear to the vocalists and musicians, making for an inspiring start. Fryeburg incorporates a wide range of music from classical to jazz to country and gospel. They have active adult and children's choirs who are accompanied by an array of musicians who play acoustic and electric guitars, piano, bass, drums, and sometimes flute, trumpet, and pipe organ.

Maine's Swedenborgians are fortunate to have accomplished ministers. Reverend George Dole from Bath is a leading translator of Swedenborg's original Latin works and has degrees from Yale, Oxford, and Harvard. The Portland church is served by Reverend Wilma Wake, who has published four books, is an adjunct faculty member at the Pacific School of Religion, and a licensed social worker. Reverend Ken Turley in Fryeburg has been a parish minister for twenty years, has produced seven CDs of originally composed and arranged music for worship and Sunday school, and along with his wife, organizes and directs the music for the Swedenborgian's National Conventions.

The New Age movement emerged onto the cultural landscape in the 1960s, but its roots trace back to Spiritualism, Theosophy, Transcendentalism, New Thought and thus, Swedenborg. His message introduced ideas that were once radical but have been absorbed into the culture through various religions and fields of thought. Swedenborg and New Age theology dovetail in several ways, which is why Swedenborg is often referred to as the Father of the New Age. In *Roots and Wings,* Reverend Wake states her belief that people who have explored New Age avenues will want to discard its excesses, and desiring a place for worship and community, they will find Swedenborg churches welcoming.

Historically, Swedenborgians were freethinkers who found answers to their most profound spiritual questions in his writings. Today, freethinkers will still find Swedenborg worth exploring. Those who are experienced in metaphysical practices will find thought-provoking theology, while those who are comfortable with Christianity and the Bible will find themselves in familiar territory.

Contact Information:

Portland Swedenborgian Church
302 Stevens Avenue, Portland, ME 04103
Mark Allen
Telephone: (207) 772-8277
Web site: *www.theportlandchurch.org*
E-mail: info@theportlandchurch.org

Church of the New Jerusalem
4 Oxford Street, Fryeburg, ME 04037
Reverend Ken Turley
Telephone: (207) 935-3413
E-mail: Fryeburgnewchurch@yahoo.com

Church of the New Jerusalem
876 Middle Street, Bath, ME 04530
Reverend George Dole
Telephone: (207) 442-8323

Unity Church of Greater Portland

Windham

"Unity is a link in the great educational movement inaugurated by Jesus Christ; our objective is to discern the Truth in Christianity and prove it. The Truth we teach is not new, neither do we claim special revelations or discovery of new religious principles. Our purpose is to help and teach humankind to use and prove the eternal Truth taught by the Master."

—Charles Fillmore
Cofounder of Unity

Most New Englanders are not prone to public displays of affection, so when Reverend Judy James arrived at Unity Church of Greater Portland in 2002, she had a difficult time convincing parishioners that hugging was a pleasurable option to shaking hands during the neighbor-greeting segment of the service. Now, she can hardly restrain them as young and old alike spill from their seats traversing the church in wonderful anticipation of bear hugs. Whether people choose to shake hands or hug, the warmth is contagious in this friendly and upbeat community.

Each week approximately eighty people, out of a membership of one hundred thirty, travel distances as far as an hour away for worship. First time visitors receive a welcome packet with information about Unity as a religion and a movement. Unity has been slow to arrive in New England, where there are only fifteen established churches, with one in Maine. In comparison, there are over fifty in Florida, and California has more than seventy churches and centers. According to the Association of Unity Churches, there are more than six hundred and fifty Unity churches, centers, and study groups in the United States and Canada.

Unity is based on the teachings and beliefs of Myrtle and Charles Fillmore, who, in 1889, founded the organization that grew to be Unity. The five basic and often repeated principles of Unity are as follows:

1. God is good and is present everywhere.
2. The spirit of God lives within each person, therefore all people are inherently good.
3. We create our life experiences through our way of thinking.
4. There is power in affirmative prayer and meditation, which increases an awareness of God in our lives.
5. Knowledge of spiritual principles is not enough. We must live them.

It is a Christian faith that believes the historical Jesus was both human and divine. In Unity, Jesus is distinguished from Christ, who represents the divine God-seed that exists within all people. Unity believes that Jesus expressed the perfection of divinity, thereby becoming the Christ who showed humanity the way to their perfection.

The Bible is the basis for Unity and is read in the traditional manner but also translated metaphorically. Charles Fillmore wrote *The Metaphorical Bible Dictionary*, which interprets Biblical text symbolically. For example, the cross is seen as a symbol for resurrection and the "crossing out" of old beliefs. The blood of Christ symbolizes spiritual energy used for redemption, and the virgin birth stands for the birth of Christ Consciousness born in a purified soul.

Unity interprets the trinity of Father, Son, and Holy Spirit metaphysically to be Mind, Idea, and Expression. The Mind, or the Divine Mind, is another name for the Father, or God. The Idea is the ability to create as shown by Jesus, who is humanity's prototype. Humanity is made in God's image; therefore, everyone has the ability to create. God created the greater universe, and people create their personal universe by linking with the Divine Mind. The Holy Spirit, or Expression, is the whole spirit of God expressing itself through humanity.

Evil is considered an incomplete expression of God, with ignorance at its root, and sin is the separation from God. Heaven and hell are states of consciousness created by thoughts, words, deeds, and actions. Salvation is not found in the afterlife but is reached each time negative thoughts are overcome.

Unity describes itself as "practical Christianity" because of the life-changing benefits of health, happiness, and prosperity that result from a commitment to spiritual practices that call for positive thinking and prayer. Prayers are conscious communions with God using statements that are either affirmations or denials. The affirmation prayers replace faulty or negative thinking patterns with positive possibilities. Conscious self-observation reveals how one shapes one's own life. The following is an example of an affirmative prayer:

> I trust in God. I know whatever I do, wherever I go,
> God is the wisdom that guides, the power that governs,
> the love that blesses, the presence that protects, and the
> substance that prospers me. For this I am grateful.

It is surprising that Unity does not have a stronger presence in Maine since the Fillmores were active in the New Thought Movement that originated in Portland, Maine, with Phineas Quimby. Quimby was a well-known healer who lived from 1802 to 1866. He was convinced that negative beliefs and thought patterns were connected to poor health and claimed that seventy percent of people's illnesses were related to faulty thinking, most of which originated in dogmatic religious beliefs and destructive medical advice. Though he criticized institutional religions, he had a deep relationship with God and believed he had discovered the technique Jesus used in healings. Quimby is said to have healed over twelve thousand people through a method he could describe only by using a daguerreotype as a metaphor. Like the camera, he received images of the person's illness and the thoughts that caused it, and then energetically he replaced those images with positive beliefs that led to healing.

Quimby's healings were inspirational to many people of the time who were exploring unconventional spirituality. New Thought developed some of its principles from his healing techniques and integrated others from a variety of sources. New Thought proposed the ideas that the mind is capable of healing matter, humanity is divine, evil is the absence of good, creative powers are infinite. Other beliefs of New Thought include a progressive revelation of Truth, non-sectarian religion, and the merger of science and religion. At the time, these ideas were threatening to a religious public that was denouncing both Darwinism and science as contradicting the Bible and waging a war on Christianity.

The mid- to late-nineteenth century generated an enormous amount of spiritual dialogue, with New Thought providing speakers, teachers, and leadership. Conversations were influenced by Transcendentalism, Swedenborg, Spiritualism, and metaphysics. The consistent refrain was that God was within each individual and science would eventually offer proof for timeless religious truths. New Thought never developed into a religion, nor did it want to, but its influence is found in Unity, Divine Science, Science of the Mind, and Christian Science.

The Fillmores were very interested in the ongoing New Thought dialogue and often went to hear speakers. Charles was particularly active in New Thought and, on his own, studied an array of religions and philosophies such as Spiritualism, Buddhism, Theosophy, and Western occult.

Emma Curtis Hopkins was an important influence on the Fillmores and a close friend of Charles'. Hopkins was an editor for the *Christian Science Journal* and held an important position in Mary Baker Eddy's budding Christian Science religion. She left Eddy's organization and opened the Christian Science Theological Seminary in Chicago. (Christian Science was a commonly used term during this period.) The leading teachers of the time studied basic metaphysical principles with Hopkins, who was the teachers' teacher. In 1886, Hopkins recommended that the Fillmores attend a lecture series by Dr. E. B. Weeks on Christian Science, New Thought, and Divine Science. Attending the lectures dramatically altered the Fillmores' life path.

At the time, they were well established in Kansas City where Charles had a real estate business. Myrtle was very ill with tuberculosis and was advised by her doctor to seek a different climate. Charles, who had been having profound dreams, dreamt that he should stay and felt the dream was prophetic. Shortly thereafter, they attended Weeks's lecture in which he said, "I am a child of God, and therefore I do not inherit illness."

Weeks's words profoundly affected Myrtle, and they served as her inspiration for self-healing. Everyday she spoke to her organs with words of praise and gratitude and asked forgiveness for years of being critical and taking them for granted. She prayed every hour and monitored her thoughts to guard against anger and pettiness. Within two years, Myrtle healed herself of a condition that had been deemed fatal. She attributed her success to recognizing that the healing power of Christ was within her. As word spread of her healing ability, a steady stream of people found their way to her door.

Charles was initially skeptical, but the overwhelming evidence of his wife's recovery led him to apply her techniques to his own infirmity. When he was a child, Charles had endured a serious hip injury and was in agonizing pain for two years, during which time he was the recipient of incompetent and damaging medical care. Disease and lack of use shriveled his leg, which stopped growing, leaving Charles with lifelong pain. Following Myrtle's example, each night for months he practiced silent meditation but experienced no change except that his dreams were increasingly vivid and rich with spiritual guidance. Eventually, his meditations bore results, and he healed the chronic pain in his leg, which actually increased in length and strength. The healing transformed Charles' beliefs on many levels, but he was most passionate about his realization that his healing was evidence of a scientific order to life that includes religion.

In 1889, the year considered to be the founding of Unity, Charles became an important voice in New Thought with the publication of his magazine *Modern Thought*. The magazine was "Devoted to the Spiritualization of Humanity from an Independent Standpoint" and provided a mouthpiece for "all honest souls earnestly seeking for the spiritual light." *Modern Thought* was not wedded to any particular school of thought, and articles from all traditions appeared between its covers, though in time the Fillmores repudiated Spiritualism, the occult, and elements of New Thought.

The ideas that emerged from New Thought provided fertile ground for the Fillmores' beliefs to take form, but Charles steadily formulated his beliefs around the life and teachings of Jesus Christ. To reflect his evolving views, he changed the magazine name to *Christian Science Thought*. Soon after, Eddy sent out notices that she wanted exclusive rights to the Christian Science name. Charles freely relinquished the name, and in 1891, *Unity* magazine was published. The name Unity was chosen to signify the inclusion of the best aspects of many religions and movements. It also signified that the Fillmores were not interested in establishing a religion but wanted to encourage people to integrate these beliefs into their own religion.

In 1890, Myrtle established the Society of Silent Unity. It originated with a group who met nightly to hold troubled people in silent prayer and communion. The practice was based on distance healing made available through an omnipresent God. It soon proved to be so popular that their magazine printed affirmation prayers that people could hold in their hearts for fifteen minutes every night at 9:00. In time, prayer requests from across the United States poured in, requiring a staff to pray and write letters of encouragement, which resulted in the birth of Silent Unity.

Unity Church of Greater Portland has a simple and peaceful interior.

The Fillmores were in demand as both teachers and healers. They held frequent meetings where all faiths came together for discussion. The Fillmores responded to the ever-increasing number of seekers by opening the Unity Training School in order to teach people from all faiths metaphysical laws, which they could in turn teach to others through Unity Centers. Charles was uncomfortable with doctrine, strict organization, and hierarchy, but he understood the importance of having set standards for teachers and ministers in order to maintain the integrity of the teachings. In 1933, the Unity Ministers Association was established, creating a constitution and bylaws for churches, centers, and schools. Unity has grown to be the second-largest—behind Christian Science—religious community stemming from New Thought.

Myrtle died in 1931 at the age of eighty-six, and Charles followed her in 1948, at the age of ninety-four. By all reports, they were warm, friendly, and down-to-earth while never wavering in their desire to serve others. Though they had no ambitions to start a religion or church, their wisdom touched too many people to be left as a historical movement.

Their legacy lives on in Unity Village, Missouri, where the Unity Institute offers education and retreats. After more than one hundred years, *Unity* magazine has a circulation of over 50,000. The *Daily Word,* first appearing in 1924, has one million readers in one hundred and seventy-five countries, and is printed in seven languages. Unity Publications has an extensive list of book titles they publish. Currently, Silent Unity receives two million prayer requests each year and is staffed by three hundred trained personnel. Prayer requests are taken twenty-four hours a day, seven days a week by E-mail, mail, or telephone. Approximately three hundred thousand individuals are involved in Unity ministries worldwide.

Unity first appeared in Maine in 1942 as the Unity Church of Truth. Initially, the church moved from location to location in the Portland area, and though it bought a site on High Street in Portland in 1946, it was not until 1967 that it secured its first fully outfitted Unity Center. With the purchase of the house on Columbia Road in Portland, it was able to supply housing for clergy, and used the first floor rooms for a sanctuary, bookstore, and library, while the Children's Church met in the basement. In the 1980s, the congregation once again found itself in several temporary locations. From 1986 to 1994, Reverend Audrey McGinnis served the church and grew the membership to one hundred seventy-five. With those strong numbers, the congregation was able to purchase a permanent home. The present church in Windham was secured in 1992. Originally a dance hall, the building underwent extensive renovations, done almost exclusively by church members.

The Windham Unity is unassuming from the outside, but inside it is lovely with a chapel that is clean, clear, and open with simple stained glass windows. The largest of these sits at the center point and depicts Unity's symbolic winged globe with hands releasing a dove and the words "Be still." The facility has a large meeting room, full kitchen, children's rooms, library, and a fairly large metaphysical bookstore.

Church services in Windham are joyful, lively events that include meditation, prayer, sharing, greeting, music, and the lesson. Visitors will find familiar Christian hymns with an emphasis on the upbeat. "Surely the Presence of the Lord is in this Place," "We are All Friends Here," and "Weave" are congregational standards. Each week a special song is offered by the choir or by a parishioner who has a musical talent to share.

As in many contemporary services, children are asked to the front of the church for a short discussion on what the adults will hear later in the service. Unity children are asked to bless the congregation by holding up their hands and saying, "We love you. We appreciate you. We behold the Christ in you." The adults then bless the children in the same manner, and they are led out to age-appropriate Children's Church.

Thirty minutes before service begins, the chapel doors are closed for those who wish to meditate in silence. Guided meditations are scheduled during services that are linked to the day's lesson. After services, Reiki practitioners are available for energy healing.

On most Sundays, Reverend Judy asks people to share the ways that God is at work in their lives. She gracefully blends the experiences into reflections on Unity teachings, which demonstrates a deep level of comprehension on her part. Unity ministers must take fifteen core courses through the Unity Institute before being accepted as a candidate for the Ministerial Education Program. This is a mandatory full-time, two-year program that runs year-round. Students are immersed in the teaching and spiritual life of Jesus Christ.

Unity Church of Greater Portland is doing a fine job at creating community. Services are followed by coffee time and once a month, by a well-attended potluck lunch. Ongoing ways to be involved include educational classes, workshops, discussion groups, ministry teams, choir, retreats, and Reiki healings for both the public and practitioners. Every Wednesday at noon, Unity in Windham joins other Unity churches and centers around the world in healing prayers for Silent Unity. Special celebrations include Thanksgiving Eve when people come together to speak about gratitude, and New Year's Eve when a ceremony guides participants to let go of the qualities that are no longer needed. On the second Thursday of September, the congregation joins an interfaith prayer vigil founded by Unity in 1994, in which people pray on a pre-selected theme for twenty-four hours.

Reverend Judy attributes the success of the Unity Church of Greater Portland to the manner in which all paths to God are honored and enhanced by the clear principles that Unity offers. Believers bring to the church a tangible feeling of love and acceptance that is rooted in their sincere desire to have direct experiences with the Divine. It is a well-organized church with a warm, loving community filled with a faith that truly speaks to the dedication of Reverend Judy and the parishioners.

Contact Information:

Unity Church of Greater Portland
54 River Road, Windham, ME 04062
Rev. Judy James
Telephone: (207) 893-1233
24 hour Dial-A-Prayer: (207) 893-0984
E-mail: Unity4angels@juno.com

For more information on Unity:
Web site: *www.unityonline.org*
1901 NW Blue Parkway
Unity Village, MO 64065-0001

Northern Lights: A Metropolitan Community Church

On January 1, 2004, Northern Lights Church, in Vassalboro, celebrated its tenth anniversary as a Metropolitan Community Church. Metropolitan Community Churches have 300 congregations in 22 countries with an approximate membership of 43,000, yet Northern Lights is the only one that is licensed and credentialed in Maine, New Hampshire, Vermont, Quebec, and New Brunswick.

Metropolitan Community Churches is a Christian denomination that was founded in 1968 by Rev. Troy Perry, a Pentecostal minister defrocked due to his homosexuality. In the early years, outreach was directed at the gay, lesbian, bisexual, and transgender community, but it has evolved past the "church for gays" label and welcomes all who feel disenfranchised by mainstream religions. Visitors to Metropolitan Community Churches will find a mixed congregation in most places, and services that range from conservative to progressive depending upon the clergy.

Northern Lights is also affiliated with The Center for Progressive Christianity, an organization that serves progressive Christian churches by providing guiding ideas, opportunities for networking, and resources. The Center for Progressive Christianity advocates religion that encourages inquiry and is opposed to exclusive doctrine that purports to be the only way to God. As a Christian organization, it holds that Jesus Christ is their gateway to God, but emphasizes that they recognize and accept other faiths.

Northern Lights consider itself liberal in some areas and progressive in others. They have defined progressive to mean a place of prayer where everyone is welcome—"Come as you are and bring your whole being." The language used during services is inclusive, and everyone who chooses is welcome at the communion table.

The twenty-five members do an extraordinary amount of mission work and are deeply committed to service. Throughout the fall and winter months, they collect toys, socks, and food; and for residents in Western Maine who depend on wood-burning stoves for heat, smoke detectors and batteries. In the spring, they collect the barely used clothing thrown out by Colby College students, and in the summer, backpacks for needy students.

In the first ten years of Northern Lights, their openly gay minister Reverend Bill Gordon guided the members by creating a safe and inviting place of worship that honors all people and all paths to God. Gordon has moved on, but this small church continues to welcome all to an informal and intimate place of acceptance and faith.

For more information:

Northern Lights Church
Web site: *www.northernlightsmcc.org*

Metropolitan Community Churches
Web site: *www.mccchurch.org*

The Center for Progressive Christianity
Web site: *www.tcpc.org*

Practicing Mindfulness: East Meets West

Hridaya Hermitage

Meetingbrook Dogen and Francis Hermitage

Morgan Bay Zendo

Shambhala Center

Sufi Order International

Hridaya Hermitage - Hinduism

Industry

It is a bit surprising to find a guru-led ashram in Maine, especially when it is located twenty miles north of Farmington and several miles into the woods in a town left off most maps. The ashram is snuggled on forty acres in the western hills, an area the Wabanaki referred to as the "top of the Turtle's back." Its settlers are a like-minded group who have fallen in love with a lifestyle that is secluded, simple, and close to nature. They are here to pursue a path that will bring them closer to union with the Divine. As part of that path, they welcome others to their community through two retreat offerings. The Kaya Kalpa retreat is traditional Ayurveda and Hatha Yoga healing, and the Kaya-sadhana is the opportunity to experience immersion in a yogic lifestyle.

The question remains. Why Industry, Maine? Another surprise—their guru, Bahagavan, formerly known as Mark Lescault, had a healing practice in Farmington. In 1989, he established Hridaya Hermitage as a place dedicated to spiritual pursuits and sometimes as a healing retreat for his clients in need of a space for prolonged treatment. Through the years, people came and went, and then in the early 2000s, an influx of people moved to the hermitage to be under the guidance of Bahagavan.

In 2004, twenty adults and eight children called Hridaya Hermitage their home. The community bustles with activity as new houses are built to accommodate the growth. That being said, they do not solicit for new members, are not affiliated with any group or organization, and have no interest in converting anyone. Those who join the community do so with a full understanding of the commitment required.

44

Nine buildings dot the landscape, including a straw-bale house, an authentic Mongolian ger, a log temple, a sauna, and two retreat cabins, plus residential houses. The community does all of its own building and provides the labor for self-sustenance. This is a considerable feat considering they are off the power grid, have no running water, heat with wood-burning stoves, use candles for light, store food that does not fit into the single propane refrigerator in a fifty-foot root cellar, and home-school the children. Vanquish any thoughts that this is a ragtag settlement—the buildings are professionally constructed, environmentally friendly, clean, and very attractive.

Hinduism is one of the world's oldest religions, dating back to 3000 BCE. The word Hindu refers to the people and culture of the Indus Valley, which borders on India and Pakistan. Hinduism is an umbrella term for those who follow any of the different practices that worship a pantheon of gods and goddesses. Hatha yoga and Ayurveda are rooted in the teachings of Hinduism, and the two have always been closely aligned and complementary. Yoga means union, and Hatha yoga prescribes an ascetic lifestyle and specific techniques that act to unite inner polarities, thereby banishing dualism and the false ego more quickly than is possible on a casual spiritual path. Ayurveda, "the science of life," is a system of preventive medicine and health care that dates back thousands of years. The goal of both practices is to cleanse and purify the body in order for the Prana, or life force, to be fully experienced. The ultimate goal is enlightenment and union with Braham, the One Supreme Reality.

Enlightenment is reached by piercing the veil of the illusion of separateness. It results in freedom, compassion, and contentment. To reach enlightenment takes "heroic effort" and discipline. Traditionally, an ashram allows the space and time to pursue enlightenment because the seeker is removed from the busyness and distractions of life on the outside. The natural setting supports spiritual growth, allowing the studies to take root.

Bahagavan, or Baba as he is affectionately called, and his wife Amma are both enlightened Masters. As the guru, Bahagavan imparts spiritual knowledge, lessons, and practices to the group. The ashram carefully follows a traditional model where the guru is released from the management of the ashram and from the responsibilities of providing for his family so that his time can be spent strictly on the spiritual welfare of the community. By limiting his hand in finances and management, power is not consolidated in one person. For the system to work, the followers must have faith that Bahagavan is enlightened, but also must remain aware to insure they are growing under the Master.

Gopala Krishna manages the Kaya Kalpa retreats and is trained in healing by Bahagavan. Gopala grew up in Manhattan and New Jersey, majored in psychology, studied Chinese and Ayurvedic herbs, and learned from a variety of healers during his travels in India. Several women at the hermitage have studied healing modalities and assist in the retreats. Gopala's role is to make a diagnosis based on Ayurvedic methods, create an individualized treatment plan, apply treatments, and monitor guests regularly. He consults every day with Bahagavan on courses of action.

Hridaya Hermitage has an environmentally-friendly retreat cabin. All structures are built by the community.

The classic Kaya Kalpa is a ninety-day process entailing thirty days each for cleansing and purifying, rejuvenation, and integration. Few modern people can commit to ninety days, so the basic formula is maintained within whatever timeframe is feasible. At Hridaya, a one-week minimum is required, and longer stays are encouraged for deeper healing.

The Kaya Kalpa methods developed over thousands of years of practice as a way for sages and yogis to slow aging, maintain perfect health, delay death, and theoretically avoid physical death completely. The idea of physical immortality is shocking to most Westerners, but conceivable in Hinduism. Deepak Chopra has subtly introduced the concept to the West with his books on Ayurveda that include *Grow Younger, Live Longer; Perfect Health;* and *Ageless Body, Timeless Mind.*

One of the assumptions of Kaya Kalpa is that toxicity is the ultimate cause of the body's demise. A cleansed, purified, and rejuvenated body creates a homeostasis for top-level functioning. The more purified a body is, the more Prana is available to it. The Prana positively affects the health of the physical, subtle, and causal bodies. The physical body is a container for the subtle body, which consists of 72,000 arteries that saturate the entire physical body with life and light force. These arteries are energetically similar to meridians in acupuncture. The seven chakras, or energy centers, are also part of the subtle body. The causal body is the force that connects spirit and matter. Prana keeps the three bodies in balance.

The Kaya Kalpa treatment begins two to three weeks prior to

guests' arrival time. Gopala makes dietary suggestions depending on the reason for their visit, and everyone is requested to refrain from eating meat or poultry for at least two weeks beforehand. The first process is cleansing, and meat slows the process considerably because it creates mucous and putrefies in the large intestine. When cleansing is slowed, a healing crisis occurs, causing the patient to feel physically ill as toxins are released from the cells but not eliminated from the body quickly.

Upon a person's arrival, cleansing is initiated with fruit and vegetable juices, herbal formulas, and traditional Ayurvedic bodywork that combine to release stored toxins. They are removed from the body using saunas, gentle purgatives, and herbal enemas. Mornings start with independent cleaning of the ears, eyes, and nose. After the initial period of cleansing, the treatments focus on purifying the body through herbs, oils, foods, and bodywork. In the final stage, rejuvenation occurs by adjusting to a building diet.

Each day there are several hours of treatments. A daily diagnosis is made using Ayurvedic tests for pulse, palpitations, spinal check, and skin. Every day a sauna is followed by a dip in the stream behind the treatment cabins. Other methods employed are skin brushing, poultices, and spinal adjustments. Head, foot, and body massages are done using medicated oils imported from Kerala, India. Herbal formulas are tailored to a guest's needs and are imported from a reputable source in India that Gopala has a relationship with through his visits. Medicated ghee (clarified butter) softens the stools and minimizes digestive actions.

Meals are vegetarian and organic. The offerings change throughout the retreat and are determined largely by a person's dosha. Simply put, the doshas are where the mind and body communicate; every thought and action leaves a mark on the physiology. The three doshas are Vata, Pitta, and Kapha. They have thousands of functions in the mind-body. Each individual has a dosha type and is dominated by one, or is a blend of two or three. Once a person's dosha is determined, the Ayurvedic practitioner will prescribe certain foods and lifestyle adjustments that will keep the dosha in balance, which is the key to perfect health. For example, a Vata tends to be thin, cold, constipated, cheerful, excitable, enthusiastic, and sleep lightly. Balance is achieved through regular habits, quiet periods, rest, warmth, and food that is warm, fairly heavy, and soothing. Meals at Hridaya are tailored both to the stage of healing and to a guest's dosha.

Soma is an integral part of Kaya Kalpa healing. The term is frequently debated; at Hridaya, it refers to an elixir of fresh juices taken with herbs. Soma is imbued with Prana for rejuvenation when it is ingested properly.

When guests are not in treatments, they are actively pursuing health. There are two one-hour sessions of Hatha yoga, which is often supervised to insure that the proper technique is followed. Independent breath work is essential. The process of healing is enhanced exponentially by the proper use of breath and postures. Meditation, consultations, free time for rest and walking, and education are scheduled into each day.

Gopala states that to the best of his knowledge there are no other healing facilities in North America that are offering authentic Kaya Kalpa. The knowledge is quickly being lost or compromised.

Hridaya values allopathic medicine and does not discourage its clients from purusing and following medical advice. Clients visit due to an illness, to heal after surgery, or as preventive action. People are not good candidates if they have terminal illnesses and are seeking a miracle cure or have unrealistic expectations. Hridaya is spiritually based, but guests can be of any religious persuasion or none at all. They come from all over the country, are equally male and female, and are over forty, which is an appropriate age to practice cleansing. Gopala asks that everyone make a commitment to the process, as well as to the pre- and post-recommendations.

Kaya Kalpa treatments are also available in the home for people who cannot travel due to illness or special circumstances. Two practitioners stay in the home for a minimum of one week. Several hours of treatments are given daily along with supervision for Hatha yoga, breath work, meditation, and personal cleansing techniques. Vegetarian meals are prepared, and the home is transformed into an environment conducive to healing.

The second type of retreat offered at Hridaya is the Kaya-sadhana, which refers to the cultivation of the body through yoga. This Yoga Lifestyle retreat offers aspiring yogis opportunity to focus on achieving their highest potential. The instruction, practice, and healing are derived from the ancient Natha Siddha tradition in India, and guests are under the tutelage of Bahagavan. The teachings are enhanced and supported by seclusion, nature, diet, meditation, worship, and community.

Practice includes specific techniques such as kriya (purification), asana (posture), banda (energetic locks), madras (energetic seals), and pranayama (extension of the life force). When these techniques are properly performed, they initiate kundalini rising, which is an energetic force that begins from the root chakra at the spine's base and moves up through each chakra to the crown chakra at the top of the head. Rising kundalini purifies and transforms the physical and subtle bodies.

Both retreats demand a ratio of three practitioners to each

guest, thereby ensuring instruction, monitoring, and attention. Due to the nature of their retreats, only two guests are accommodated at a time. The cedar retreat cabins are constructed to be chemical free—the insulation is cotton batting from recycled blue jeans; wall paint is all-natural and clay-based. The cabin has an aesthetically warm practice space with a wood burning stove, a slate hearth, pillows, and candles. On either side are the entrances to two comfortable, private bedrooms, each with its own bathroom. There are composting toilets and a sink, but water is brought in from one of the ashram's five wells. Each bedroom has a private entrance and deck.

The treatment cabin is across the road and has the same type of construction and pleasing warmth. Here guests receive massages, herbal treatments, and poultices. Close by is the sauna. Guests are encouraged to take advantage of nature by exploring the grounds and hiking the spiraling trail that leads to the hilltop where many of the ashram's ceremonies take place. Just walking through the grounds is a pleasure, with the gurgling streams, a tiny bridge, the sounds of undisturbed nature, and the many shrines that decorate the landscape.

Hridaya is sustained completely by the donations of the retreat guests. The community felt uncomfortable charging set rates and decided that each person should decide what the service is worth and pay at the end of their stay. Practitioners at Hridaya vow to give the best care to their highest ability and, in return, they trust in the law of reciprocal giving and receiving. The average donation for Kaya Kalpa in 2003 was $300 per day depending on the length of stay, while Kaya-sadhana guests donated $150–$200 per day.

Imagine the restorative value of being removed from the hectic distractions of everyday life, the relief of being able to commit with singular focus to growth and healing, the benefits of having experienced practitioners attuned to specific personal needs, and the peace found in the beauty of nature. Hridaya Hermitage offers the rare opportunity for authentic Kaya Kalpa and immersion in a Yogi lifestyle that cannot be duplicated.

Cost: 2004 - Suggested donation is $150–$300 per day, depending on the length of stay.

Contact Information:

Hridaya Hermitage
243 Greenwood Brook Road
Industry, Maine 04938
Telephone: (207) 542-6606 (cell phone)
Web site: *hridayahermitage.com*
E-mail: info@hridayahermitage.com

Meetingbrook Dogen and Francis Hermitage – Zen and Christian

Camden

Tourists flock to Camden by the thousands, drawn to its scenic harbor, good food, and shops. If they happen to wander into the eighteenth-century cape that is home to the Meetingbrook Bookshop and Bakery, they would immediately recognize it as a place where locals find community. On any given day, the bulletin board overflows with announcements of art, music, and religious events. People relax on cozy seating, sip organic coffee, and munch on homemade snacks while chatting about books, the news, or each other. Discussion groups gather on the deck overlooking Camden Harbor to explore spiritual topics, while lingerers browse through bookshelves filled predominantly with spiritual titles. This appealing and unique gathering place is sister to the Dogen and Francis Hermitage four miles away on Ragged Mountain, and the two make up a single nonprofit, tax-exempt religious organization.

The cofounders Saskia Huising and Bill Halpin are lay people following a religious calling. At Meetingbrook they have created a place for the side-by-side practice of Zen meditation and Christian contemplative prayer, conversations that enrich religious life, and correspondence through spiritual books, letters, poetry, and journals.

When Huising and Halpin moved to Camden in 1992, they knew their life path was one of monastic spirituality, which is the single-hearted pursuit of God. They opened the bookshop in 1996 and held silent sittings, while their home was their personal hermitage. In 1998, they expanded their goals by obtaining tax-exempt status and developed plans to turn their homestead into a hermitage that welcomed visitors.

The hermitage consists of a farm-house, barn, and cabin, and sits on two-and-a-half acres of land. There are long-range plans to turn the barn into a space for conversations and meditation, to build solitude huts, and to acquire additional property. Currently, the cabin serves as a chapel and zendo. It is located on a path leading into the woods and is small and charming with a screened-in porch. Inside, it is sparse, clean, clear, and adorned with a simple Buddhist altar. Further along the path is Meetingbrook's namesake—a brook that divides around an island and rejoins itself to form a single brook once again.

The simple chapel-zendo at Meetingbrook is adorned with an altar featuring Buddha.

Shortly after Meetingbrook became a nonprofit organization, Huising and Halpin chose vows that are loosely derived from the Rules of Benedict: poverty, chastity, and obedience. Their vows are contemplation with the promise of simplicity, conversation with the promise of integrity, and correspondence with the promise of faithful engagement. These vows, based on their roles as lay people, inform the intentions and activities of Meetingbrook and are renewed each year.

The two traditions that form their religion are Christianity and Zen Buddhism. Halpin was a Franciscan monk for five years in the early 1960s and has practiced Zen since 1965. Huising has been practicing since the mid-1980s. Both were inspired by Thomas Merton, who was one of the most prominent Christian contemplatives of the 20th century and is recognized for taking his values out of the monastery through social and political activism. Merton was largely responsible for opening intermonastery dialogue between Buddhists and Catholics, and he forged the way for the sharing of ideas between faith traditions.

The models that Huising and Halpin chose for the integration of Christianity and Buddhism are Saint Francis of Assisi (1183–1226) and Dogen (1200–1253). Francis is the patron saint of animals and the environment. He is honored for his closeness to nature, his belief that God is felt and found in the natural world, and his desire to be of service. Dogen brought Soto Zen from China to Japan, where it was stripped to the essentials of silent sitting, stilling the mind, and receptive attention, all of which lends itself to dovetailing with other traditions.

At the Hermitage, Zen and Christianity inform and infuse each other. The dogma, doctrine, and ritual of Catholicism are downplayed while the monastic traditions of mysticism and contemplation are held in high regard. Though Zen is not mystical and does not speak of God, it comes to the same place through present-time awareness, an empty, clear mind, and observation of the conditioned responses of the ego. The Christian practice of contemplative prayer, which is resting in the presence of God and intuitively looking inward with a listening heart, is practiced side by side with the emptying and stillness of Zen.

Everything that Meetingbrook Bookshop and Hermitage have to offer is open to people of all paths. No formal membership is required to use the cabin for meditation or attend retreats and/or discussion groups. All of the offerings are free, open, and informal. A loose-knit association of people forms their local community, though visitors from away are welcome.

The cabin is open at all times for meditation, prayer, or contemplation. The only requirement is that guests enter, sit, and leave in silence. On Saturday mornings from 6:45 a.m. to 8:00 a.m., the practice is *Lectio Divina* (reading of scriptures and sutras), and on Sunday evenings from 6:00 p.m. to 8:00 p.m., the practice includes sitting and walking meditation, heart sutra chanting, table reading, silent eating, conversation, and compline chanting.

The bookshop hosts conversations five days a week. Books are discussed on Saturday mornings, and in the afternoon, "Tea, Poetry, and Literature" is on the agenda. The topics from Tuesday through Friday, 5:30 p.m. to 6:30 p.m., are Buddhism, Christianity, personal paths and practices, and inter-religious dialogue, respectively.

Meetingbrook offers mindfulness retreats once a month from 6:00 a.m. to 2:30 p.m. The retreats entail six sittings, a work period, readings, mealtime, and circle reflection. Occasionally, longer retreats are scheduled, though seldom with a specific theme, allowing people to come to their own wisdom through practice and conversation. In suitable weather, a twenty-six-foot sailboat is used for spontaneous retreats lasting several hours or planned retreats with overnight camping on a Penobscot Bay island.

Each day Huising and Halpin follow a disciplined practice that they invite those present to join. Their daily practice entails silent sitting, liturgy of the hours (reading psalms throughout the day), conversation, *Lectio Divina,* walking meditation, and engaged service (intentional daily interaction).

The Meetingbrook Bookshop and Bakery feeds the mind and

spirit with a wide array of books specializing in traditional and non-traditional spirituality, philosophy, world religions and scriptures, contemplative and meditative traditions, poetry, prayer, art, ecology, nature, myth, and folklore. They also carry religiously themed music, art, icons, and magazines. Delightful pastries, cakes, muffins, soups, and breads nourish the body.

Huising and Halpin have created an original and inviting community that is accessible to all individuals; people do not have to be rooted in Zen and/or Christianity to feel welcome. The Meetingbrook Dogen and Francis Hermitage encourage uniting with God through contemplation and meditation, and provide people with a hospitable environment to connect with one another through sharing insights, experiences, and personal paths.

Costs: 2005 - All activities are free and open.
Donations are gratefully accepted for the continuance and deepening of Meetingbrook.

Contact Information:

Meetingbrook Bookshop and Bakery
50 Bayview Street
Camden, Maine 04843
Telephone: (207) 236-6808
Web site: *www.meetingbrook.org*
E-mail: mtgbrook@midcoast.com

The cabin at Meetingbrook Dogen and Hermitage serves as both a chapel and a zendo.

Morgan Bay Zendo – Buddhism

Surry

The footpath through the woods leading to Morgan Bay Zendo is well worn by those visiting this place of exceptional beauty and calm. The first indication that there is a commitment to quiet contemplation is that all vehicles are left at the street-side parking lot. Upon emerging from the woods, one enters a cleared area with two low-lying buildings that gracefully merge with the natural surroundings.

The Zendo (or meditation hall), a meeting hall, five cabins, and twelve campsites sit on ten acres of land. The acreage holds an apple orchard, moss garden, and paths to the cabins, but is otherwise left untouched. The buildings border a pond, and unobtrusive sculptures dot the landscape.

The Zendo is designed with the clean simplicity that is the hallmark of Asian architecture. An ambience of serenity and balance is created by the use of wood and tile. A simple altar marks the front, and elevated platforms with cushions ring the perimeter of a center island. A reception area has shelves for belongings and shoes, along with information introducing newcomers to the expected behavior, manners, and practices of the Zendo.

The meeting hall has a large room, kitchen, composting toilets, showers, and an apartment. Scattered throughout the woods are five rustic cabins. The cabins offer few amenities beyond shelter from the elements, but are inviting nevertheless.

The sculptures found throughout the grounds were created by Lenore Thomas Strauss, one of the early students of the Zendo, which was originally named Moonspring Hermitage. It was founded in 1971 by Walter Nowick. Nowick taught Japanese Zen and created a full-time residential community that had forty students at its peak.

Today, Morgan Bay Zendo is a non-profit corporation administered by the Zendo Sangha and Board. (Sangha refers to a community of people.) The board shares responsibilities and decisions. Upkeep and expenses are derived from retreat fees, membership dues, and donations.

Morgan Bay Zendo integrates elements from Ch'an, Vipassana, and Zen Buddhism. Buddhism seeks to understand the nature of suffering and the path away from suffering towards a more balanced life. The practice of keeping present with breath or moment-to-moment experience leads to a gradual awakening. Vipassana simply means insight meditation and comes from the Buddhist traditions in Burma and Thailand. Zen developed in Japan, and Ch'an is Chinese Zen. All of these elements bring practitioners into a silent space and encourage mindfulness in meditation as well as in daily life. Practice brings contact and engagement with the world as it exists.

Though the emphasis is on those three forms of Buddhism, people from all traditions are welcome. A distinctive aspect of the Zendo is that there is no single teacher. Programs and their implementation, beginner instruction, and discussion leaders are all responsibilities that are fulfilled by the board and the membership. This creates fertile ground for learning as the variety of retreat offerings indicate.

On Sundays, from 8:00 a.m. to 10:00 a.m., the Zendo is open for meditation practice. Visitors do not enter once practice has begun but wait until a bell is rung to announce the end of sitting and the beginning of walking meditation. Walking meditation begins slowly and like other Buddhist practices, calls for concentration and awareness. The instructions recommend that focus be directed to the body sinking into the foot if grounding is desired, or to be aware of the lifting of the foot to decrease feelings of lethargy. The walking meditation balances periods of sitting and shakes off sleepiness. It starts slow and gradually moves to a jaunt that is just quick enough to increase heart rate. Walking meditation is followed by twenty minutes of sitting meditation.

Afterwards, the Prajanaparamita Heart Sutra is handed to each practitioner in a methodical and ritualized manner. The Heart Sutra is chanted each Sunday to the beat of a large fish drum. The power of the Heart Sutra is derived from the chanting, though this does not discount the written words, which contain the often-read phrase, "form is emptiness, and emptiness is form." Its beautiful and hypnotic paradoxical text has served as a mantra for many different traditions.

Each week a reading drawn from different Buddhist traditions closes the practice period and is the basis for a thirty-minute discussion in the main meeting hall. The end of the practice involves bowing while seated, standing and dusting off the cushion, then bowing twice more. Movement is always clockwise around the room and upon exiting, a final bow is made to the Buddha at the altar. Tea is served in the meeting hall as people gather to discuss the reading.

The Zendo opens each year on the first Sunday in May to celebrate Buddha's birthday. A conscious decision has been made to include children and young adults in the sangha's activities, so this event is geared to children. Families chant together and may offer flowers to the baby Buddha or wash him in sweet tea. A procession of banners and drumming adds to the celebration as does cake, cider, and a potluck brunch.

In early November, a memorial service honoring the deceased is held. After the morning practice, the Heart Sutra is chanted and daffodils are planted in the apple orchard. Buddha's enlightenment is marked in early December with eight days of more intense practice. The year ends on New Year's Day with a celebration that is open to the public. During the winter months, sittings continue at a local United Methodist church.

When open, a workday is scheduled for the first Sunday of every month. Families are encouraged to volunteer their time for the upkeep of the grounds and buildings. Working mindfully is considered an integral part of Buddhism and is a way to show generosity and an open heart. The teaching of being present in each moment includes being present during tasks that can be considered tedious. One is taught to approach each task as if washing the baby Buddha.

Retreats occur approximately seven times a year from May through August. They range from one to three days in length, and up to thirty-five people can be accommodated. People may choose a cabin, a campsite, or local accommodations with a daily commute. Some retreat topics are: *Introduction to Zen, Zen Meditation, Zen and Yoga, Advanced Zero Balancing, Being Present with Our Children, Zen and Native Americans, Loving Kindness, Write Meditation, Young Adults age 14 to 22,* and *Women's Retreat.*

Thich Nhat Hanh said the next Buddha will be the sangha. Commitment to that prophecy is evident at the Morgan Bay Zendo where sincere effort is made to include families, the greater community, and people from all traditions. The serenity of Surry coupled with the natural beauty and stillness of the Morgan Bay Zendo create an atmosphere in harmony with retreats and mindful practice.

Prices: 2005 - Membership is $45.00
Retreats vary in price depending on their length and the number of meals. They range from $10.00 for one day to $165.00 for three days.

Contact Information:

Morgan Bay Zendo
532 Morgan Bay Road
Surry, Maine 04684
Telephone: (207) 374-9963
Web site: *www.morganbayzendo.org*
E-mail: info@morganbayzendo.org

About the Area:

Surry is a small Down East town that is approximately thirty minutes from Mount Desert Island. Much closer is Blue Hill, where visitors can find high quality art and craft galleries, and a decidedly alternative culture. The area has an abundance of natural beauty without the crowds.

Sculptures are found along the trails at Morgan Bay Zendo.

The Morgan Bay Zendo gracefully merges with its natural surroundings.

Shambhala Center - Buddhism

Brunswick and Portland

The romantic name of Shambhala is from the legendary king-dom found in Tibetan folklore. In the ancient stories, the king of Shambhala was visited by Shakyamuni Buddha, who taught him the path of meditation and compassion. Shambhala became a place where peace, prosperity, and wisdom reigned. This utopian world was the inspiration for a unique type of Buddhism inspired by the vision of its founder, Chögyam Trungpa Rinpoche, one of the first teachers to bring Buddhism to the West. He based Shambhala on Tibetan Buddhism, but geared it specifically to people who lead secular lives and did not have the time or the inclination to study Buddhism aca-demically in order to achieve deeper levels of understanding. To insure that all would feel welcome, he stressed that Shambhala teachings were not limited to any one religion, culture, or era, and that humanity would move forward as individuals learned to access their innate wis-dom and basic goodness.

Today, Chögyam Trungpa's vision has become manifested in Shambhala International, which has approximately six thousand members, one hundred fifty meditation centers, six residential centers, a monastery, and a prolific publishing house. The Shambhala Centers in Brunswick and Portland are authorized by Shambhala International to offer instruction and support.

Chögyam Trungpa's idealistic goals were realized only after a series of events that started with his harrowing escape from Tibet in 1959 at the age of twenty. The young monk was already the head of a group of important monasteries and a highly regarded teacher of a form of Tibetan Buddhism that stressed meditation. The 1960s was a defining period for him. He was a scholar at Oxford University in England, was partially paralyzed in a car accident, gave up his monastic vows, married, and moved to North America. The next decade proved to be even more eventful as he traveled extensively laying the groundwork for what would become Shambhala and wrote a number of books on his teachings.

The experimental mood of the 1970s provided Chögyam Trungpa with enthusiastic and receptive students, and he is often credited with introducing Tibetan Buddhism to Westerners. His teachings combined meditation, spiritual training, and traditional Tibetan Buddhism in a way that his Western audience found easy to understand. During this period, he established Karmê Chöling, a meditation center in Vermont that offers advanced programs, internships, and retreats. He also opened Naropa University in Colorado, an accredited university with an emphasis on contemplation, and in Cape Breton, he founded Gambo Abbey, the first Tibetan-style monastery in North America. The number of local meditation centers grew with the number of interested practitioners.

As his ideas developed, he created a system for study and practice called Shambhala Training. The intent was to bring a deep level of contemplative practice to a large number of people. With the establishment of the Nalanda Foundation, he encouraged students to integrate activities into their daily lives such as Japanese archery, calligraphy, flower arranging, tea ceremony, dance, theater, psychology, and health.

Chögyam Trungpa died in 1987, shortly after moving the organization's operations to Nova Scotia. This highly productive, complex man wrote fourteen books. His oldest son, Sakyong Mipham Rinpoche is leading the Shambhala International society, a role he had been preparing for since childhood.

Philosophically, Shambhala is basically Tibetan Buddhism. It differs in that the Shambhala Training stresses the ancient Tibetan secular tradition of warriorship. In Shambhala, the warrior is brave and courageous with a heart that is so soft and vulnerable that a mosquito landing on it would cause pain. Bravery is needed to face and defeat self-deception, and a tender heart requires sensitivity to life, including both the sorrow and the joy. Therefore, the warrior is capable of fearless action based on awareness, gentleness, and kindness.

The first five levels of Shambhala Training are called *The Heart of the Warrior*. During weekend workshops, the foundation of meditative practice is established, and the basics of practicing warriorship in daily life are taught. The following are descriptions of the first five levels of Shambhala:

Level One: *The Art of Being Human*. Experiencing the world as sacred and seeing basic goodness as a birthright.

Level Two: *Birth of the Warrior*. Recognizing habitual patterns and discovering fearlessness.

Level Three: *Warrior in the World*. Developing confidence in all aspects of daily life.

Level Four: *Awakened Heart*. Allowing the heart and intuition to open so that one communicates fully with the world.

Level Five: *Open Sky*. Trusting one's self and one's existence and genuinely caring for others.

The next level, *The Sacred Path of the Warrior*, entails six weekend workshops and is followed by *The Warrior Assembly*, which is a two-week residential program. Students interested in intensive study attend seminary, which is three months of training and practice. Shambhala International offers a number of workshops and retreats throughout the year for all levels of students.

A unique aspect of Shambhala is Nalanda, which evolved from the Nalanda Foundation established by Chögyam Trungpa, and integrates secular activities into daily life for their contemplative value. Students can choose from four major categories that encompass a variety of interests: art, health, education, and business. They may learn an array of artistic skills or chose from offerings such as contemplative psychotherapy, early childhood education, or leadership training. Course work, programs, or workshops at Naropa University, Shambhala institutes, and in local or regional meditation centers support all four areas.

In order to become an authorized Shambhala Center, a potential center applies to Shambhala International, and guidelines must be strictly followed. To maintain the integrity of the teachings, the new center's teachers must fulfill training requirements that generally take two years to complete. The center must provide members with a Meditation Instructor who meets with them individually to discuss their practice, what classes to choose, and their general progress. This service is free of charge, as is the meditation instruction to newcomers or to drop-ins who visit the center out of curiosity.

The Meditation Instructors begin students with instruction on how to physically and mentally prepare for meditation, which is practiced in the traditional manner of either sitting in stillness or walking, while focusing on the breath. The eyes stay open, but relaxed and directed to the floor at about a ten-foot distance. As thoughts arise, they are labeled as such, and released. Shambhala teaches that meditation, when practiced regularly, allows for the recognition of the ego. As that occurs, the practitioner learns to quiet the ego and see more readily his or her

60

projections onto the world. Eventually, meditation leads to more conscious living, which results in self-acceptance and ever-expanding compassion, wisdom, and virtue. As higher levels of practice are reached, the meditation becomes devotional, an equivalent to prayer.

Buddhism teaches access to the world without projecting onto it, which is conditioning that is difficult, if not impossible, to avoid completely. Everything rises and falls, change is ceaseless, and suffering arises from attachments. A Buddhist practitioner hopes to move beyond the ego. The continued practice of Buddhism can lead to an inner transformation that can be at times quite dramatic. Students are therefore encouraged to periodically consult with an experienced meditation instructor as they develop their own regular meditation practice.

The Brunswick Shambhala Center has followed the strict guidelines of Shambhala International to create a serene and lovely meditation space. Tibetan traditions are honored by the Eastern decor, the conscious use of space, and the altar, which is a work of art. Pillows used for meditation are designed especially for Americans who have difficulty sitting cross-legged for long periods of time.

Both the Brunswick and Portland Shambhala Centers offer *Heart of the Warrior* training, which is an introduction to meditation offered in a series of five weekend programs (Levels I through V). Participants are given the tools needed to establish a personal meditation discipline and to incorporate the principles of warriorship—gentleness, fearlessness, precision, and humor—into daily life. Each weekend includes meditation instruction and practice, talks, discussion groups, individual interviews, and selected meals.

Excluding the summer months, weekend workshops are regularly scheduled on a variety of interesting topics including flower arranging, Japanese archery, meditation practice, and the *Art of War*. They also celebrate significant days throughout the year, such as the Tibetan New Year. Most of the workshops ask that participants have had some introduction to meditation or the permission of the instructor, but others have no prerequisites. The centers are open on Sundays from 9:00 a.m. to noon for group meditation, and the public is welcome.

Shambhala offers a path for students to follow and supportive individual guidance. Students move through the levels at their own pace, have a wide range of learning options, and workshop fees are very reasonable.

Prices: 2005 - Shambhala Training's *Heart of the Warrior* programs are two-and-a-half days and are $100, $80 for members, and $50/40 for repeats. Special events are listed on the web site and can last several hours, one day, two days, or occur in a series. Most workshops are priced at $35 with some ranging up to $75.

Contact Information:

Co-Director Eunice St, John
Shambhala Center
19 Mason Street
Brunswick, Maine 04011
Telephone: (207) 582-2203

For information about the Portland Shambhala Center:
Alan Holt
Telephone: (207) 780-6017
E-mail: alanaia@aol.com
Brunswick-Portland Center
Web site: *www.shambhalabp.org*
General information
Web site:*www.shambhala.org*

Sufi Order International - Sufism

Centers in Portland, Brunswick, and Portsmouth

The Sufi Order International (SOI) is an interreligious organization with the broad aim of reaching out with the Sufi message of love, harmony, and beauty. But, what exactly is Sufism? A Sufi will respond that it is a religion of the heart. Perhaps it is best exemplified by the whirling dervishes whom Americans will recognize from the pages of National Geographic. In their conical hats and swirling white gowns, dervishes spin on their axes in a ritual ceremony that symbolizes their rotation around God just as the planets circle the sun. Music, singing, chanting, and drumming accompany the dervishes as they dance and transform their bodies into doorways that receive the Beloved. In a state of trance prayer, they enter ecstatic communion with God.

Jeladuddin Rumi, the thirteenth-century Sufi poet, writer, and mystic also speaks to the heart of Sufism. His sensuous, inner-directed poems are saturated with love, longing, joy, and ecstasy directed at the Beloved. (Incidentally, Rumi is one of Americans' most popular poets.) Rumi's son founded the whirling dervishes, properly known as the Mevlevi dervishes, based on his father's teachings. Both Rumi and the dervishes had a profound impact on the classical music, art, and poetry of the Ottoman Empire. It is this essence of joyful celebration informed by spiritual discipline and the longing for direct experiences with the Divine that is embodied by SOI.

Sufism developed in the 9th century and is the mystical path of Islam. Possibly, it arose as a way to maintain simplicity as the Ottoman Empire gained wealth. Sufis believe that God resides in each soul and, in their early history, that belief led to their persecution as heretics. Their goal is to be close to the Beloved in life, as opposed to waiting for the afterlife, and to create a personal and passionate relationship with

God that imbues each moment.

Throughout its history, Sufism has been open to other religions, and influences from the Gnostics, Kabbalists, Knights Templar, and mystic Christians can be found in its teachings. This openness is reflected in Western Sufism, which is a universal religion that is less linked to Islam. Sufism arrived in the West in 1910 with the teachings of Hazrat Inayat Khan, who set the foundation for the SOI. Hazrat Inayat Khan, referred to as Murshid (teacher/guide), was initiated into the lineage of the Chishti Sufi Order of India. All legitimate Sufi schools have a chain of transmission that links students to the spiritual power of their antecedents. Murshid's teacher enjoined him to bring the Sufi message to the West by using his musical talent as a vehicle. He was a distinguished musician of classical Indian music and traveled extensively in Europe and America during the 1910s and '20s performing and spreading what he referred to as the Sufi Message.

Through his writings, classes, lectures, and interviews, Murshid introduced the West to the key elements of Sufism. He believed that the practices leading to self-knowledge, awakening, and love could be integrated into any religion. Western students were trained as spiritual guides, for in Sufism the path can be walked only with a teacher. The teachings convey that prayer, concentration, contemplation, and meditation bring an inner awakening of consciousness and conscience, which includes a desire to awaken all of humanity. The goal is to work towards unity through the realization that God is within each individual and connecting all of humanity.

Murshid left a body of knowledge and a structure in place that grew into SOI. His son, Pir Vilayat Inayat Khan (Pir refers to Teacher), assumed his father's work after years of formal education followed by training and study with the son of his father's grandmaster. Pir Vilayat passed away in 2004, leaving his son Pir Zia Inayat Khan to lead SOI.

Today, SOI continues to foster Murshid's philosophy that this is not the time to advance any single religion, belief, or church but to come together to recognize the oneness of humanity. Members of SOI are encouraged to explore their religious roots and to continue practicing the religion of their choice as they move forward on the Sufi path. Through schools, centers, retreats, and seminars, SOI is not teaching religion as much as it is teaching a point of view that recognizes the truth found in all major traditions.

Murshid established Ten Sufi Thoughts that act as a container for an interreligious philosophy. (SOI is very sensitive to gender-based language and changed its prayers to be gender-neutral but have not changed the words of Murshid, who wrote at a time when the masculine form was universal.)

1. There is One God, the Eternal, the Only Being, none exists save He.
2. There is One Master, the Guiding Spirit of all Souls, Who constantly leads His followers towards the light.
3. There is only One Holy Book, the sacred manuscript of nature, the only scripture that can enlighten the reader.
4. There is only One Religion, the unswerving progress in the right direction toward the ideal, which fulfils the life purpose of the soul.
5. There is One Law, the law of reciprocity, which can be observed by a selfless conscience, together with a sense of awakened justice.
6. There is One Brotherhood, the human brotherhood that unites the children of earth indiscriminately in the Brotherhood of God.
7. There is One Moral, the love which springs forth from self-denial and blooms in the deeds of beneficence.
8. There is One Object of Praise, the beauty which uplifts the heart of its worshippers through all aspects from the seen to the unseen.
9. There is One Truth, the true knowledge of our being, with and without, which is the essence of all wisdom.
10. There is One Path, the annihilation of the false ego in the real, which raises the mortal to immortality in which presides all perfection.

As a basis for training and study, Murshid established five concentrations: Esoteric School, Healing Order, Ziraat, Universal Worship, and Kinship. A senior member of SOI heads each concentration and is assigned by Pir Zia. There are no gurus in SOI, as no one is infallible. Spiritual guides go through a two-year training and are tested and certified by SOI.

All of SOI's offerings are open to non-members, but when the student, or mureed, is ready to make a serious commitment, he or she is initiated, and then a SOI spiritual guide is invited to work with the mureed. The initiation connects and attunes the mureed to the lineage of masters. The guide does not advise or direct the life of the mureed but prescribes specific spiritual practices and teachings that lead the mureed towards reliance on his or her own inner guidance. At the time of initiation, the spiritual guide gives the mureed a name that relates to an attribute of God. The names are often chosen from the Ninety-Nine Names of God, which are the attributes of the Divine. Examples of names are ar-Rahman for all-Beneficent, al-Karim for the Generous, al-Wahid for the Unique, an-Nur for the Light, and al-

Muqsit for the Equitable. The Arabic name has an energetic effect that allows the mureed to develop that attribute more fully. Much of Sufi practice emphasizes glorifying and exalting God's attributes, thereby arousing those qualities within oneself.

The Alchemical Retreat is central to the spiritual development of the initiate. It is done in solitude for three to forty days under the direction of a certified SOI retreat guide and at a designated retreat center. A curriculum directs the guide and initiate through practices that require discipline and fortitude. The retreats are not relaxing vacations away from the rat race but are intended to assist in the intense and difficult work of self-examination, a rehearsal for life.

Initiates have the option of choosing one of the five activities to which they are most drawn. In the Esoteric School, mureeds focus on personal transformation and, through meditation practices, discover attributes that are dormant and break habitual habits of the false ego. All guides and teachers are from the Esoteric School.

Murshid developed the Healing Order for those who have a divine calling to heal others. Healings are primarily done from a distance using prayer, attunement, breath, and concentration. Requests for healings are free and open to anyone. The Sufi Healing Order serves fourteen countries and has organized twenty-six national conferences on integrating science and spirit.

The religious activity of SOI is through the Universal Worship or Church of All Churches concentration whose chief function is to ordain ministers after a long process of training and study. Once ordained, ministers can perform marriages and other sacraments. Universal Worship Services are performed by SOI ministers and are open to all. The services are held whenever Sufis come together for retreats, camps, or school and are offered on a regular schedule in many communities. In the service, a single altar holds a candle and a sacred text of each of the world's major traditions: Hinduism, Buddhism, Judaism, Christianity, and Zoroastrianism. In recent years, Earth, Goddess, and Native American Spirituality have been added to many altars. There are also two candles, one for the Spirit of Guidance and one for the God of Light. Each service has a theme and is divided into three parts. To begin, the candles are lit and an invocation is stated. This is followed by attunement to each of the traditions through prayer, music, dance, and/or performance. A reading from each of the sacred texts that illuminates the theme closes the service.

In Ziraat, farming is a metaphor for cultivating the soul by nourishing the divine seed found within each person. Plowing, sowing, reaping, threshing, and gathering have significance for blossoming self-awareness that seeks balance between the spiritual and the material.

Initiates to Ziraat perform daily practices and express reverence for air, fire, earth, water, and ether through breathing exercises, meditation, and initiation rites.

The Kinship activity focuses on compassion and responsibility to one another. Kinship provides the public with community services, schools, retreat centers, food banks, soup kitchens, transformational theater, counseling, birthing, and health clinics. The Prison Book Fund in the United States and the Hope Project in New Delhi are just two of the major ways they serve humanity.

One does not have to be a member in order to visit SOI Meditation Centers, and visitors should not feel pressured in that direction. Individual Sufi Centers develop their own variety of offerings: meditation, book discussions, poetry, chanting, song, prayer, and discussion. One can expect to find traditional Sufi practices and prayers that are done universally, such as Zikr and Wazifa. In Zikr, a phrase that glorifies God is repeated thirty-three or ninety-nine times as an act of remembrance. A divine quality is used in wazifa, a mantra, where the mureed attunes to the quality by first repeating it aloud, then silently, then letting it go and listening within.

The Northeast Region of SOI provides services for Maine, New Hampshire, Vermont, and Quebec. Teaching and retreat centers are sprinkled throughout the region and are led by trained and certified representatives. Meditation and Message classes are held weekly and/or monthly for all who wish to attend. Annual camps and twice-yearly retreats provide the opportunity to meditate, pray, and socialize.

In 1975, Pir Vilayat founded the Abode of the Message on four hundred acres in New Lebanon, New York. It is an intentional community of approximately seventy people who live within the complex or have built houses on the property. The Abode offers programs throughout the year, has regular meditation sessions, healing circles, esoteric classes, and Universal Worship Services. The retreat and conference center has accommodations ranging from campsites to bed-and-breakfast-style rooms. Guest rooms are available for $25 to $60 per day including meals, and guides are available to give tours.

The Suluk Academy, located at the Abode, was founded in 2003 to provide an intensive four-year program of study for individuals exhibiting a high level of commitment.

The studies are rooted in the Esoteric School and the legacy of Murshid. For those restrained by time, geography, or money, SOI provides E-mail classes, though they are not related to Suluk Academy.

Women may find SOI a particularly welcoming organization compared with other traditions that have not adjusted their outdated patriarchal views and language, or examined their practices for masculine bias. Murshid was a visionary who used the term "planetary consciousness" in the 1920s and spoke of the coming years as a time when women would lead humanity to higher evolution. He initiated women to the highest positions of his organization, and the high regard for women's spirituality is carried on in SOI. The Crystalis Connection: The Feminine Council of Sufi Order explores the effects of practices on women, experiments with various practice techniques, organizes retreats with female themes, and integrates feminine perspectives into Sufism.

The Sufi Order International offers meditation and teaching to all who are interested, but it is through a serious commitment that deep spiritual benefits are reaped. Initiates are attuned to a lineage of Masters, Saints, and Prophets from all traditions and are exposed to a wealth of esoteric and metaphysical teachings. They move toward understanding the true purpose of life while being assisted by trained guides who support and encourage their development by prescribing practices designed to bring progressive awareness and awakening.

Guided retreats allow for profound transformation, while camps, workshops, and Universal Worship Services provide community. Women will find a responsive organization that is forward looking and flexible. Above all, mureeds will find a personal and passionate mystical path leading to a joyful, divine heart.

Costs: 2005 - All activities are free and open.
Donations are gratefully accepted.

Contact Information:

Sufi Order International Web site: *www.sufiorder.org*

Call of the Beloved Meditation Center
70 Main Street
S. Berwick, Maine 03908
Malika Serrano
Telephone: (207) 384-4828 or (603) 433-5525
E-mail: onebismillah@msn.com

The Divine Light Center
31 Bostwick Road
Brunswick, Maine 04011
Nur Allah Sarah Wood
Telephone: (207) 729-7906
E-mail: woodbess@yahoo.com

The Dances of Universal Peace

    The Dances of Universal Peace celebrate the sacred found in spiritual traditions throughout the world and were started in the 1960s by Samuel L. Lewis, who was a Sufi Murshid and a Rinzai Zen Master. He was inspired by the feminist modern dancer Ruth St. Denis and by the Sufi Message of Hazrat Inayat Khan. In the 1970s, the collection included fifty dances; today there are over five hundred.

    There are no audiences as the dances are participatory. They focus on the themes of peace, healing, community, harmony, and the unity that underlies all traditions. Sacred phrases, chants, music, and movements from around the world and across time are used to bring people together and attune them to their spiritual essence.

    The Dances have spread throughout the world and are performed in North and South America, Europe, Eastern Europe, the former Soviet Union, Japan, India, Pakistan, Australia, and New Zealand. In the United States, forty to sixty grassroots groups meet weekly or monthly. Gatherings are regularly held in Portland and Portsmouth, New Hampshire.

More information can be found at *www.dancesofuniversalpeace.org*

Coming Together: Communities

Amish

Shakers

St. Anthony's Monastery
and Shrines

Wabanaki Confederacy

Amish - Anabaptist

Smyrna

Route 2 in Smyrna has not been the same since five Amish families arrived in 1996 to begin a settlement. The steadily growing community has rural Smyrna humming with activity. New farms dot the rolling hills, and at least a half dozen businesses provide Amish and locals alike with goods and services. The newcomers have not disrupted the slow pace of life in northern Maine; in fact, they have enhanced it with their horse-drawn buggies and their rejection of even the most elemental of modern conveniences—electricity.

The Amish's desire to be separate from the world dates back to their early history. The group emerged from the radical changes that were brought on by the Protestant Reformation, which was sparked by Martin Luther in 1517. Luther was appalled when the Catholic Church sold "indulgences" that were purchased to shorten the time souls spent in purgatory. He wrote his "Ninety-Five Theses Upon Indulgences" and, within ten years, established the basic principles that formed the foundation of Protestantism. Luther rejected the notion that priests were needed as intermediaries to God, believed that salvation came through God's grace and not the church's sacraments, and relied on the Bible as the sole religious authority. Initially, Luther had not intended to start a church but wanted to reform the Catholic Church.

In Zurich, Ulrich Zwingli was strongly influenced by Luther but took a radical stance that called for a break with the Catholic Church and for the division of church and state. In 1525, a small group of dissidents re-baptized one another, believing that only adults were capable of vowing to dedicate their lives to Christ. They became known as the "Re-baptizers," or Anabaptists.

The Anabaptists were a threat to the social order because, with the Bible as their authority, they refused to take oaths of allegiance, serve in the military, or baptize their infants. By not baptizing infants, they denied the state its means of conferring citizenship and, therefore, taxation. At a time when there was a close alliance between church and state, re-baptizing was a capital offense and thousands of Anabaptists were executed through burning and drowning. They fled to remote areas where they were hunted down, tortured, and persecuted.

Menno Simons left the priesthood in 1536 to join their movement and became an important leader of the Anabaptists. Due to his influence, Anabaptists came to be called Mennonites. Simons continued to define Anabaptist principles: separation of church and state, pacifism, re-baptism, religious tolerance, separation from the world, simplicity, God as Love, and refusal to take oaths or serve in political office.

In 1693, a small group led by Jacob Amman left their Mennonite community, which they considered to have lost much of its discipline, to adopt more rigorous practices. The group settled along the Southern Rhine in Switzerland and became known as the Amish after their leader Amman.

The first Amish migrated to Pennsylvania in the 1720s, lured by William Penn's promise of a colony based on religious tolerance. Today, there are Amish communities in twenty states and in Canada. Though their numbers are difficult to verify, it is estimated that there are between 150,000 and 180,000 Amish in the United States.

The settlement in Smyrna is Old Order Amish, a conservative Anabaptist branch. They have chosen this remote spot—Smyrna's population, including approximately 100 Amish, is 415—to remove themselves from a world that was getting difficult to separate from in their former location. "Be not conformed to this world" (Romans 12:2) is scripture that they strictly adhere to. They do not drive cars or have electricity, telephones, or modern conveniences in their homes. Their clothing harkens back to another age; they wear long sleeves, long skirts or pants, and keep their heads covered. All clothing is plain, homemade, and utilizes hooks and eyes instead of buttons.

In their desire to hold themselves separate from the world, they have developed an impressive self-sufficiency. Children do not attend public schools but are taught in a one-room schoolhouse until eighth grade, at which time they start on-the-job training within the Amish community. In 1972, the Supreme Court exempted the Amish from compulsory education after eighth grade. Though they pay other taxes, the self-employed Amish do not pay Social Security tax because they choose not to collect Social Security benefits, preferring to take care of their own. Each Amish community maintains a mutual aid fund that assists members in need.

Maintaining equality among community members is highly valued and is the reason for many of their practices. Amish may ride in cars but do not own them, as they are a means to show off wealth and status. Musical instruments are prohibited because learning the skill may lead to a lack of humility. Clothing is kept unassuming, subdued, and uniform. Funerals are simple, without eulogies or praise for the deceased.

The focus of Amish life is to walk in complete faith with the Lord Jesus Christ, and all of their practices are based on the Bible, which is considered inerrant. Shunning is the practice of not talking to or eating with those who break their baptismal vow of complete obedience to God and the church. This is based on scripture passages that call for believers not to keep company with or eat with sinners (I Corinthians 5:11) and to avoid those who are contrary to Christian doctrine (Romans 16:17). Their belief in nonresistance is based on scripture, as is their admonition against photography, which is considered a "graven image."

The long winters in northern Maine made farming difficult, so the Amish started a variety of businesses to support themselves. Sturdi-Built constructs wooden buildings used for camps, barns, or storage sheds. The business has exceeded expectations, and a concession was made to technology by allowing gas-fired engines to run air compressors.

The Metal Shop provides metal roofing and siding to contractors. A popular stop for outsiders is the Country Store, which sells old-fashioned general merchandise such as canning jars, homemade soaps, bulk food, cast iron fry pans, books, bolts, lanterns, and even rustic log tables and beds. Merri-Gold Greenhouse sells high quality perennials and annuals, while the organic farm stand sells seasonal bounty. Other businesses include a bike repair shop, bakery, and harness and leather goods shop.

The Amish are welcome in Smyrna, where their farms and businesses have revitalized the area. Locals consider them well mannered, honest, industrious, and private—all attributes valued and shared by Mainers.

Contact Information:
The Amish of Smyrna prefer not to become a tourist destination.

The Shakers at Sabbathday Lake - The United Society of Believers in Christ's Second Coming

New Gloucester

The Shaker Village at Sabbathday Lake is bustling with activity. The four Shakers who call this home are busy managing and maintaining the only active Shaker community in the world. An enthusiastic interest in all things pertaining to Shakers brings thousands of people to their museum, store, and library. Correspondence from around the world arrives from the curious or those hoping for spiritual guidance. Each year dozens of inquiries into joining the community are received. During the summer, up to one hundred people attend Sunday worship meetings. Historians, authors, artists, academics, craftspeople, genealogists, herbalists, theologians, reporters, journalists, and filmmakers seek the Shakers' attention. Though the demand on their energy is great, the Shakers consider the exposure to be a blessing that will attract new members to their church, which is their highest priority.

In addition to outreach activities, the Shakers manage 1,750 acres that include an apple orchard, tree farm, two-acre herb and vegetable garden, hayfields and pastures with sheep and livestock. Eighteen antique buildings are lived in, put to use, and/or preserved as historically significant. Income-producing businesses include commercial herbs, Shaker boxes, yarn production, knit and sewn goods, candy, printing, weaving, and basket making. Special events such as the Christmas Fair and craft workshops are planned throughout the year.

Fortunately, the Shakers have employees and volunteers to assist in their responsibilities. Seasonal workdays bring in sixty volunteers to do minor repairs, paint, and help with planting and harvesting. The Friends of the Shakers was established in 1974 to provide donations, organize fundraisers, and volunteer for assorted duties and workdays.

During the tourist season, 10,000 visitors pass through Sabbathday Lake Village and approximately 3,400 take the guided tour. On the tour, visitors step back in time to 1794, when nearly one hundred people made Sabbathday Lake a Shaker community and consented through an oral covenant to live a life dedicated to God. In the covenant, then as now, Shakers vow to give all they own to the collective commune, to be celibate, and to freely confess their sins to a witness.

Shaker theology is based on the indwelling Christ. It is believed that the Second Coming of Christ occurred in 1747, not as a physical resurrection, but as the spirit of Christ who descends and dwells within the heart of those who confess their sins and open themselves to the spirit of love and truth. (Emanuel Swedenborg believed the Second Coming occurred in 1757. See page 25 for more information.)

The three Cs—community of goods, celibacy, and confession—allow for a life with the indwelling Christ. By choosing to live in community, Shakers emulate the early church in which all things were held in common. In community, they die unto the self to establish a way of life that is firmly rooted in seeking perfection through God's work. Living with like-minded people, away from the world, makes a difficult path easier. The celibate individual imitates the life of Jesus and is free to make God his or her only responsibility. Confession of sins to an Elder or Eldress cleanses the heart and readies it for baptism of the Holy Spirit.

Ann Lee, called Mother Ann by believers, is the guiding spirit of the Shakers. She announced the arrival of the second coming and that she was one of the first people to receive the indwelling Christ. She taught that God had attributes of both male and female and that no good could ever be achieved through violence and war. It is Mother Ann's founding principles of community, celibacy, confession, gender equity, and pacifism that have informed Shakerism throughout its history.

Shakerism arose in Manchester, England, from the religious upheavals of the 1740s. Mother Ann was a spiritual child and young woman who felt unfulfilled by the Anglican Church. At the age of 23, she began to attend religious meetings led by James and Jane Wardley. Their meetings focused on direct contact with God that expressed itself in spontaneous dancing, singing, body tremors, and testimony. The Wardleys came from a tradition of dissent that began in 1662, when the Church of England passed the Act of Uniformity deeming that all clergy must accept everything within the Book of Prayer. Those who refused were referred to as dissenters. The Wardleys' group was influenced by the early Methodists and Quakers, which earned them the contemptuous label of Shaking Quakers in reference to the agitated movements that occurred at meetings. It is theorized that the French Prophets, who were expelled from France for religious reasons, may have influenced them as well. The radical Protestants proclaimed an imminent Judgment Day and millennium and were known for ecstatic dancing when receiving the Spirit. Both groups held that women and men were equal in the eyes of God, with the French Prophets believing women were more spiritually attuned than men.

The Shakers manage 1,750 acres including sheep, livestock, pastures, and hayfields.

Mother Ann was one of eight children born into a working-class family. The family's struggles intensified after their mother's early death. Mother Ann was an uneducated child laborer in the textile mills. Though she did not want to marry, she bowed to her father's wishes in 1762. In the following years, she gave birth to four children, all of whom died young. After the death of her children, Mother Ann ceased having sexual relations with her husband.

This period appears to have radicalized Mother Ann; she became increasingly more vocal and emerged as a leader in the Wardleys' group. They disrupted congregations by threatening imminent judgment and calling for repentance. Their activities provoked mobs to violence and brought incarceration, fines, and beatings. Mother Ann was beaten and stoned several times and jailed at least twice.

In 1770, while Mother Ann was jailed for two weeks under torturous conditions, she had a profound experience of Christ. She received visions, revelations, and momentously, the indwelling Christ. Mother Ann claimed to be made complete by the transformation and told her followers, "No soul could follow Christ in regeneration while living in the works of generation."

In 1774, Mother Ann, her brother William Lee, her faithful friend James Whittaker, her husband, and four others set sail for America to fulfill Mother Ann's vision of a church awaiting her there. She and her husband secured employment in New York City, though he left her after she nursed him through an illness. Three people from the group traveled to Albany where they leased land in nearby Niskayuna. It was there that the group reunited after two years of separation and quietly bided their time while Mother Ann awaited a sign to begin her evangelical work.

The sign she was waiting for arrived on May 19, 1780, known as the Dark Day. The morning began with an ominous sky colored a strange hue of yellow. By mid-morning, New England was plunged into darkness. Thunder, flashing light, and a fireball witnessed off the coast of Rhode Island contributed to the eerie effects. The darkness was caused by a rare combination of atmospheric conditions and fires, but to early New Englanders, the event was an omen of the impending millennium. The Dark Day occurred at the height of the New Light Stir, a revival that was sweeping New England with predictions of Christ's return. Millennium fever was stoked by radical evangelical preachers who found a receptive audience in rural areas and used the Dark Day to convert countless numbers to their charismatic groups.

After the Dark Day, Mother Ann excited and engaged people with the news that there was no need to wait for the Second Coming; it had already arrived. The indwelling Christ was available to all who confessed their sins, denounced lust, and opened their hearts to love. Rejecting the Calvinist notion of predestination, Mother Ann spoke of free will and of direct experiences of God. The Dark Day brought many curious people to Niskayuna, and often they were baptized in the Spirit after Mother Ann listened to their confessions. Meetings were exuberant events of ecstatic dancing, testimonies, singing, spinning like tops, and speaking in strange tongues.

An important group of converts was a New Light Baptist congregation from New Lebanon, New York, especially their leader, Joseph

Meacham. Shaker tradition states that Mother Ann prophesied his conversion by saying, "The first man in America is coming," and prepared food for his visit. He would become a pivotal leader in the coming years.

Mother Ann, William Lee, and James Whittaker traveled throughout New England spreading their ministry and rapidly attracting followers from 1781 to 1783 during the closing years of the Revolution. Whittaker did much of the speaking and biblical interpretations. William Lee is said to have led the ecstatic dancing and singing, while Mother Ann was the charismatic personality. In *The Shaker Experience in America,* Stephen Stein revealed that Mother Ann was a woman of few words. She was described as tender, nurturing, and deeply concerned with her followers, which she demonstrated through frequent touching and a desire to serve them. Mother Ann was also capable of firmness and brought attention to people's mistakes while encouraging perfection. Together, the three conveyed a consistent message: confess your sins, turn away from the ways of the world, and accept the love of the indwelling Christ.

Tragically, the missionaries were often subjected to frequent mob violence and beatings by those who suspected them of witchcraft and satanic behavior. On several occasions, Mother Ann was dragged from her bed, verbally and physically abused, and examined to see if she was a man, woman, or witch. Houses where they stayed were shot at, and they were repeatedly forced to move on by threats of violence. In Harvard, Massachusetts, a particularly brutal beating is marked with a monument that states, "On this spot a Shaker was whiped [sic] by a mob for religious views in 1783."

One year later, on July 24, 1784, William Lee died at the age of 45. Mother Ann was grief stricken and weakened from years of beatings and work. She announced, "I see Brother William, coming in a golden chariot, to take me home." On September 8, just weeks after her brother's passing, she died at age forty-eight. During an exhumation years later, it was found that her skull had been fractured, leading to speculation that her death was the result of mob violence.

After her death, James Whittaker continued her work until his death three years later. Joseph Meacham then took the helm and is responsible for providing a structure to the Shaker religion by establishing a uniform framework for the organization, for the governance of the newly formed communities, and for worship meetings. Meacham stressed unity in meetings by using set dances and songs. Energy was directed away from missionary work and into gathering converts into communities. Women's equality was affirmed when he appointed Lucy Wright as his ministry partner.

After Meacham's death in 1796, Wright led the Shakers through their period of greatest growth and development. Under her strong leadership, missionary work was renewed, resulting in western expansion. None of Mother Ann's teachings was recorded during her lifetime, nor was a doctrine or theology formalized, as they felt there was no need to rationalize direct experiences with God. Wright oversaw the move away from anti-intellectualism by improving children's education and by formalizing and publishing Shaker doctrine. Mother Ann was brought out of obscurity and recognized as the "founder and pillar" of the Shaker faith. Hymns, songs, and dances continued to be unified.

The hard work of Meacham, Wright, and hundreds of committed Shakers was clearly visible by 1827 at which time there were eighteen communities in New England, New York, Ohio, and Kentucky. In the decade preceding the Civil War, approximately five thousand Shakers were living in Shaker communities.

A fascinating period in Shaker history began in 1837 and continued for fifteen to twenty years. The Era of Manifestations, or Mother's Work, was marked by thousands of gifts from the Spirit and was experienced throughout the Shaker villages. The gifts came as testimony, song, dance, marching forms, visions, revelations, art, and sermons. The channels, or instruments, were usually young women who brought forth gifts from Mother Ann, the founders, saints, historical figures, Native Americans, and pagans. Feast grounds were set aside in each community after an instrument revealed a location. Believers walked reverently to the spot where elaborate rituals were performed around monuments referred to as fountain stones. For a time, the meetings became so long, so spirited, and so emotionally powerful that they were closed to the public.

Approximately two hundred spirit paintings from the era of Mother's Work have been located. The paintings defy labeling, as they are unlike other art from the period. In some, there are elements of quilts, samplers, and folk art. Others have free-flowing elements that are contained in organization, order, and symmetry. Multiple meanings are derived from the elaborate use of symbols, animals, figures, plant life, geometric shapes, stars, moons, and esoteric symbols.

The spiritualist experiences of the Shakers were mirrored in the outside world in the second half of the century. It is interesting to note that in 1904, the progressive Shaker Anna White wrote in *Shakerism: Its Meaning and Message* that the Shakers were the first "Modern Spiritualists." Certainly, Spiritualism confirmed what Shakers had asserted since their beginnings—connecting with the spirit world is possible and happens frequently. (For more on Spiritualism, see page 16.)

After the Civil War, membership steadily declined. The Industrial Revolution created opportunities for men in industry and business. Young men learned their skills with the Shakers then moved on. Shaker life offered women equality, work, and security, so few left, leading to a female majority in the communities. The population loss continued into the 20th century regardless of the vision and strong leadership of many elders and eldresses.

The history of Sabbathday Lake follows that of other communities with the exception that their hardships were more severe. In the last third of the 19th century, the changing economic landscape brought realities that the Shakers were not equipped to handle. All of the societies were plagued, in one way or another, with lawsuits, embezzlement, or the costly revenge of apostates. Sabbathday Lake was saddled for years with debt incurred from embezzlement and contracts with unscrupulous business people. Their reaction, under the conservative leadership of Elder Otis Sawyer, was to retrench by focusing on their agricultural and spiritual roots.

Elder Sawyer is often credited with the lasting success of Sabbathday Lake because he was temporally progressive but spiritually conservative. He encouraged contact with the outside world, yet used his authority to ensure that the Sabbathday Lake believers kept their spiritual commitments. Contemporary Shakers believe that his influence, coupled with years of poverty, strengthened them and is one of the reasons their population declined more slowly than that of other societies. It can also be argued that Yankee independence, their rural location, and the hardships inherent to Maine's climate combined to create a tradition of strong faith and willful determination.

When other societies had disappeared or had numbers in the single digits, Sabbathday Lake experienced a renewal. In the 1960s, two strong leaders emerged from the group of fifteen: Sister Mildred Barker (1897–1990) and Brother Ted Johnson (1930–1986). Sister Mildred joined Sabbathday Lake with twenty others when the Alfred, Maine, community was sold to the Brothers of Christian Instruction in 1931. Brother Ted was an adult convert and highly educated. Both of them put their "hands to work and hearts to God." The meetinghouse was open to the public in 1963 after being closed for seventy-six years. The museum was expanded, and exhibits focused on their faith-based lifestyle as opposed to their material culture. Work was begun to turn the library into an important research center and to safeguard its priceless documents. A flock of sheep was purchased for yarn production. The herb business was successfully resurrected using tins and labels that were replicated from the 1860 originals. In 1974, they shipped 1,100 tins to Bloomingdale's for the holiday season.

This antique shaker barn remains in full use.

The hard work of outreach, education, and renewed traditional industries brought public support, and most importantly, new converts. Unfortunately, the revival was not sustained. Due to deaths and attrition, in 2000, there were nine Shakers. The following year proved to be traumatic with the deaths of two members and the loss of three who left the community after a trial period.

The Believers are determined to build their community once again and offer seekers a religion that is not out of step with modern life. Brother Ted clarified Shaker theology for the contemporary seeker in *Life in the Christ Spirit: Observations on Shaker Theology.* He wrote that the foundation belief of the indwelling Christ expresses itself in Shakerism through the two concepts of unity and simplicity. In unity, the believer practices the "spontaneous forgetfulness of self." Mother Ann taught that the spiritual sickness of one member is capable of causing sickness throughout the community; therefore, unity calls believers to build the spiritual health of all the members. The expression of Christ's spirit is revealed through oneness with the world and a willingness to serve in love. By living in simplicity, in both the physical and spiritual realms, Shakers are prevented from thinking too high or too low of themselves. Brother Ted writes that through simplicity a person realizes their "basic Christian right and responsibility of self-fulfillment," which has been of vital importance to Shakers throughout their history.

The Shaker Father-Mother-God is pure spirit, the Creator, and "omniscient, omnipotent, and omnipresent." As a way to understand God more clearly, Shakers view God as having the masculine qualities of strength and power and the feminine qualities of mercy and compassion. With modern day mystics calling for the return of the divine feminine, it is apparent that the Shakers were far ahead of their time.

Mother Ann did not claim to be the female Christ as has been frequently reported. She was imbued with the spirit of Christ and was called to make known the feminine dimension of God, as well as to announce that the second coming of Christ is the church.

An interesting departure from mainstream Christianity is the Shaker belief that Jesus was not born divine but was anointed by God at his baptism by John. The early years of Jesus are offered as evidence that He was pre-chosen to receive the divine spirit, just as Mother Ann had been.

In Shaker theology, heaven is an eternal, incorporeal state for those who were united with God during life. Hell is the eternal separation from God based on choices made with free will. An intermediary state exists where souls can benefit from prayers. The Bible is not considered inerrant, but acts as a guide to God's laws and should not be confused as being God's laws. It is not the culmination of God's communication with the faithful, as revelations are continually expressed to followers. The Shaker God speaks constantly through gifts that are revealed through Spirit and can occur at any time.

The public is welcome to witness and participate in the gifts of the spirit at worship meetings on Sunday mornings. Benches line either side of the meeting room and face each other—men sit on one side and women on the other. Each week three Bible readings are posted on the blackboard so that believers can contemplate them before the meeting. There are two set songs from the hymnal, and the rest of the worship is open to gifts of the spirit, which comes in the form of testimony and song. Several moments of contemplation follows each testimony, and then one of the believers begins a fitting song. In their brief history, there were over ten thousand songs and hymns written, making for an astounding number of choices. In the earliest years, this was a time of ecstatic frenzy, which gave way to ordered dances and marches. As the population grew older, the dancing was discontinued because the elderly could not join in, therefore breaking the unity of the service. Unwilling to sit still, believers clap and gesture to accompany many of the songs. The gifts of the past have been replaced with quieter gifts of contemplation and testimony.

The Shaker Library is appropriately housed in the former schoolhouse built in 1880. It has an estimated 100,000 items, including books, periodicals, manuscripts, ephemera, scrapbooks, photographs, microfilm, an audio/video collection, maps, and two beautiful spirit paintings. There are special collections on herbs and agriculture and the radical religious sects of America. The Shaker Museum offers guided tours Monday through Saturday from Memorial Day through Columbus Day. Six of the eighteen building are included on the tour but are not open to visitors to explore on their own. The museum has changing exhibits that chronicle Shaker life, and both the museum and the store offer authentic Shaker goods for purchase.

The public can find seemingly unlimited information about the Shaker way of life, daily routines, history, inventions, herbs, furniture, and industries. In much of this information, their faith is overshadowed by the visible results of their labors. Their religion is often subjected to tedious amounts of psychological interpretation and projection. They are romanticized and mythologized, some of which is well deserved, as they have a formidable history of productivity, idealism, and faith. The risk of romanticizing their lives is that the discipline and difficulties are ignored. All scholars of religion know that walking a path dedicated to God does not exempt the faithful from grief, disappointments, betrayals, and descents into the dark night of the soul. However, the Sabbathday Lake believers are fully cognizant that the path also brings ecstasy, joy, and gifts that far outweigh the pain. Each day they pray in hope and faith that others will follow the Shaker way of the indwelling Christ.

Contact Information:

Sabbathday Lake Shaker Library, Museum, and Herb Departments:
United Society of Shakers
707 Shaker Road
New Gloucester, ME 04260
Telephone: (207) 926-4597
Web site: *www.maineshakers.com*
Library E-mail only: brooks1@shaker.lib.me.us
Office E-mail: usshakers@aol.com

St. Anthony's Monastery and Shrines - Franciscan Friars

Kennebunk

St. Anthony's Monastery and Shrines has been a cherished landmark since its purchase in 1947 by Lithuanian Franciscan friars. Approximately sixty thousand visits are made per year to this sanctuary on the Kennebunk River that is a short stroll to Gooch's Beach and the village of Kennebunkport. For years, locals have endured persistent rumors of its imminent sale to developers with plans for luxury condominiums, an exclusive resort, or even President George Bush's library. Fortunately, the friars are committed to keeping their sixty acres of natural beauty out of private hands.

The relocation of Lithuanian Franciscans to Maine was precipitated by the communist take-over in 1940 of Lithuania, a country geographically smaller than Maine with a population of three-and-a-half million. After the communists closed churches and monasteries, forcing the religious underground, Father Justin Vaskys was granted permission by the Vatican to begin a relocation order in the United States, even as it was fully expected that the communists would be gone within two years. Father Justin hoped to start the order in Chicago, which had a Lithuanian population of nearly one hundred thousand. When that failed, he explored New York and Pennsylvania, also to no avail. In 1946, a priest from Hartford, Connecticut, brought Father Justin to Maine, where the Bishop granted him permission to relocate as long as he could secure his own place.

Father Justin settled temporarily in Greene but was determined to be in southern Maine in order to be closer to Boston's Lithuanian community. A "providential arrangement by God" brought together Father Justin and William Campbell, the millionaire owner of the estate that is now St. Anthony's Monastery. Though Campbell was not Catholic, he was impressed with the Franciscan order after his visit to Assisi, Italy, where the order's founder St. Francis was born and is honored in the Basilica of St. Francis. Campbell, believing he was near death, sold the property to the Franciscans for a reasonable price to be paid in installments.

The history of the property can be traced back almost three hundred years. After the Native Americans were forced out, it was possessed by Sir William Pepperell until 1740 when he sold two hundred acres to John Mitchell, a theology professor and seaman. Mitchell's family controlled the estate until 1900, at which time William Rogers, Esq., a wealthy industrialist, purchased it and built the handsome tutor style mansion. Campbell bought the estate in 1937, and in 1947, it was officially dedicated as St. Anthony's Monastery.

Technically, St. Anthony's is not a monastery, but a friary. Friars are semi-cloistered, in contrast to monks, who live in cloistered self-sustaining communities with little or no contact with the outside world. The Franciscans are a contemplative order that traditionally has been accessible to lay people through their work within the world. St. Francis (1181–1226) founded three orders: the Franciscan order for men in 1209, Poor Clares for women in 1215, and Secular Franciscans for lay people and priests in 1221. He is the patron saint of animals and the environment and is revered among Roman Catholics for his compassion, love of creation, and veneration of Mary, Mother of Christ, who is of great importance to the Franciscans.

During the fifty years that communists ruled Lithuania, St. Anthony's played an important role in the formation (religious education that entails four years of college and four years of theology) of Lithuanian priests and friars. Formation was not the only education offered at the monastery; from the late 1950s until 1969, it was a boarding high school for Lithuanian boys from Chicago, New York City, Hartford, and Boston. The school never exceeded more than one hundred students yet, thanks to the regulation size gymnasium, the school made it to the state basketball semi-finals one year. The school closed when it became unaffordable for the friars to continue, and in the mid-1970s, it was remodeled as the Franciscan Guest House.

In the 1950s and 1960s, St. Anthony's Monastery was a vacation destination for thousands of Lithuanians, mostly from

Boston, who arrived in early July for the Lithuanian Festival Day, which consisted of picnics with ethnic food, traditional folk dancing, and religious services performed in Lithuanian style.

Through the years, the friars have added a number of shrines on the grounds and within the monastery. Upon entering the grounds, a visitor can see the Grotto of Our Lady of Lourdes on the expansive lawn framed by a backdrop of pines. The architect Jonas Mulokas constructed the shrine in 1953, and people from throughout the United States attended its dedication. The large shrine is intended to be reminiscent of the appearance of Mary to Bernadette Soubirous in Lourdes, France, in 1858. Inside the cave-like structure of granite blocks, Mary is elevated and encircled with lights. The structure is topped with a delicate Lithuanian shrine.

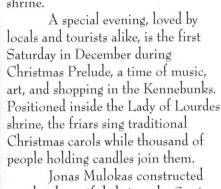

St. Anthony's Shrine is found inside the monastery entrance.

A special evening, loved by locals and tourists alike, is the first Saturday in December during Christmas Prelude, a time of music, art, and shopping in the Kennebunks. Positioned inside the Lady of Lourdes shrine, the friars sing traditional Christmas carols while thousand of people holding candles join them.

Jonas Mulokas constructed another beautiful shrine, the Stations of the Cross (1959). Four brick buttresses come together to support each other and the graceful pagoda-style roof. The Stations of the Cross are depicted in four Lithuanian shrines topped with metal crosses.

Close to the monastery is the Monument to the Triple Church sculpture, created by the Lithuanian artist Vytautas Kazimieras Jonynas. The sculpture, which was transported to the monastery in 1967, was originally the façade for the Vatican's pavilion in the 1964–'65 World's Fair in New York City. The piece represents the Church Militant on Earth, the Church Suffering in purgatory, and the Church Triumphant in heaven. It is dedicated to the Silent Church and to those who are persecuted for their faith. The piece is rich in symbolism—the all-seeing eye of God, a dove, a lamb, keys, a rooster—and uses delicate yet powerful vertical lines of gold and glass tile mosaics to move the eyes upward. In 1992, the artist visited the monastery and, upon seeing the sculpture, advised that it be torn down due to its poor condition. Unwilling to allow that, the friars had the work restored and renovated by York, Maine, artist Ron Hayes.

There are two shrines to St. Anthony: one on the outside depicting St. Anthony holding the child Jesus and the other just inside the entranceway of the monastery. The newest section of the chapel is named after him as well. St. Anthony is a well-loved saint who is known as a miracle worker. He lived at the time of St. Francis and left his wealthy family to become a Franciscan. Within his order, he performed menial tasks until an occasion arose when there was no speaker available for a planned event. St. Anthony stepped in and so impressed the audience with his oratory skills and knowledge that he was sent to preach throughout Italy and France and to teach theology to friars and priests.

Other shrines on the property include the Fatima Shrine, St. Francis Fountain, Tekakwitha Shrine, and niches found along the nature trails that meander through the property and to the waterfront.

Inside the monastery, traces of the elegance of the former mansion are evident in the moldings, windows, and flooring. The former foyer has been transformed into a shrine to St. Anthony and is partially lined with stunning stained glass windows picturing St. Anthony, St. Francis, St. George, Our Lady of Mercy, and St. Casimir, the patron saint of Lithuania. The St. Anthony Chapel dates to the early 1960s and is in a modern style with elements of Lithuanian architecture. Jonynas, the artist of the Triple Church Monument, designed and produced the chapel interior, including the stained glass windows, bas-relief wall ornaments, altars, flooring, lighting, candlesticks, pews, and textured walls. The scene behind the altar is of special significance to Franciscans. It portrays St. Francis praying in Our Lady of Angels Chapel at Porziuncola. The ancient chapel, which is now inside the Basilica of St. Mary of the Angels close to Assisi, was known for its angel apparitions. St. Francis lived in the chapel as he restored it and dedicated it to Mary. It is said that he loved that place beyond any other, and his request that all who prayed there would receive a special blessing was granted during a vision of Christ and Mary. Also within the chapel are depictions of the Stations of the Cross, a shrine to St. Therese, and an Infant of Prague Chapel.

In 2005, there were eight friars living in the monastery, down from a peak of fourteen. Father Justin and all of the original friars have passed away. The establishment is overseen by Father John Bacevicius, who immigrated to the United States at the age of ten in 1946, after four years in a refugee camp. Father John joined the Franciscan order at seventeen years old, during a time when many chose religious life at a young age. Today, most of the friars at the monastery are older and lead a contemplative life of prayer and self-education. Though the friars are less active in the outside world, there is still a lot of activity at the monastery. The friars offer daily services with three on Sundays, healing services, spiritual guidance, and seminars on faith. They conduct devotions and hear confessions. The theology is very conservative. Due to the increasing interest in the monastery, the number of special events planned is steadily growing—icon painting classes, Lithuanian Cultural Week, Family Day, and self-directed retreats.

Father John and the friars enjoy considerable material assistance from the St. Anthony Monastery Association, which handles financial concerns, renovations, and upkeep. The Franciscan Monastery Capital Campaign Fund and Franciscan Monastery Operations Fund address long-term care and ongoing expenses, respectively. Both funds are managed by the friars, volunteers, and the Secular Franciscans, an area group of approximately twenty-five who offer extensive help to the monastery.

The Franciscan Guest House has been completely renovated in recent years, leaving behind the austere rooms of its past. There are sixty-five comfortable rooms with air conditioning, television, full baths, and a Lithuanian breakfast is included in the price. The facility is open from May to October and is increasingly becoming a desirable location for self-directed retreats. Many of the boys who attended high school here return each year with their families.

St. Anthony's Monastery and Shrines is a treasure for Roman Catholics, Lithuanians, and people of all religious persuasions who can appreciate its sacred shrines and grounds.

Contact Information:

Franciscan Monastery
P.O. Box 980
Kennebunkport, ME 04046
Telephone: (207) 967-2011
Web site: *www.framon.net*

Tax free donations can be sent to:
Franciscan Monastery Capital Campaign Fund or Franciscan Monastery Operations Fund
P.O. Box 273
Kennebunk, ME 04043

Franciscan Guest House
Telephone: (207) 967-4865
Web site: *www.franciscanguesthouse.com*

Wabanaki Confederacy

The Wabanaki Confederacy is an alliance of Maine's four Native American tribes: the Penobscot Indian Nation based at Indian Island, the Passamaquoddy Tribe based at Pleasant Point, the Houlton Band of Maliseets, and the Aroostook Band of Micmacs. There are approximately 5,500 Wabanaki people in Maine. The tribes, which are culturally and linguistically related, have been political allies for several centuries. Like Native Americans across the continent, Wabanaki spirituality is grounded in nature and a love of the Creator.

Native American religion is not a religion in the European sense. There is no single doctrine, holy book, church, clergy person, founder, or savior. It is not evangelistic, and people cannot join. Native American spirituality is seamlessly woven into all aspects of daily living; culture and spirituality are inseparable. Life is permeated with the Creator, who is central to the inner self. The Creator is extant in all of creation, infusing every animate and inanimate form with spirit. Rocks, plants, elements, living beings, and natural phenomena have specific qualities that are both physical and spiritual. The Creator is revealed through nature, which is the source of health, learning, and wisdom. Humans, who are born spiritual, have the ability to communicate with the Creator and the creations.

With nature being the highest teacher for Native Americans, the elements hold a sacred place in daily life, ceremonies, creation stories, and traditional wisdom. Fire transforms, energizes, and purifies. It is used to burn the sacred herbs of sage, sweet grass, cedar, and tobacco, the smoke from which is sent prayerfully to the Creator. Sacred fires are built for prayers and ceremonies by first purifying the ground with sweet grass. Tobacco is held in the hand while praying, and then thrown onto the fire where it is transformed into smoke, which carries the prayer to the Creator. Stones heated in fire are used in sweat lodges, where they create the heat that purifies the body and spirit, and it is fire that ignites the tobacco in the sacred pipe ceremony.

The beginning and ending of life is defined by the powerful element of air. It is the breath of the Creator, and is the four winds from the four directions that carry spirits. The eagle is closely aligned to air and is sacred to the Wabanaki, who send many prayers to it and sing many songs in its honor. Of all the birds, eagles fly the highest, bringing prayers to the Creator and messages from the Creator to Earth. The eagle represents clarity, strength, courage, and spirit. Eagle feathers arrive as gifts from the Creator and are used to connect to Spirit.

Wabanaki culture is closely linked to the waters of the Kennebec, Androscoggin, and Penobscot Rivers. For thousands of years, the rivers provided nourishment, transportation, material resources, and recreation. An early connection with the Jesuit priests who arrived in the 17th century was the mutual use of water for spiritual blessing, healing, and cleansing. Almost all ceremonies involve water in some manner.

In the 20th century, the rivers were heavily polluted by sewage and industrial waste. By the 1980s, swimming, fishing, or eating plants along the rivers' edges was made impossible due to the high levels of dioxin discharged into the waters from the bleaching process used by paper mills. This caused severe disruption to the Penobscot Nation in particular because much of their land holdings incorporate the Penobscot River, including two hundred islands in the river north of Old Town. The river has been the lifeblood of the Penobscot people since time immemorial, and protecting it is an ongoing struggle. Since the 1980s, the Penobscot Nation, frequently joined by the other Wabanki tribes, has been at the forefront of an environmental battle with state and federal government to force stricter industrial discharge laws and dam removal. Though enormous gains have been made, the Penobscot people have no plans to cease their efforts until the river is restored to its original state.

The element of earth is the Mother, who is connected to all things in nature. Nothing should be taken from the Earth without returning something, and she must be treated as one would treat his or her own mother.

The creation stories of the Wabanaki people best express the reverence for Mother Earth. Native American mythology often includes an individual who is sent by the Creator to learn how to best live on Earth and then to teach humans how to proceed. For the Wabanaki, this man is Gluskabe. Each of the four tribes has a different spelling and story, but in all of them, Gluskabe creates the first man and woman and teaches them the right way to live in creation. In at least two of the stories, Gluskabe is made from dirt. The Penobscot

Gluskabe forms himself from the dust that the creator shook off his hands after forming the Earth. In the Micmac myth, Gluskap was brought to life when the Creator sent a bolt of lightening to Earth. The largest mountain in Maine, Katahdin, plays a central role in Wabanaki spirituality and is home to mythological spirits. In the Maliseet creation story, Glooscap is a very large spirit who has made Katahdin his wigwam.

The creation story of the Penobscot people is told in the *Life and Traditions of the Red Man,* written in 1893 by Joseph Nicolar and reprinted by the Penobscot Nation Museum. In one part of the story, the first mother becomes extremely distraught when her tribe faces starvation. Her husband returns from a journey to find her in despair and follows her in an attempt to find out what is wrong. He observes her singing cheerfully in the river, and watches as she steps on land and takes a long green blade from her ankle and casts it back into the river. Immediately her sadness returns. When he approaches her to ask what he can do to make her happy again, she replies that he must slay her so that she can show her love in such a way that people for all time would love her. Her shocked husband responds that he needs seven days to make his decision. After seven days of deep prayer, he knows he must grant her wish. The first mother directs him to slay her with a stone, drags her body back and forth across the ground until the flesh is gone, and buries her bones in the center of the area.

After seven moons passes, her husband returned to the spot and saw that it was filled with tall plants with blades like the one his wife had cast in the river. Inside the blades was a sweet tasting food that came to be called corn. Where her bones lay was the large broad-leafed plant, tobacco.

The man had been in despair since slaying his wife, but now he understood the importance of her sacrifice. He spoke to his people about the first mother being the embodiment of love whose great power would be felt the world over. From then on, it was understood that when eating the food granted by the Mother, it was her flesh that gave strength. The tobacco from her bones was a gift of inspiration and sacred to her memory. That is why offerings must always be made to Mother Earth in gratitude for her sacrifice and love.

Seven and four are sacred numbers to the Wabanaki. Seven is a magical number that indicates wholeness: north, south, east, west, above, below, and center signifying the omnipresence of the Creator.

Native Americans speak frequently of "seven generations," which refers to the impact of choices made in the present on the next seven generations of children. It is believed that no decision should ever be made that would harm tomorrow's children. Environmental issues are extremely important in this context, making the care of Mother Earth and ensuring future resources a moral obligation.

The sacred number four is the number of creation. There are four seasons, four elements, four stages of life, four races, and four qualities in humans: emotional, mental, physical, and spiritual. The medicine wheel is divided into four parts and is a physical representation of the above qualities and much more. It has multiple layers of meaning and is a powerful and sacred tool.

Due to the rich diversity of the Wabanaki Confederacy, an attempt to write about each tribe's specific ceremonies would likely offend the Wabanaki people through misrepresentation, inaccuracy, or an intrusive violation of their private practices. Therefore, what follows is a general description of ceremonies that are practiced in most Native American communities, including the Wabanaki Confederacy.

Ceremonies are performed collectively or individually and are carried out for a wide range of reasons and occasions: to celebrate the seasons, to connect with Spirit, as social celebrations, for favorable hunting or planting conditions, for healing, and for all of life's passages. No matter what the occasion, prayer, expressing gratitude and humility, and honoring the Creator are always part of the ceremony.

Tools are gifts from the Creator that assist in communication with the spirit world during ceremonies. Herbs, rattles, drums, tobacco, and the sacred pipe bring focus, expand consciousness, and attune energy during prayer, meditation, and ceremony. Sweet grass is called "the hair of the Mother" and is braided before it is burned. In a ceremony called smudging, sweet grass, cedar, and/or sage are burned to clear away negative energy and bring in all that is positive. Drumbeats are the heartbeats of Mother Earth, and rattles are the vibrations of creation.

Tobacco is an offering to express gratitude and, when used in a sacred pipe, it brings wisdom and healing. (Many Native Americans believe that the health issues caused by cigarette smoking are brought on by the selling of the sacred plant for profit.) A sacred pipe is a holy object used to communicate with the Creator and the spirits of nature. Only natural materials are used to make the pipe. The bowl is round like Mother Earth and the womb, while the stem represents the Father and a phallus. When the stem and bowl are joined, masculine and feminine are united in wholeness.

Each tribe has a pipe carrier who is chosen by Spirit. The tribe's elders come to recognize this person by the quality of his actions. The potential pipe carrier stands out to the elders because he makes a full effort to learn Native American ways; he has powerful prayers; and he displays wisdom, generosity, respect, and honor. After being informed of his potential by the elders, he must embark on several sweat lodges, fasts, and visit the elders to increase knowledge. The pipe must be given by another pipe carrier; one cannot claim oneself to be a pipe carrier.

The pipe is usually presented in a ceremony and is considered a great honor as well as a great responsibility as the first pipe received is to help all people and Mother Earth. (Many pipes may be received during a lifetime.) The pipe carrier leads ceremonies, teaches, assists in healing, and is honored at intertribal ceremonies. The pipe grants the spiritual powers of vision and healing. If the pipe carrier's morals lapse, the pipe loses its powers. Often it is expected that the pipe carrier abstain completely from alcohol and drugs, and touching the pipe under their influence is forbidden.

It is important to understand that the pipe is not a symbol of knowledge; it is knowledge. For example, when a person visits the pipe carrier seeking a healing, an offering is made, prayers are said, and the tobacco is lit. When the pipe carrier draws in the smoke the needed knowledge for the healing is received. Upon exhalation, the knowledge enters the atmosphere as healing energy. The seeker is healed by the energy in the smoke, but it is also the seeker's responsibility to act on the knowledge given by the pipe. Words are inadequate for expressing the full meaning and depth of esoteric ceremonies; therefore, the above example is an incomplete explanation of a sacred healing experience.

The sweat lodge ceremony is for spiritual and physical purification. The lodge, usually temporary, represents the womb of the Mother. It is dome shaped, built low to the ground, and covered with leaves and blankets. The door is low, necessitating that participants crawl through it on their hands and knees as if entering or exiting the womb. On the day of the sweat lodge, indigenous rocks, referred to as grandmothers and grandfathers, are heated on a sacred fire. When ready, they are placed in a fire pit in the center of the lodge. Once the ceremony begins, the door is covered and the interior of the lodge is pitch black except for the red glow of the grandparents, onto which sacred herbs are sprinkled. Water is then poured over them creating steam and intense heat. All four elements are used during a sweat: earth, fire, water, and air. Usually there are four rounds, each hotter than the last. In between each round, grandparents from the fire are brought in along with air and light, while water and the sacred pipe are passed around the circle.

Drumming, chanting, prayer, and spirit communion are powerful contributors to the expanded consciousness that many experience in sweats. The body sweats profusely, releasing both physical and psychic toxins. It is a potent form of prayer invoked in part by being brought to the edge of physical tolerance.

Women who are menstruating, or "at their moon time," do not partake in sweats because their bodies are being purified through their menstrual cycle. Moon time is when a woman is considered most spiritually powerful, and during ceremonies, she is asked to stand outside the circle to protect the others from negative energies.

The vision quest entails spending one to four days in nature while fasting in hopes of receiving a vision. The fast acts to cleanse impurities enabling the individual to be open to the gifts from Spirit. In Native American culture, it is essential to have a reciprocal relationship with the Creator so, on a vision quest, food and comfort are sacrificed as an offering. A vision quest may be done many times for many reasons, but it must always have a spiritual intention. The quest may be to find wisdom, meaning, purpose, or healing, and the knowledge often arrives through the study of nature. When the vision appears, it may be physical, such as the appearance of a wild animal within close proximity, or it may arrive in a waking or sleeping dream. The vision is real energy, not fantasy, and must be honored upon returning to daily life.

The Wabanaki are called the People of the Dawnland, and they have occupied northern New England and the Maritimes for at least ten thousand years. Prior to the 17th century, their population is estimated to have been between twenty and thirty thousand.

The first regular contact with Europeans began in the 16th century, when explorers seeking the legendary kingdom of Norumbega found furs instead and established the first permanent outposts. Early relationships between the tribes and the traders were peaceful and profitable for all parties, but nevertheless, the contact turned fatal to the Wabanaki people in what is referred to as the Great Dying. Between 1616 and 1619, an estimated 75% of the Native American population died when a pandemic raged throughout New England. The Great Dying was caused by diseases introduced by Europeans, presumably small pox, cholera, measles, hepatitis, and whooping cough. Throughout the 17th century, sporadic epidemics coupled with intertribal wars continued to decimate the Wabanaki population.

The Wabanaki Confederacy stayed neutral in the battle between the French and English for control of North America until the Iroquois Confederacy formed an alliance with the English. The Wabanaki Confederacy then viewed an alliance with the French favorably, as it would address their concerns about the growing number of English settlements. The series of wars that ensued, known in American history as the French-Indian Wars, were fought from 1690 to 1763, and continued to sap the population and strength of the Wabanaki Confederacy.

Jesuit priests lived with the Wabanaki tribes as soon as there were permanent French settlements in North America. Though they were there for the sole purpose of conversion, their approach was far more respectful than that of the English, who thought the Indians should be assimilated or eliminated. The first Catholic conversion was in the Passamaquoddy Tribe in 1604. In 1610, the Grand Chief Membertou and twenty-one family members from the Micmac Tribe converted as an act of goodwill. Intermarriage between French men and Wabananki women led to a heritage of integrating Catholicism with traditional Native American beliefs.

By the 1800s, the Catholic Church had established permanent churches in all of the Wabanaki communities, and schools soon followed. Throughout most of the 20th century, the only primary education available on Indian Island was Catholic. Some of the Wabanaki people converted to Catholicism, some combined Catholic and traditional beliefs, and some held on to their original faith. No matter what their personal belief system, Wabanaki spirituality and culture are the same, and their spirituality finds continuity through canoe building, basket making, traditional arts, gardening, hunting, fishing, and honoring the natural world.

The policies and practices of governmental and religious institutions in the 19th and most of the 20th century attempted to systematically assimilate Native Americans into the mainstream Christian culture. Practicing their traditional religion was illegal until the passage of the Indian Religious Freedom Act in 1978. The grinding poverty on the reservations did not allow for fully retaining traditional Wabanaki lifestyles, and for many decades ceremonies were not held. Cultural changes of the 1960s brought a growing awareness of Indian heritage to reservations, and in the 1970s, events evolved that brought Native Americans across the United States to a renewed sense of pride and political fight.

The resurgence of Native American culture and spirituality was inspired by the Civil Rights Movement and energized by the 1973 occupation of Wounded Knee by the American Indian Movement and its supporters. The seventy-two day occupation by several hundred protestors called attention to the deplorable conditions on Pine Ridge Reservation in South Dakota, the endless federal treaty violations, and corrupt tribal governments. Wounded Knee was chosen for the occupation because it was the location of the last military action against Native Americans. In 1890, between 150 and 300 men, women, and children were massacred by the United States 7th Calvary, which lost thirty soldiers. In 1973, the United States government once again responded with a military assault, resulting in the deaths of two Native Americans, the wounding of twelve people, including two federal agents, and the arrest of twelve hundred.

There is no consensus among Native Americans on whether or not the occupation was the best approach, but it brought the nation's attention to the American Indians' history and hardships, and it acted as an important catalyst to the rebirth of culture and dignity for Native Americans.

After the Wounded Knee occupation, members of the Wabanaki Confederacy traveled to meet with western tribes and realized how much of their original ceremonies had been lost through time. On their return, research of Wabanaki history began in earnest, and much of their heritage was uncovered. Traditional ceremonies that honor the rivers, Mount Katahdin, the ancestors, and nature were revived and continue to unfold today. Pride, political activism, and a spiritual renewal have energized communities.

A prophecy states that healing between Native Americans and those of European descent will begin at the Eastern Door. The Wabanaki are the Keepers of the Eastern Door, and it is here in Maine, at the first point of contact between the two races that the healing will begin. In time, all of the Doors in each direction will be opened, ushering in creativity, peace, and unity for the entire world.

Elder Arnie Neptune is the pipe carrier and respected spiritual leader of the Penobscot Nation. In hopes of facilitating the healing, he invites the people of Maine to learn the Wabanaki teachings in hopes that it will bring healing to the earth by stopping pollution and beginning a concentrated effort by all people to give back to Mother Earth whenever something is taken. The teachings are committed to a deep understanding that all of creation is One. As the Eastern Door opens, Maine can set an example of unity for the rest of the country to follow.

Not all Wabanaki people are pleased by Elder Neptune's invitation, and not without just cause. The past twenty years have been marked by an increased interest in Native American spirituality that has led to its appropriation by those who take bits and pieces, who practice ceremonies without full understanding, or who charge fees for teachings and healings (legitimate Native American healers do not charge money). Unwittingly rude people attend ceremonies uninvited or act inappropriately during them. Unless a ceremony is open to the public, as many powwows around the state are, people must approach the pipe carrier with an offering of tobacco and ask politely to attend. If there is any doubt as to protocol, ask someone how to proceed. Do not ever touch jewelry, clothing, instruments, or sacred objects without asking. For those new to Native American ceremony, the Mawiomi of Tribes, held in August and hosted by the Aroostook Band of Micmacs,

is a three-day open celebration in Caribou that includes singing, dancing, drumming, traditional meals, children's games, ceremonies, and
open sweat lodges.

Wabanaki spirituality teaches respect, honor, reciprocity, and
generosity. Their lives entail an abiding love of creation, respect for
elders and ancestors, and concern for the seventh generation. Most
importantly, they know that all of humanity is connected to each other
and to creation.

Contact Information:

Check local newspapers and the Internet for powwows, seminars, and
activities.

Seeds of Peace International Camp

Since its inception in 1993, the internationally recognized Seeds of Peace International Camp has been bringing teenagers from regions of conflict to Otisfield, Maine. The nonprofit organization is secular and nonpolitical, but religion and politics are at the root of the conflicts that brings the youth to the remote and neutral camp for three-week programs designed to foster dialogue, understanding, and tolerance. Seeds of Peace began with forty-six teenagers from Israel, Palestine, and Egypt. The focus remains chiefly on the Israeli-Palestinian conflict, but it has been expanded to include delegations from eight Middle East countries, plus India, Pakistan, Afghanistan, Greece, Turkey and divided Cyprus, and the Balkans. Maine Seeds, specifically for Maine youth, and Beyond Borders, for Arab-American relations, are the most recent additions.

The campers, called Seeds, are fourteen to sixteen years old. In the highly competitive acceptance process, applicants must demonstrate proficiency in English, have strong leadership skills, and write an essay on why they want to attend the camp. Leadership is especially stressed, as it is hoped that the youth will assume leadership positions in adulthood and be "Seeds of Peace."

Each summer, four hundred fifty Seeds share living quarters with those who are considered their sworn enemies at home. Campers from regions in conflict are deliberately matched for discussion sessions and camp activities: Israelis and Palestinians, Indians and Pakistanis. Dialogues are led daily by professional facilitators who guide campers through discussions about their experiences, views, and feelings surrounding the conflicts disrupting their countries. The dialogues promote honesty, openness, and respect. Other activities include Cultural Night, when Seeds share their heritage; Group

Challenge, which promotes teamwork and cooperation; and Color Games in which the entire camp is divided into two multinational teams that compete in a range of activities including sports, music, fine arts, cooking, and computers. Throughout their stay, campers canoe, swim, dance, create art, participate in drama, play sports, and take computer classes.

Several times during the three weeks, delegates and their adult leaders meet to discuss concerns and impressions. It is the only time the campers speak their native language; all other times English is the common tongue.

In 2000, Seeds of Peace began its first exclusive American Project to address racial tensions between Maine teenagers and Asian and African immigrants. The program quickly expanded to other Maine cities and became known as Maine Seeds. According to Seeds of Peace, Portland and Lewiston are two of the largest refugee resettlement cities in the country. Campers are middle school students who are chosen through a series of interviews and an essay competition. Facilitators conduct daily conflict resolution dialogues that focus on race, religion, culture, and economic disparity. Police, youth agencies, and schools cooperate to continue the program throughout the school year by having the Maine Seeds attend meetings and give presentations throughout New England.

On October 28, 2003, Portland Seeds presented Governor Baldacci with the "Youth Charter for the State of Maine." Fourteen campers, inspired by Governor Baldacci's inaugural address, in which he called for a Youth Summit, wrote the document, which covers how diversity, education, economics, and media affect Maine youth.

Beyond Borders began in 2004 to address Arab-American relations by bringing together sixty-five campers from diverse regions, religions, geographies, and cultures in the United States and the Arab world. The most frequent topics discussed are the Iraq War and September 11, 2001.

Eleven years after its first summer, nearly three thousand Seeds have graduated the program, with most continuing to be involved with the program as leaders.

For more information:
Web site: *www.seedsofpeace.org*

Pursuing Higher Wisdom: Degrees, Certificates, and Programs

Bangor Theological Seminary

Chaplaincy Institute

Iseum of Divine Feminine

Rudolf Steiner Institute

Spirit Passages

Standing Bear

Bangor Theological Seminary – Christian Religious Education

Bangor and Portland

"Bangor Theological Seminary is an ecumenical seminary in the Congregational tradition of the United Church of Christ. It is committed to equip men and women for the work of Christian ministries; to serve as an intellectual center for the continuing sustenance and transformation of the church and the world; to provide for the study of religion; and to embody a public ministry within the local communities of northern New England."

"Here am I. Send me!" –Isaiah 6:8

—Mission Statement

Imagine a seminary where diversity is an actuality and everyone is welcome. Consider a student body comprised of various ethnicities with religious backgrounds that include Congregationalist, Baptist, Catholic, Jewish, Bahá'í, Salvation Army, Unitarian Universalist, Episcopalian, and Christian Science, among others. The age span is from twenty-two to seventy-two, with most students in their forties. They are from all over the country, work in different professions, and arrive with diverse understandings of their call to ministry. Now put these mature, enthusiastic, and curious students into small classes with excellent professors. The instructors are scholars, preachers, or theologians and are committed to interactive, flexible teaching methods. This imaginary classroom is the reality at Bangor Theological Seminary, and the outcome is invigorating discussions and open, in-depth learning.

Bangor Theological Seminary is unique in many ways. It is the only accredited seminary north of Boston, it is ecumenical, and its programs are designed for working adults. Today's students come to seminary for reasons such as enhancing their secular professions, personal growth, or choosing ministry as their first, second, or third career. Bangor Theological Seminary has worked hard to develop programs to address these diverse needs while maintaining the spiritual calling of the students.

The mission of modern seminaries is profound and complex. Bangor Theological Seminary aims to address global economic, social, and political realities but in connection with the local church. The small, community church has been a dominant part of its mission since its founding in 1814—it is the third oldest institution for theological study in the United States. At that time, populations were spreading north and west into unsettled territories, and the seminary sent ministers into the frontiers to build, serve, and civilize the struggling communities. It is still educating both ministers and lay people to serve in the small church but is now challenged by the spread of the consumer culture that is eroding the traditional small-town values of service and sharing. The seminary seeks to educate people who can bring awareness of world issues to small churches while also revitalizing them.

A prayer garden graces the front of the David Nelson Beach Chapel at Bangor Theological Seminary.

President William Imes is proud that Bangor Theological Seminary is considered progressive, and he stresses its tradition of being open and affirming to all people. It has welcomed women since 1904, with the enrollment of Lenora Hawles Jones. Today women comprise 60 percent of the student body. In the early 1980s, the seminary fully supported an openly gay professor. Imes predicts that as more churches accept gays and lesbians, the seminary will see an increased enrollment of that population just as it did with women in the past twenty years.

At Bangor Theological Seminary, they strive to connect faith to social injustice, be open about human sexuality, expose people to the trials of the third world, and deal with life as global, pluralistic, and multicultural. In the classroom, faith and spirituality are emphasized, and though that may seem self-evident in a seminary, many theological schools are mired in academic language and scientific research that seldom alludes to living a life immersed in God.

To address contemporary issues and the needs of students, Bangor Theological Seminary has developed a variety of learning options. Programs of study include:

- The Master of Divinity prepares students for ordained ministry and religious leadership programs in congregations.
- The Master of Arts is an individualized degree in which the student develops a program of study geared toward their personal objectives. Preparation for public ministry and/or professional and spiritual development are typical outcomes.
- The Doctor of Ministry is designed for experienced professionals from ministry settings.
- The Bangor Plan is an innovative and popular program for non-college-graduates. In a period of five to seven years, a student can complete a Baccalaureate and a Master of Divinity.
- Mentored Practice includes rigorous training, allowing students to gain field experience in churches, domestic violence shelters, hospitals, homeless shelters, hospices, and prisons.
- Continuing Education offers ecumenical mini-courses open to all people. The courses tend to focus on leadership training, professional development, spiritual enrichment, ethical questions, and global concerns.
- Also offered is a Church Leadership Program.

Courses of study include Old Testament, New Testament, Hebrew, Greek, Church History, Theology, Ethics, World Religions, Preaching, Worship and Spirituality, Congregational Life, Small Church Studies, Practical Theology, and the usual liberal arts programs.

The progressive position of Bangor Theological Seminary is evident in some of its courses: *Sexual and Domestic Violence, Sexuality and Social Order, Economic Justice, Feminist Theology and Spirituality,* and *Imagination, Ritual, and Art.* Cross-cultural courses may involve travel to France or Turkey.

Bangor Theological Seminary has deep roots in Bangor, and its distinctly beautiful chapel steeple is a landmark in the heart of the city. Thanks to donations and fundraisers, the front entrance to the David Nelson Beach Chapel (1859) is graced with a prayer garden holding an elegantly sculpted dove at its center. Services are held on Wednesdays at 11:00 a.m., and often, local clergy take advantage of attending a service they do not have to conduct.

Services are not held on Sundays so as not to compete with local churches; the Seminary believes it is there to serve the community, not to compete with it. A Worship Committee coordinates campus religious activities that utilize local religious figures, faculty, and students in events such as art shows, panel discussions, lectures, seminars, or special services.

In 1985, the Ruth Rich Hutchins Center was constructed connecting the chapel with the Wellman Commons (1895). The commons houses the dining room, lounge, and a second story balcony, which had a faculty art exhibit when I visited. The Hutchins Center contains classrooms, a meeting room, kitchen facilities, and lounges. All classrooms are set up with tables for seminar style learning.

The impressive library has ninety thousand volumes and subscribes to three hundred journals, making it one of the largest theological libraries in New England. Over one thousand books date prior to 1820, and there are over two thousand pamphlets of early nineteenth-century sermons.

To better serve older students, Bangor Theological Seminary offers one-, two-, and three-bedroom apartments, making it possible for families to live on campus. Shared living units are available for one to three people.

Maine Hall (1833) is the oldest building on campus and houses the administrative offices and the bookstore. An interesting aside for history buffs is that Joshua Chamberlain's former dormitory room is now the admissions office. The bookstore goes beyond supplying course textbooks and has a large amount of retail space given over to books on a wide range of spiritual and religious topics. There are sections on grief, fiction, theology, faith, global ecology, sexuality, women's issues, violence, and children's books.

Bangor Theological Seminary has a branch in Portland that was established in 1991 and is quickly growing. It is located in the historic State Street Congregational Church. The facilities include a library with thirty thousand volumes, a classroom, conference room, and administrative offices.

The priorities of Bangor Theological Seminary are to offer flexible, meaningful programs for working students, to engage in community support and service, to re-energize small churches, and to help communities understand how everyone is affected by global issues. The hope is that students will leave the seminary with an open, broad view of the world and with a set of beliefs that are fully thought out and truly their own. Bangor Theological Seminary presents to students the tools to transform religious life through education, faith, and acceptance.

Prices: 2005

Tuition – Degree or non-degree	$328.00 per credit
Tuition – Doctor of Ministry	$1,983.00 per semester
Student apartments	$341.00 to 645.00 per month
Shared living units	$261.00 to 341.00 per month

Contact Information:

Bangor Theological Seminary
Two College Circle
P.O. Box 411
Bangor, ME 04402-0411
Telephone: (800) 287-6781 extension 126
          (207) 942-6781
Web site: *www.bts.edu*
E-mail: enrollment@bts.edu

About the Area:
Historically, Bangor has been the gateway to Maine's north woods. In the 1850s, it was one of the world's largest lumber ports. Sights to see include historic points of interest, Stephen King's house, and a great metaphysical bookstore called Silo 7. A wonderful trail meanders through the city's historic highlights and along the Penobscot River. Bangor is an hour from Mount Desert Island and two and a half hours from Baxter State Park.

Chaplaincy Institute
of Maine
Interfaith Seminary

Portland

"The Chaplaincy Institute of Maine is an interfaith wisdom school and open community committed to transformation of the self and planet Earth though education, ordination, support, celebration, and service. ChIME will not discriminate based on race, color, religion, sex, marital status, beliefs, age, national origin, sexual orientation, physical or mental ability. ChIME is a non-profit educational organization governed by a Board of Trustees."

—Mission Statement

ChIME ordains planetary chaplains. The seminary's founder and abbot Reverend Jacob Watson reserves that intriguing term to describe those who are living their vision of community and healing through the arts, ministry, and the pursuit of justice. Radical theologian Matthew Fox, mystic and scholar Andrew Harvey, poet Mary Oliver, spiritual leader and teacher Dali Lama, scientist Brian Swimme, and Maine's own peacemaker George Mitchell are examples of "planetary chaplains" that walk among us.

To become a planetary chaplain, students must go beyond studying the mystics and become a mystic. At ChIME, mystics are not recluses but are active agents delivering their gifts of service to the world. First, students must delve into their emotional and spiritual life in order to discover their authenticity and gifts. They then bring this spiritually aware self to the world. Rev. Watson believes strongly that all ministers must be emotionally and spiritually mature before they have the privilege of working in the greater community as models of authenticity, sincerity, and integrity.

Interfaith seminaries are gaining popularity, and presently there are approximately a half dozen in the United States. Studies at interfaith seminaries encompass the world's great wisdom traditions, which are honored and respected, while also acknowledging the underlying connections between all faiths. In general, coursework tends to be more experiential, with the arts, meditation, ceremony, and ritual offered along with skill-based courses required of pastoral life such as grief counseling and sermon writing. At this point in time, interfaith seminaries are not geared toward producing ministers for churches, but toward chaplains for prisons, hospitals, hospices, and other institutional settings.

Interfaith education appeals to adult learners who are seeking a deeper relationship with God, and as is often the case, a second and more meaningful career. Some students simply want the knowledge and choose not to be ordained at graduation. They tend to be independent thinkers who wish to avoid the emphasis on church history, doctrine, and theology that is stressed in mainstream denominational schools. To them, interfaith ministry is relevant to America's growing pluralism and the emerging global community.

Reverend Watson's students enroll for the above reasons but also to be part of a strong spiritual community that offers support and connection, along with knowledge. It was the desire for community that was a major motivation for opening ChIME in September 2002. The seeds were sown over many cups of coffee with friends, colleagues, and associates who were looking to either share or seek spiritual knowledge. Watson was the obvious choice as abbot; in fact, his experiences were a tailor-made prelude to opening a chaplaincy institute.

In 1969, Watson founded Collins Brook School in Freeport. The school offered an alternative education for grades kindergarten through twelve. During his seven years as schoolmaster, he found he was well suited to counseling, as much of his time was spent in that task. He continued his education with intensive postgraduate work and a Master of Arts in Human Psychology with a specialty in grief counseling. He then worked as a senior staff member of the Elisabeth Kubler-Ross Center where he led Life, Death, and Transition workshops nationally and overseas. In 1988, Watson brought his expertise back to Maine when he became a founding director of The Center for Grieving Children, which offers community support, education, and outreach for children, teenagers, and families who are dealing with loss. It has grown into an invaluable asset to Greater Portland.

After a time, Watson felt the need for change, but he disregarded his inner longing until a fire destroyed his office and forced his hand. He left for California to pursue a new calling in religion. There he earned a Doctor of Ministry degree from the University of Creation Spirituality, an innovative program founded by Matthew Fox, who is best known as the author of *Original Blessings* and for the creation spirituality movement. The University of Creation Spirituality combines Western religious wisdom, art, science, and indigenous spiritual traditions to produce a unique educational experience. Watson was ordained through the Chaplaincy Institute for Arts and Interfaith Ministries, which ChIME is modeled after.

Over thirty years, Watson opened an alternative school, became a counselor, founded a specialized social service center, studied at two visionary religious schools, and became a minister. Certainly this compassionate and focused man could bring an interfaith school to Maine. In Watson, the group of colleagues had the spiritual guide that could make ChIME a reality, and together they committed to create a community for sharing and growing, which remains one of the highest values of the program.

ChIME is an intentionally demanding and intense program. Complacency, wherever it is hiding, is challenged on a multitude of levels by two years of immersion in spirituality. Deep exploration of the entire self brings with it both painful and powerful revelations—peace of mind is not one of the promises of spiritual life. Building a spiritual community with a diverse student body requires relationships that are honest, trusting, and open. Prayer is an essential ingredient in the education.

The commitment of time is also demanding. In two years, students must complete five hundred hours, consisting of sixty weekly evening classes, thirty-six one-day weekend workshops, two residential retreats, and independent study. The school year begins in September and ends in June. Additionally, three hundred hours of volunteer work and a contracted internship must be completed. After the obligations are met, students submit a minister's manual as their thesis. The manual includes commitment ceremonies, funeral services, naming ceremonies, three rites of passage rituals, guided visualizations, and uses for art in ministry.

Students are given considerable support as they move through the program. Once a month each student has contact with a core teacher. Four to six core teachers do a large percentage of the school's instruction. Each semester a student is assigned new teachers so that he or she is exposed to a variety of insights. A mentor is chosen by the student and may or may not be an instructor at the school. The student's interests drive the choice of mentor, and contact occurs monthly.

The first year is called "The Way of Contemplation," and learning involves inner exploration, researching a planetary chaplain, experimenting with a daily meditative prayer practice, exploring art in relationship to spirituality, comparative religions, creation spirituality, dream work, communication, ceremony, and ritual. In the first year, students do volunteer work and are encouraged to make choices that offer new experiences.

The second year is referred to as "The Way of Action," and is when more skill-based courses are taught. Studies in world religions, ceremonies, and rituals continue but with an emphasis on public involvement. Classes are offered in reinventing work, writing sermons, leadership, ethics, grief counseling, prayer / body prayer, healing with art, and community service. Students explore putting their gifts into action as chaplaincy interns, serving in places such as the Center for Grieving Children, Cumberland County Jail, Longcreek Youth Development Center, Barron Center, and hospice programs.

Students who are in circumstances that prohibit the full-time two-year schedule can enroll in the five-year extended program. Weekend workshops are taken anytime within the five years, but weekly classes must be completed with the same group of students in keeping with the commitment of a supportive community.

The impressive faculty includes fourteen instructors. Reverend Watson is reported to be a wonderful teacher and a wise abbot who has a gift for allowing events to unfold while providing guidance to move things along. Though the core teachers are the most involved, the others step in to teach their area of expertise. They are an eclectic group that includes the expected scholars and ministers, but also a Nigerian priest, art therapists, artists, performers, and counselors. Most staff members live in Maine, but guest instructors do visit for weekend workshops or classes. The well-known teachers and authors Philip Goldberg, PhD, author of *Road Signs: Navigating Your Path to Spiritual Happiness,* and Andrew Harvey, who wrote *The Direct Path,* have made guest appearances at ChIME.

The fledgling school of under twenty graduated their first class of five and ordained four ministers in the spring of 2004. Before the ordination service, the school year ended with a two-day residential retreat at Old Orchard Beach for all students and staff. The loosely scheduled days included drumming, meditation, silent beach walks, reflection, and sharing. The goal of community had been maintained by these individuals who grew to trust and respect one another in their preparation to be planetary chaplains.

ChIME students leave the program with a larger sense of the many avenues people take to God. Most people pursuing post secondary degrees are comfortable with a curriculum that appeals to the intellect and assignments that involve reading and writing, but limiting spiritual growth and expression to the written word disregards the multitude of ways that worship and healing occurs. Those same students are initially uneasy with art as a fully integrated part of their studies, or with body prayer that involves singing and dancing as prayer. However, these are the areas that allow them to stretch and that are found to be the most rewarding as they redefine themselves as artists and creators within God's world. Likewise, artists who spent years in educational systems that stressed the rational intellect can blossom fully in an environment that honors their expressive strengths and talents. ChIME attempts to bring their students, and therefore society, to a clearer understanding of wholeness and balance.

The public may enjoy the benefits of having ChIME in their community by attending workshops or interfaith afternoon worship services on the third Sunday of each month at the Swedenborgian Church on Stevens Avenue in Portland. ChIME is sure to become a growing and influential part of Greater Portland's community, and we can all be thankful for its service and ministry.

Requirements:
All applicants must have a Bachelor of Arts or Science

Prices: 2005
Tuition for the two-year program: $4,800
Tuition for the Extended Program: $5,200

Contact Information:

ChIME
P.O. Box 3833
Portland, ME 04104
Telephone: (207) 347-6740
Web site: *www.chimeofmaine.org*
E-mail: chime@gwi.net

About the Area:
Portland is Maine's largest city and its most sophisticated. There is an abundance of cultural attractions: an excellent art museum, several theater groups, countless galleries, a symphony, and diverse music offerings. The Old Port and downtown have interesting architecture, superb restaurants, bars, and shops.

Iseum Musicum and the Temple of the Feminine Divine – Goddess Religion

Bangor

"Priestess/priest training is more than a study group; it is an intensive program of work. I foresee there being lots of fun as well, but an earnest commitment to study and development is essential … It is imperative that our children and our children's children see and feel the divine feminine energy equally with the divine masculine energy. Women's spirituality must come out of the groves and secret circles to dance in the open. Its beauty, gentleness, and power will influence generations."

—The Vision
By Kay Gardner

The Iseum Musicum, or "Hearth of the Goddess," is a course of study for exploring personal spirituality, heritage, activism, and service through a three-year curriculum in Goddess religion. At the program's conclusion, students may choose to be ordained as priestesses or priests.

The Iseum exists in collaboration with the Temple of the Feminine Divine, and is located on the second floor of a downtown office building. The dreary hallway opens into the Iseum, a bright, warm room with comfortable chairs, a library of five hundred books, and all the comforts of home, including a nearby kitchen. The adjoining room is the Meditation Room, which is a room used specifically for meditation, prayer, ritual, seasonal rites, and offerings. The main altar in the Temple changes with the seasons and a smaller altar, the altar of the ancestors, is dedicated to Kay Gardner, one of the founders, who passed away in 2002. It is evident that the priestesses are creative and artistic as the rooms have a lovely assortment of feminine art, though the dominant theme is Egyptian with a significant nod to Isis, the Goddess of Ten Thousand Names.

The priestesses' talents are also expressed in their love of singing, and they readily break into song when requested. Music plays an important role in the Iseum's history, which explains "Musicum" in the title. In the early 1990s, before there was an Iseum, some of the founders bonded at a retreat where Kay Gardner taught them chants in a circle, rounds, and songs from around the world. Gardner was an internationally known musician who studied the impact of music on healing. In 1990, she wrote *Sounding the Inner Landscape: Music as Medicine*. The retreat participants convinced her to lead a singing group in Bangor that came to be called Women with Wings. Each week since 1994, between ten to seventy women have rehearsed songs that they have written themselves, as well as songs written by others. They even have a CD—"Hand to Hand and Heart to Heart."

The Iseum's birth was in 1998 with the "Magic, Music, and Mystery Tour" to southeastern Ireland where Gardner, who had been initiated as a priestess twenty-three years prior, was ordained. Seven women from Women with Wings joined Gardner and witnessed her ordination as a high priestess in the Fellowship of Isis by the Honorable Olivia Robertson at Clonegal Castle, in Enescorthy, Ireland.

In Goddess religion, the Fellowship of Isis is a large and well-known organization, and Lady Olivia Robertson is one of the four founders. It began in 1976 at the Clonegal Castle in Ireland and is dedicated to the worship of the Goddess with an emphasis on Egyptian and Celtic goddesses. They claim to have approximately 12,500 members from 81 countries, and over 450 Iseums in 37 countries. People from all religious alliances are welcome, leading to a diverse membership base. They provide education, standards, and principles to members and have a worldwide directory of Iseums.

During the tour, Gardner initiated two of the women at the Chalice Well in Glastonbury, England, known as a sacred spot that has attracted pilgrims for centuries. When the travelers, some of whom were newly ordained or initiated, returned to Bangor, they were invigorated and inspired by their trip. A group was formed to create an Iseum based on the guidelines set forth by the Fellowship of Isis. A curriculum committee studied programs from around the world, and designed one tailored to their philosophy and needs. In February

1999, the first class of students entered the Iseum Musicum and were ordained in November 2001. The first group of priestesses immediately opened the Temple of the Feminine Divine.

The three-year program entails eighteen weeks per year, twelve in the spring and six in the fall. Classes meet once a week for three-hour sessions. In addition to class time, initiates complete forty hours of independent study.

For the independent study, initiates specialize in one or more of seven paths that resonate with them: leading and creating ritual, creating art, physician and spiritual healing, teaching and scholarship, administration and organizing inspirational events, ecological and earth-based studies, and public speaking and activism. In the past, students have learned a healing technique such as Reiki, studied shamanism, or attended workshops.

The program is designed to transform students' lives on multiple levels. All students are required to pursue good physical health with a form of movement, such as yoga, dance, or regular walking. Creativity is shown through a port-

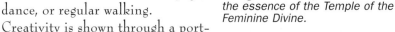

This graceful sculpture captures the essence of the Temple of the Feminine Divine.

folio of artistic projects. One woman who felt artistically challenged found she had a talent for making altar cloths and ritual clothing. Inner exploration is expressed through journal keeping, be it in the form of writing, scrapbooking, or even keeping clippings from magazines and newspapers.

Students arrive for their first class having read *Peace and Power* by Peggy L. Chin. The book is a feminist version of the classic text for conducting meetings, *Robert's Rules of Order,* which first appeared in 1896. In a peace and power procedure, people sit in a circle so everyone has eye contact, it is non-hierarchal, everyone contributes, and all dissension is thoroughly explored. The emphasis is on integration, consensus, unity, and sharing. All classes begin with the peace and power process, and though students find it difficult and frustrating in the beginning, with time, some claim that their perceptions are transformed as they adopt ways that conform to feminine qualities.

Classes are learning circles, and there is an aversion to using the word "teacher." Administrators guide students and assist in facilitating classes, but students are active participants. Part of each class is a student presentation on a goddess.

The course of study is guided by the group and includes goddesses as archetypes of the feminine divine, environmentalism, psychic skills, feminism, creative expression, healing, divination, conflict resolution, ethics, and ritual. A small sampling of courses includes: *Meditation, Music, and Movement; Pandora's Box: Expressing Creativity through Gender; Unlearning Racism (and Other 'Isms); How to Serve the Goddess; Trance I and II;* and six classes on *Life Passages.*

The fall semester of the second year is dedicated to planning and producing a public event. A major goal of the Temple and Iseum is to bring the feminine divine to Bangor as a visible force with the intention of broadening people's horizons and increasing their awareness. In its grandest project, the Iseum organized Goddess 2000, which was in conjunction with an international week of celebrating Earth religions, nature, and the Goddess. Events took place in thirty-three countries. In Bangor, the six-day festival included an interfaith panel discussion, films at the library, two art workshops, a lecture on "Rooting Out the Green Man," a community drumming circle, a performance by Portland's Veronica Sacred Arts, and an exhibit featuring altars and artistic celebrations of the feminine divine. One of the highlights was an eight-foot paper mache Gaia. The festivities were capped with a chemical-free Goddess Ball where all those age twelve and over were invited to attend dressed as their favorite deity.

During the last semester, initiates prepare for their ordination by studying Fellowship of Isis rites, creating tools, and planning the event. The ordination is a sacred ceremony and each graduating class designs its event through consensus. Five years after the opening of the Iseum, fourteen priestess have been ordained. The following is the Iseum's statement of purpose:

> We make a commitment to embody the Feminine Divine
> in our lives and in the community at large through individual study, group work, and community action. We agree to
> confidentiality, honesty, compassion, trust, love, and joy.

Paganism has been recognized as a legal religion since 1985 (Dettmer v. Landon), and as the religion grows, the desire for clergy has grown as well. Followers have always had priestesses and priests, and some argue that official status matters less than lineage, training, experience, and wisdom. However, there is a demand for trained, professional clergy that are held to certain standards and can perform

114

weddings, funerals, rites of passage, and initiations. Clergy may also be adept at divination and healing.

Priestesses who are ordained at the Iseum Musicum have the option of registering with the Maine Pagan Clergy Association (MPCA), which provides licenses, recognition, and support to pagan clergy. The council of priestesses and priests carefully screens applicants with a thorough interview process before licensing or adding them to a state directory of pagan clergy. The MPCA is registered with the state, which brings advantages such as legal status, community outreach, and legitimacy in the eyes of those who are unfamiliar with paganism. (For more on Paganism see page 9.)

The Iseum is remarkably affordable, charging only $20.00 per class, insuring it is accessible to most people. (In general, Pagans are sensitive about not profiting from their teaching.) The priestesses offer an assortment of interesting fundraisers that compensate for the low enrollment cost and allow them to maintain their space. On one occasion, David Trobisch, a graduate professor from the Bangor Theological Seminary, presented "Traveling with Paul in the Footsteps of the Goddess," which was a fascinating exploration of cities that had temples dedicated to feminine deities at the time of Paul. They regularly offer learning circles open to the public on a variety of topics: symbols, herbalism, massage, Tarot reading, sound therapy, goddess arts and crafts, and Celtic art, among others. There are also film nights and benefit concerts by Women with Wings. Several times a year, they hold a "Red Tent Day" in the Temple. Inspired by the book of the same name by Anita Diamant, women who drop by are treated to foot baths, neck and back rubs, sweets, tea, stories, and laughter.

The public is welcome to become members of the Temple and is entitled to the use of the library, discounts on workshops, rent of the Temple for special events, attendance at open rituals, and eight newsletters a year. It is open at regular hours for prayer and meditation. Women are in the majority, but there are male members, and there have been male students at the Iseum. At times, those involved with the Temple and Iseum are misunderstood as "anti-male" because of their emphasis on the Goddess. They stress that they honor men and masculine energy, but believe that feminine energy needs extra attention to make up for years of neglect due to the patriarchal nature of society. By focusing on the Goddess, they are seeking to rectify the imbalance between masculine and feminine energy. One of their long-term goals is to assist in bringing balance to Bangor by creating a public meditation garden that would include sculptures and be a place to honor the feminine divine. (In a sad commentary on the depths of the patriarchy, the priestesses had to be very careful in choosing a name that would not be interpreted as a place for illicit massages.)

Most of the priestesses at the Iseum Musicum and the Temple of the Feminine Divine say they practiced honoring the Goddess, even before they had a name for what they were doing. Now, they have found a community that supports and respects their beliefs. They invite all people who have a hunger for knowledge of the Goddess to join their community and bring balance to their lives.

Costs: 2005
Classes are $20.00 per week, for 18 weeks per year. Payments are made at class meetings.

Contact Information:

Iseum Musicum
Temple of the Feminine Divine
Suite #203–205
31 Central Street
Bangor, ME 04401
Telephone: (207) 941-0261

About the Area:
See Bangor Theological Seminary, page 101.

Rudolf Steiner Institute - Anthroposophy

Locations in Northern New England

"Every insight you seek only to enrich your own store of learning and to accumulate treasure for yourself alone leads you from your path, but every insight you seek in order to become more mature on the path of the ennoblement of humanity and world evolution brings you one step forward. This fundamental law must always be observed. Only if we make it the guiding principle of our lives can we call ourselves genuine seekers after higher knowledge."

—Rudolf Steiner
How to Know Higher Worlds

Since 1974, the Rudolf Steiner Institute has provided coursework for curious newcomers and for those who have studied Steiner for years. For three weeks each summer, students from around the world come together in community to learn from the teachings of Steiner, an Austrian who lived from 1861 to 1925 and was the founder of anthroposophy.

A coherent discussion of the Rudolf Steiner Institute is not possible without first outlining the teachings of Steiner himself. This is not an easy task as the man was a prolific scientist as well as a clairvoyant and visionary whose many ideas conceivably could reshape and renew our culture. Steiner referred to his teachings as anthroposophy, which is derived from the Greek *anthropos,* meaning human, and *sophia,* meaning wisdom. He taught that direct experience with the spiritual world is attainable when human wisdom is directed along a prescribed path of self-discipline.

In anthroposophy, the intellect is balanced with the needs of the heart. The intellect is generally considered masculine while the heart is feminine, symbolized by "sophia." Steiner believed that much of the negativity found in the world was the result of the excesses of patriarchal institutions that emphasized intellect, repressing the feminine and, therefore, the demands of the heart.

Reincarnation was an integral part of Steiner's beliefs, and he spoke of the "I" as the kernel of the self that does not die and allows each being to be a unique individual. In karma loca, the Buddhist term for the period between lives, life is re-experienced from the "I" vantage point and also from the point of view of anyone who had contact with the individual. He taught that divinity manifests itself through humans who are evolving toward perfection. The best way to achieve perfection is through relationships that are provided by community. As the "I" transforms, the community and the world transform as well.

In anthroposophy, evil exists to allow for freedom through individual choices. People choose to evolve toward perfection or to stagnate. Spiritual beings are evolving along with those in physical form. Steiner disagreed that humans are one step up from the apes; he considered humanity to be a step down from angels. In his view, humans are not physical beings on a spiritual path, but spiritual beings on a physical path.

Steiner was adamant that anthroposophy not be characterized as a religion. It is better understood as the teachings that direct one toward spiritual awareness. He predicted that self-directed development within the sphere of community service is the next stage in humanity's spiritual evolution. He wrote, "The healthy social life is found when in the mirror of each human soul the whole community finds its reflection, and when in the community the virtue of each one is living."

Thinking, feeling, and willing are the hallmarks of Steiner's teachings. He urged meditation as essential for spiritual growth but did not discount the ego, which should be developed, nor did he deny the power of trained cognition as necessary for transformation.

It is difficult to find an area of culture that Steiner did not expand on. He established initiatives in art, dance, drama, architecture, science, education, agriculture, medicine, economics, religion, care for the dying, and social organizations. He also found time to write forty books, four mystery plays, give seven thousand lectures, and hold thousands of consultations.

His initiatives were triggered by questions. For instance, his agricultural practices were inspired by questions from farmers who were concerned about the degeneration of cultivated plant and seed strains. Steiner researched the question scientifically and developed an innovative plan of action. He invented biodynamic agriculture, which went beyond organic farming because it addressed the interdependence of soil, plants, livestock, weather, lunar cycles, and seasons. He included in his plan an herbal compound referred to as "medicine for the earth." To this day, biodynamic agriculture is practiced and has been particularly successful in wine production. Benzinger Estate winery in Sonoma, California, is committed to Steiner's biodynamic techniques. There are also two lines of personal grooming products that adhere to his production standards.

People are most familiar with Steiner through the Waldorf schools, which were started in 1919 when he was asked by the Waldorf-Astoria Cigarette Company to establish a school for its workers' children. His model for education has grown into nine hundred Waldorf schools worldwide, one hundred fifty in the United States, with five in Maine. The philosophy that education is an art and should be geared toward human growth and development is now standard even if it is not regularly practiced in many public schools. In Waldorf schools, the curriculum is based on the developmental stage of the child with a focus on hands-on activities. Rhythm, believed to create harmony and balance, is stressed holistically through observing things like body movement, the time of day, and the seasons of the year.

The Rudolf Steiner Institute began as a forum for anthroposophy professors from around the United States to share their knowledge and insights. Their vision was to create college-level courses about spiritual science. The first session was six weeks long and included intense coursework with evening performances and lectures. The free-flowing exchange of ideas, lively conversations, and the sense of community that prevailed convinced the organizers that they had tapped into a demand for sharing the teachings of anthroposophy. In the following years, the program was shortened to three weeks.

From the beginning, the institute was designed to reflect a balance of thinking, feeling, and willing. To that end, classes in art, dancing, drama, and music were offered along with geometry, philosophy, nutrition, science, and history. Due to the poor quality of food found in most institutional kitchens, the Rudolf Steiner Institute decided to provide its own food program. In Steiner's philosophy, nutritious food produced and prepared with care and eaten in community, is essential to good health. The food program also provided working scholarships for students who otherwise would be unable to attend.

After thirty years, the integrity of the institute is intact. Course offerings are a blend of academic and artistic. Early morning movement, afternoon music, mealtime, and exciting evening programs address the social and community-building aspects of Steiner's philosophy. Families are welcome, with children attending a Waldorf-based camp during the day and appropriate evening activities.

Days at the institute begin with a morning warm-up based on Bothmer gymnastics. Count Fritz von Bothmer, who was a gymnastics teacher at the Stuttgart Waldorf School, worked closely with Steiner to create healthful movements that enhanced balance and coordination. It appears similar to Tai Chi in that the movements are slow and graceful yet clearly defined.

There are four periods in each day, and students choose up to three courses. The following is a description of a course that is typical of a philosophical offering. *What did Steiner Bring to Esotericism? A Comparative Approach,* which was taught by Robert McDermott, PhD, and Sharon MacCabe. Academic and art instructors often co-teach classes. McDermott is the former president of the Rudolf Steiner Institute, President Emeritus and Professor of Philosophy and Religion at the California Institute of Integral Studies, and President of the Owen Barfield Graduate School of Anthroposophical Studies. MacCabe teaches music at the Kimberton Waldorf School, has a degree in Organ Performance and a Master in harpsichord. The five-day course met for one and a half hours twice a day. The course material explored and compared the spiritual traditions of Rudolf Steiner, the Dali Lama, and Sri Aurobindo. Steiner is from the esoteric, Christo-centric and Rosicrucian traditions. It is probably safe to assume that definitions are needed. Esotericism is spiritual knowledge that was previously secret. Christo-centricism is the belief that Christ was the supreme historical avatar, the physical embodiment of a spiritual master. Rosicrucianism refers to an occult organization that passed information orally through generations for the spiritual development of humanity. Steiner broke with this oral tradition by recording the teachings, making them accessible to everyone.

The Dali Lama also brought esoteric knowledge to all when he left Tibet. He taught that Tibetan Buddhists do not have a god in the Western sense but focus on buddhas, the "awakened ones," who transcend ordinary physical life. The buddhas bestow blessings on humans. Tibetan Buddhists integrate astrology, oracles, and mediums into their practice. Their focus is to evolve to an awakened state through mantra, prayer, ritual, and meditation. There is no word for religion in Tibetan Buddhism, though the concept closest to it is dharma.

Sri Aurobindo lived from 1872 to 1950 and was well known in India and to people who were intrigued by his vision of a utopian community. Aurobindo was also responsible for transmitting previously secret practices to a public audience. He taught that through the practice of yoga it was possible to transcend to a higher consciousness, to discover the separate self within, and to feel the oneness of all that is. Through practice, spiritual evolution could be achieved by uniting the higher self with consciousness and the physical body. Disciples believed that he and his partner, who was called Mother, were avatars. The course included advanced reading on the teachings of the three men, combined lecture with discussion, and offered intriguing and original insights.

The Rudolf Steiner Institute offers in-depth, intensive, and high-level coursework. Students repeatedly report that their attraction to anthroposophy is based on science and research. The instructors are highly qualified and committed.

A description of the day would be incomplete without discussing the institute's excellent food program. The family-style meals are vegetarian, and whenever possible, biodynamic and organic foods are used. Accommodations are made for dairy- and gluten-free diets and they are substantial alternatives. Lunch is the main meal of the day, and a sample menu includes sautéed fresh vegetables, mixed field greens with a homemade dressing, and a pasta casserole. The alternative offering was stir-fried vegetables and brown rice with glazed carrots as a side dish. The food is hot, fresh, and appetizing.

After lunch, students are welcome to participate in an hour of choral singing under the guidance of Sharon MacCabe. All are welcome, even the musically illiterate.

The last period ends at 6:00 p.m. and is followed by a light supper. At 8:00 p.m., the evening program begins. Students and instructors share their expertise in programs with broad appeal. Dancing, puppetry, storytelling, and drama round out panel discussions and lectures. Children are welcome only at those events that will capture and hold their attention. On weekends, guests are free to explore the area, and transportation is provided for group outings.

Classes last for one or two weeks and are combined in several ways to meet individual needs. Approximately twenty classes are scheduled each year. Examples include: *Re-Imagining Geometry, Christ in a Pluralistic Age, Parzival: How Can a Fool Become Lord of the Grail?, Singing Down the Stars, Soul-Color-Images, Movement and Freedom: The Body in Play, Puppets Alive!,* and *Covering Home: The Challenges of Fathering in the 21st Century.*

Many Waldorf school teachers visit the summer program, and classes geared to their needs may include *Painting in the Waldorf Curriculum, Fundamentals of Waldorf Education,* and *Life Ways: Caring for the Young Child.*

The Rudolf Steiner Institute sets up a bookstore with hundreds of books. They also sell grooming products made using Steiner techniques, arts and crafts, teaching supplies, and toys.

People of all ages attend the programs. Ages range from the

early twenties to the nineties. In 2003, twenty-eight states and seven countries were represented. (Rudolf Steiner is better known in Canada and Europe.) Every year between two hundred and two hundred fifty students enroll.

Several other educational facilities are based on Steiner's teachings, including a full-time college. His education and dance programs are especially popular. The Rudolf Steiner Institute is independent and not affiliated with any other organization.

For eight years, the institute met at Thomas College in Waterville. In 2004, it moved to Bishop's University in Lennoxville, Quebec, and in 2005 to Green Mountain College in Putney, Vermont. The institutes chooses campuses that are in harmony with its philosophies and has no future plans of leaving northern New England.

Steiner's ideas on spirituality, culture, and science are truly dynamic and deserve attention. The Rudolf Steiner Institute is an enriching and inspiring way to explore Rudolf Steiner's anthroposophy and spread the good word.

Prices: 2005

There is a variety of options depending on whether the stay is for one, two, or three weeks, and on the number of courses. The following price is based on a three-week stay with three courses and includes tuition, lodging (double occupancy), and meals.
Tuition: $2,795.00
Work-study programs and scholarships are available.
A 5% discount is available to those who live and work in Canada.

Contact Information:

Rudolf Steiner Institute
Registrar
P.O. Box 5373
Baltimore, MD 21209
Telephone: (800) 774-5191
Web site: *www.steinerinstitute.org*
E-mail: registrar@steinerinstitute.org

Spirit Passages –
Shamanism

Yarmouth

"The purpose of Spirit Passages is to give individuals the tools to become conscious participants in their own healing, health and spiritual evolution."

—Statement of Purpose

When external values are no longer fulfilling and mainstream religion fails to provide meaningful guidance, spiritual seekers are often aroused to explore ideas and practices that appear to be at odds with our materialistic, intellectually driven culture. Shamanism is the antithesis to modern society, and its growing acceptance exemplifies a perceptual change that is redefining religion, faith, healing, and our relationship with the natural world. The founders of Spirit Passages, C. Allie Knowlton and Evelyn C. Rysdyk, are also co-founders of True North, an integrative health center that combines conventional medical care with complementary practices, such as shamanic healing. True North is the home base for Spirit Passages which, among its many offerings, has the only graduate program for shamanism in the United States. The paradigm has shifted.

Shamanism is humanity's oldest religion. Anthropological evidence of shamanic practices is found throughout the world and has strikingly similar features wherever it occurs. In shamanism, everything is spiritually interconnected—plants, animals, elements, weather, geography, and humans. The intent of practicing shamanism is to awaken our awareness of the natural world, and through states of expanded consciousness, connect with it on a deep level.

In indigenous cultures, the shaman is often chosen after

recovering from a health crisis or near-death experience. In some tribes, surviving a high-risk experience or having a spiritual transformation involving visions and/or dreams would indicate a calling. Once the shaman is identified, he or she is trained in the traditions of the tribe to become a healer and a spiritual guide who communicates with the natural world to bring information and solutions to the tribe.

Today, a transforming life experience may provoke a calling to shamanism just as it has for thousands of years, but as ancient shamanism adapts to our contemporary life, the skills and practices are no longer reserved exclusively for a chosen few, but are open to all who want to learn. Healing methods such as soul retrieval, power animal retrieval, extraction, and journeying for others require long-term study and a full commitment. However, those who want to use the skills in their daily lives and participate in their own healing can choose from many tools.

Knowlton and Rsydyk have been teaching shamanism since 1991 and offer students basic to advanced skills. They have studied extensively with Michael Harner, PhD, and Sandra Ingerman. Harner is an anthropologist who has studied shamanism since the 1960s when he turned away from his academic life and lived with tribes to train with their shamans. He introduced shamanic traditions to a modern audience with his classic book *The Way of the Shaman,* and is the founder of the Foundation for Shamanic Studies. Ingerman was formerly the director of education for the Foundation of Shamanic Studies and has authored four books on shamanism. Both Knowlton and Rsydyk graduated from the Foundation for Shamanic Studies' Three-Year Program in Advanced Shamanism and Shamanic Healing. In addition to being Shamanic Practitioners, Knowlton has a Master of Social Work and is a licensed clinical social worker. Rysdyk is an author and spiritual artist.

Journeying is as essential to shamanism as meditation is to Buddhism, and Spirit Passages offers an inexpensive two-hour workshop to introduce techniques to the general public. Each month, approximately twenty people arrive at True North to experience the Lowerworld. The intent of the journey is to leave ordinary reality, the place most of people occupy in their daily lives, and enter nonordinary reality, which is the state of expanded consciousness. During the journey, travel to another realm is initiated through sound, movement, meditation, or in some cultures, psychotropic drugs. This realm is divided into the Lowerworld, Middleworld, and Upperworld. In most cultures, the tree is symbolic of the connection between the three worlds.

Like shamans throughout the world, Knowlton and Rsydyk use drumming to make spiritual connections. They explain that the brain entrains to four drumbeats per second creating theta brain waves, which are the most conducive to altered consciousness. The theta waves produce a state of alert awareness where visual and somatic experiences are enhanced. People often experience fluctuations in body temperature, varying degrees of discomfort, and difficulty ignoring the incessant chatter and skepticism of the left brain. A journey is a trip from the left brain, which is never fully silenced, to the right brain for sensory experience, and then back to the left brain for interpretation of what occurred. The right brain allows travel to a realm that is outside of form, time, or space.

Knowlton and Rsydyk use the method for journeying that is taught by Harner. Once drumming begins, people go to a pre-chosen place to begin their journey. This is called the power place, and is a place in nature that a person remembers, or still visits, that makes him or her feel exceptionally good. While the drumming is gradually inducing a trance state, the journeyer looks for a portal in the power place to enter the Lowerworld. Examples are a foxhole, tree stump, or cave. It is important to set the intention of going downward, and to let the imagination run wild without being concerned that it is cheating or not the right way to proceed. People often travel downward in tunnels and tubes, or on ladders and ramps. As the trance state takes hold, active imagination shifts to images and actions of the spirits. On the first journey, people are encouraged to explore and, when an animal comes forward, to engage it in conversation. With successive journeys, the same animal may appear, indicating that it is a spirit helper or power animal, and it will answer questions brought to the Lowerworld.

Journeys are made to seek wisdom from spirit guides who may take the form of ancestors, mythological creatures, archetypal figures, animal guides, or power animals. The guide that appears is sometimes determined by an individual's ethnic or cultural inheritance. A person of Irish descent may meet a fairy, while a Hawaiian may have a Kahuna appear. Entering nonordinary reality to receive wisdom from personalized spirit guides sounds fun, and some people are tempted to treat it as an amusement since anyone can be taught the skill, but shamans emphasize that each journey is sacred and must be honored as such.

Spirit Passages offers nearly thirty different workshops that are two hours, one day, or two days in length. Two-hour workshops introduce participants to journeying without a large investment in time or money. The short programs include *Introduction to Journeying; Peruvian Whistling Vessels,* in which participants journey to the unique sound created by the vessels; *Ayni Despacho,* an Andean ceremony for thanking the earth; and *Visit with Grandma,* in which a wise spirit merges and speaks through Rysdyk in a traditional shamanic method for offering wisdom and healing.

One- and two-day workshops cover a wide range of topics including learning from a Peruvian shaman, building a relationship with nature, integrating shamanism into everyday life, death and transitions, divination, shamanic dreaming, connecting with ancestors, accessing past lives, the merging of science with spirituality, and creating rituals. A common theme that runs throughout the teaching is to honor Mother Earth through rituals, environmentally sound habits in daily life, and giving thanks.

The *Shamanic Journey Process* is an introductory, weekend workshop and a prerequisite for the others, unless the enrollee already has a working knowledge of the journey process. Rysdyk's book *Modern Shamanic Living: New Explorations of an Ancient Path* is the basis for a workshop of the same name in which the inner hunter/gatherer is accessed through journeys, stories, movement, and drumming. Some of the most popular workshops are those in which a native shaman is present. In the *Indigenous Spirituality of Peru,* a Peruvian shaman, Puma Quispe, teaches about building sacred places and creating a rewarding relationship with the Guiding Mountain Spirits.

For people who wish to expand their studies or to become shamanic healers, Spirit Passages offers a Two-Year Advanced Shamanic Training Program. The training involves classic techniques from around the globe, ritual work, power dances, and power songs. Shamanic skills include soul retrieval, power animal retrieval, word and sound doctoring, spirit canoe and arrow, and absentee healing. Ethics, clear diagnostic work, and following Spirit's guidance are emphasized. Students attend one-week residential intensives twice a year for two years. The intensives are held at a lakeside resort in Maine. Group size ranges from twenty to thirty people, and students come from throughout the United States and Canada to participate.

The Two-Year Graduate Program in Shamanism and Healing is open to students who have completed their apprenticeship with either Spirit Passages or the Foundation for Shamanic Studies. The program presents opportunities to expand upon shamanic healing practices and with an emphasis on integrating shamanism into daily life. The information and techniques are not offered elsewhere in the training. Like the apprentice program, intensives occur twice a year for two years.

Spirit Passages also offers peer supervision and/or personal spiritual direction for shamanic practitioners.

Some people believe that shamanism is a primitive and fantastical attempt to explain reality, but science has begun to find evidence that everything in the natural world is vibrating with the energy of subatomic particles, and shaman's believe our DNA very possibly contains the collective unconscious. Currently, there are no proven rational explanations for the spirit guides that greet people during journeys or for the effectiveness of soul retrieval in curing illnesses such as depression. Whether empirical proof exists is unimportant to those who find shamanism to be a fascinating, effective way to access intuition, wisdom, and healing, and Spirit Passages is a qualified and safe place to embark on the shamanic path.

Prices:

Prices range from $15.00 for the short programs to $150.00 for the two-day workshops. The apprentice and graduate programs are $950.00 per intensive, including lodging and meals.

Contact Information:

Spirit Passages
P.O. Box 426
Yarmouth, ME 04096
Web site: *www.spiritpassages.com*
E-mail: passages@maine.rr.com

About the Area:

Yarmouth is a ten-minute drive north from Portland, Maine's largest city. The lovely coastal town is free from tourist attractions with the exception of the DeLorme Map Store. Two-day workshops are held at Sacred Oaks, a shamanic center in Wells. Wells is a popular beach town that is full of activity in the summer months.

The Standing Bear Center for Shamanic Studies – Shamanism

Surry

"One of the major goals of shamanic practice is to bring the ego into proper alignment within the structure of the personality. One of the most effective ways of doing this consists of exploring and integrating the image and meaning of the Tree of Life as an archetypal symbol of psychological and spiritual balance between the purposes of the Divine Feminine and the purposes of the Divine Masculine. This difficult practice, which requires perseverance, patience and compassion for oneself and for others, often results in a profound spiritual experience."

—Scarlet Kinney

Shamanism predates all spiritual practices by tens of thousands of years and is experiencing a worldwide revival. Indigenous peoples are reclaiming shamanic practices, and archeological findings are evidence that most people on the planet can partake in exploring their shamanic heritage. For centuries, ethnocentric studies resisted seeing the value in practices viewed as uncivilized, while modern psychiatry dismissed transcendent religious experiences as pathology. Those attitudes still prevail in some circles where shamanism is considered crazy, eccentric, and as embodying the excesses of the New Age movement. At the opposite extreme from the skeptics are those who consider shamans to have godlike powers. Responsible, legitimate shamans are not crazy, nor do they claim godlike powers, and they do not take on the title after a workshop or two. Legitimate shamans are chosen and initiated in experiences that demand the death of the former self so that a new self can be born. Scarlet Kinney, the founding director of The Standing Bear Center for Shamanic Studies, was chosen.

How did an Irish Catholic who grew up in Ellsworth, Maine, become a shaman? The simple answer is, by catching on fire, but of course there is more to her story than that. Kinney's dramatic story is a classic shamanic initiation. In 1988, Kinney, who is a professional artist, was moving into a space that would serve as her home and art gallery. An unsecured pipe led to a propane explosion that blew the sky-light forty feet into the air and destroyed all of Kinney's possessions and art. During the explosion, Kinney had an out of body experience in which hulking spirits were evident to her and informed her she must return. She sensed that they instantaneously passed huge amounts of information to her. Upon looking down at her burning self, she felt deep compassion and in a flash was back in her body. Once back, she had total clarity and presence of mind. She removed her clothing and ran naked to a neighbor's where she got into a cold shower. Her quick thinking did not prevent a two-month stay in a burn clinic, but the healing went very quickly, with all of the initial skin grafts being 100 percent successful. The hulking spirits identified themselves as five bears who belonged to the Bear Spirit Clan. It was evident to her that they were assisting in her rapid physical healing.

When Kinney left the hospital, the psychological impact of the event made her daily life extremely difficult. She could not think of nouns and had to use elaborate descriptions for objects she wanted to name. Her dreams became tremendously vivid and were filled with bears and cobras that moved up her spine, symbolizing the Hindu Kundalini energy. She fell back on her Zen training and moved forward each day by showing up and functioning to the best of her ability. (She trained with Walter Nowick, the original founder of Morgan Bay Zendo; see page 54.)

Understandably, Kinney thought she was insane and made visits to several therapists who were unable to find an applicable diagnosis. During this period, her painting changed from the studies of light on water that had engrossed her prior to the explosion to subject matter that was radically different. A therapist who viewed her new paintings referred to them as shamanic, which was a term that was new to Kinney. Desperate for information to explain her experience, she researched shamanic material and found many initiation stories that mirrored her own.

Two years after the accident, Kinney started to receive guidance to travel to Santa Fe, New Mexico. She describes it as a constant drum beat in her mind, body, and blood. After two months, she heeded the guidance and went to Santa Fe, where she saw a poster of an Iroquois woman giving workshops on women's shamanic ways. Kinney recognized the woman from her dreams and began three years of study with her.

The Standing Bear Center for Shamanic Studies opened in 1994 and evolved gradually from offering workshops to a full-fledged apprentice program and a shamanic counseling practice. Kinney believes that the information imparted to her during her out-of-body experience was not fully integrated until the years from 2002 to 2004, and it took those fourteen years to learn to manage the shamanic energies and powers she had been given. To complement her shamanic studies, Kinney enrolled in a master's program in Mythology, with an emphasis on depth psychology, at Pacifica Graduate Institute. However, she credits the bear spirits for making her conscious of how to use her skills to teach others and to heal others through shamanic counseling, painting, music, and writing.

There are two types of shamans: traditional and creative. Traditional shamans are historically associated with planting cultures and meticulously follow time-tested traditions and ceremonial forms. Creative shamans are historically associated with hunting cultures and are visionaries who forge new paths, healing techniques, and cere-monies. Kinney refers to herself as a creative shaman because she is developing new shamanic processes. Also, she is able to bring arche-types into ordinary reality through her painting and performances. She still paints landscapes, but her shamanic paintings create the most market demand. While painting them, she moves into a trance state where her conscious sense of time is lost. Each painting has a lesson and a specific message, making it difficult for her to part with them until she feels the teaching is fully transmitted. In addition to paint-ing, Kinney has a drumming group that assists her in presenting myths that she has retrieved from shamanic reality as ceremonial healing performances. (See inset on page 131.)

Shamans travel between the physical world and the spirit world, or in other terms, between ordinary and nonordinary reality, or inner and outer landscapes. Though apprentices work with more expe-rienced shamans, it is essentially an independent process in which practitioners find their own way. For this reason, there is no uniform technique, landscape, or experience between shamans. Kinney has established practices that she refers to as the Kinney Method, which is a process used throughout her program, as well as in her counseling practice. An understanding of the medicine wheel as a mandala and a map of human consciousness is the foundation of the Kinney Method and essential to all of her teachings. She emphasizes that the medicine wheel is a living dimension where shamans experience everything as archetypal energy. In the Kinney Method, the sea turtle is at the center of the medicine wheel and all journeys are taken on its back. Drumming is usually found in shamanism, and in the Kinney Method, skilled drumming and chanting are stressed, as is a close relationship with a power animal. (See Spirit Passages, page 124, for an explanation of journeying.)

The Kinney Method stresses working with power animals, animal spirit guides, and totem animals, which she describes as living archetypal energies. Power animals reflect the essential nature of an individual and are lifelong guides that offer qualities to be embodied for success in the physical world. Each person

This artwork is a shamanic painting by Scarlet Kinney, the founding director of the Standing Bear Center for Shamanic Studies.

has one at birth, and a second and permanent one arrives at puberty. Kinney believes that only a qualified shaman has the ability to discover a person's correct power animal and place it in his or her energy field. Her concern is that unqualified people may identify the wrong animal and struggle to emulate qualities that are not beneficial.

Animal spirit guides are attracted to a person's energy field and are of assistance in developing qualities that the person needs to evolve. They often assist in journeys, provide teaching, or take possession of a person during a journey so that he or she can experience the full effect of their essences. They come and go throughout a lifetime as they are needed. Totem animals are spirits that are relevant to a group, tribe, family, or clan.

The Standing Bear Center apprenticeship is open only to women, as Kinney was trained in the women's shamanic tradition. The standing bear is "a mythic symbol for watchful protection of the dreaming earth and the Feminine process of Creation."

The Apprentice Training Program is at the heart of the Center's activities. It is a three-year program that certifies students as Shamanic Counselors in the Kinney Method. The study schedule is divided into seasonal quarters, with each quarter consisting of two six-hour workshops, a drumming workshop, and a two-day intensive retreat. The Distance Learning Program allows for communication through E-mail, telephone, or letters, but all students must be present for retreats and the four-day summer intensive.

In the first year of the program, participants are apprentice candidates. During this time, students decide if the program is the right fit, and Kinney determines if they meet the criteria to move into an apprenticeship. If it is revealed during the first year that a person has psychological problems, then they cannot continue. It is critical to establish a healthy group consciousness, and addictive or unstable behaviors can disrupt the entire group.

During the first four quarters, journeys are to the Middleworld, which is a dimension of the medicine wheel that exists on the same plane as physical reality but is beyond the periphery of our everyday ability to see. It is referred to as nonordinary reality. Students learn to stay on the sea turtle's back while journeying in the four directions. The sea turtle is used because it is the best expression of patience, perseverance, generosity, and stability, which helps beginners to maintain their emotional and spiritual balance. In advanced training, the sea turtle takes journeyers into the depths of the unconscious realms to the place of feminine wisdom. Each season's workshops focus on a direction's landscape, animal, goddess, archetypes, challenges, attributes, and skills. For example, winter classes explore Wolf Medicine while journeying to the landscape of the north. Students learn about one of the goddesses who has the dual nature of being Nurturing/Warrioress Woman. The skill is "seeing around." This refers to four types of shamanic energy scanning: seeing around, seeing into, seeing beneath, and seeing heart or what is hidden. Scanning is used to avoid intellectual projections that are often a reflection of the perceiver and not the perceived.

Kinney retrieves each student's power animal during the first year so that she can begin building a conscious relationship with it and infusing daily life with animal medicine.

Other courses teach students drumming, breathing techniques, space clearing, working with crystals, basic shamanic counseling skills, how to shield themselves with visualizations and intention, and how to establish their feminine authority in their own environment.

Those students who have shown an affinity to shamanism are accepted into the apprenticeship. In the second year, they embark on journeys to the different directions in the Upperworld and Lowerworld. Usually the Lowerworld contains the animal spirits, and the Upperworld holds the guides that are human in form. They may be ancestors or guides who are attracted to a person's energy. Most people find three to ten guides in the Upperworld. In shamanism, these guides are archetypal entities and are not aspects of the self. Healing occurs by interacting directly with these shamanic energies.

Drumming, shamanic psychology, ethics, and counseling techniques that are introduced in the first year are studied in more depth as students become increasingly comfortable with their own power.

Students begin the personal healing that intensifies during the third year when they journey in each direction to heal blocks. Each direction contains walls that hold the qualities of the direction and the life difficulties they represent. The wall of the north keeps people from claiming their own authority as it holds everything told to a person by every authority figure in her life. The southern wall contains all past childhood wounds and, once they are healed, the joy and innocence of childhood is recovered. All of the religious and spiritual beliefs formed by family and culture that hold people back from their true spirituality are in the east. The west wall contains the illusions and misconceptions of the ego, which when healed earns the practitioner spiritual power— power that Kinney insists is bestowed and cannot be attained through force of will and certainly not purchased for the price of education. She believes that humility, introspection, and the dissolution of the former egoic self attract shamanic energy to a person.

Whatever elements a practitioner fails to heal in herself may be projected onto the person she is hoping to help, therefore healing emotional wounds is vitally important. Kinney teaches that healing journeys must be planned and directed in advance. Her students know what direction they are traveling to, what animal helper or guide to call on, what their intention is, and what questions they will ask. This is a disciplined way to journey that is not subscribed to by all shamans. Third-year students learn techniques for journeying into genetic memory and have a plethora of skills and techniques they can use in their daily lives and to serve others. They have gained knowledge of how to be in the presence of and interact with archetypes. By the end of the third year, apprentices have a clear understanding of the ego within the psychological landscape and have taken steps to bring it into alignment. Ego is the glue that holds all aspects of the self together, but it is incompetent at interpreting events and must be disciplined and integrated using the feminine aspects that are intuitive and self-observant. The ego is masculine and is valuable in action and bringing things to fruition, but without feminine wisdom, the ego becomes overly inflated and destructive.

The highlight of the final year is the creation of a shield that symbolizes the student's achievements. When the shield is completed, a ceremony with family, friends, and students is held to honor the shaman practitioner and to present them with a Certificate of Shamanic Counseling, Kinney Method. Graduates cannot consider themselves shamans unless they have had an initiation experience, but they are shaman practitioners who have learned skills, techniques, and wisdom that they can use efficiently and effectively.

Kinney teaches that shamanism is an ecumenical path with room for all traditions as the medicine wheel can be experienced from various religious perspectives. There is no prayer or worship involved, so how people envision divinity is individual and not prescribed.

Kinney offers workshops that are Continuing Education Units approved for psychologists, therapists, and counselors. Topics include shamanic psychology as the precursor of the depth psychological traditions; the medicine wheel as a living mandala and map of human consciousness; and practice of shamanic counseling skills.

The Standing Bear Center is located on twenty-eight acres of woodland in Surry, which is a jaunt from Morgan Bay and some of Maine's most gorgeous coastal landscape. Workshops are open to the public, and private study opportunities are available. Kinney's initiation experience, years of practice and study, artistic ability, and shamanic counseling skills combine to create unique and comprehensive offerings in contemporary western shamanism.

Prices: 2005

The Apprenticeship Program is $375.00 per quarter, plus $575.00 for the four-day summer Shamanic Foundation Intensive with catered meals. The Distance Learning Program is $475.00 per quarter, plus $575.00 for the summer intensive. All written materials are included in the prices. A variety of payment plans are available. Private study opportunities are available and priced according to individual needs.

The Shamanic Foundation Intensive is scheduled each year in July or August and is also open to women who are not in the apprentice program. The four-day intensive is open to sixteen women and includes catered meals, all written materials, and a prayer flag kit. The cost is $750.00.

Contact Information:

Scarlet Kinney
The Standing Bear Center for Shamanic Studies
P.O. Box 272
Surry, ME 04684
Telephone: (207) 667-4772
Web site: *www.thestandingbear.com*
E-mail: scarlet@thestandingbear.com

About the Area:
See Morgan Bay Zendo on page 57.

The Turtle Mountain Drummers

    Apprenticeship training at the Standing Bear Center for Shamanic Studies includes active participation in The Turtle Mountain Drummers. The drummers assist Scarlet Kinney, the center's founding director, in presenting shamanic healing performances based upon myths she "catches" in shamanic reality. "The Stone Heart Turtle People" is a mythic tale performed to heal the generational wounds of ancestors forced to leave their homeland and suffer cultural relocation. "Journey through the Cave of the Bear" heals the loss and wounds to the heart. Trance-inducing drumming combined with the rhythmic chanting and singing creates a hypnotic effect that enhances perceptions of the shamanic archetypes. Kinney states, "Shamanic healing occurs as a result of being in the presence of, or interacting directly with specifically shamanic archetypes and archetypal energies."

Reflection and Renewal: Retreats and Camps

Green Acre Bahá'í School

Greenfire

Living Water Spiritual Center

Marie Joseph Spiritual Center

Notre Dame Spiritual Center

Seawall House Retreat

Temple Heights Spiritual Camp

Two Roads

Green Acre Bahá'í School
Bahá'í Retreat and Conference Center

Eliot

Many Maine residents are unaware of the existence of Green Acre Bahá'í School, though it is known to Bahá'ís around the world due to an unusual and highly celebrated visit in 1912 by 'Abdu'l-Bahá, the founder's son. This sacred location on the Piscataqua River has a rich spiritual heritage that the Bahá'ís continue to build on through educational programs for all ages. (For more on the Bahá'í faith, see page 2.)

The early history of the Green Acre Bahá'í School is a dramatic and compelling story. It is marked by tremendous successes and by trials that threatened its existence. Intrinsic to the story is Sarah Jane Farmer, who embarked on a new and daring endeavor that would influence many people to think more openly about religion, equality, and peace. Her enthusiasm, optimism, warmth, and grace were infectious, and many toiled under her guidance to make her vision a reality. Unfortunately, the successes were matched with personal tragedies, betrayals, and disappointments.

Sarah Jane Farmer is the heart of Green Acre, and there can be no doubt that her ambitions for it were shaped by her upbringing. She was born in 1847 to transcendentalist parents who were known for their philanthropy and progressive social beliefs. Their home was a stop on the underground railroad, and Sarah grew up knowing Harriet Beecher Stowe, Harriet Tubman, Julia Ward Howe, and Sojourner Truth. Sarah developed into a deeply spiritual woman who held a hopeful view of the world, even as she acknowledged the pain of poverty, prejudice, and war.

In 1892, while sweltering in a hot Boston lecture hall, Sarah had a vision of providing a country setting for people to learn about and discuss religion, philosophy, and contemporary issues. Two years before this, she had opened the Eliot Hotel on the Piscataqua River with several partners and knew she had the ideal spot.

From its beginning, the Eliot Hotel was a gathering place for Transcendentalists, and has since been referred to as the "last stronghold of the Transcendentalists." Almost immediately the hotel was renamed by the poet John Greenleaf Whittier, who was heard to say that he would refer to it as Green Acre. The name resonated with Sarah, and it became known as Green Acre-On-The-Piscataqua. Into this environment, already ripe with intellectual and spiritual discussion, Sarah introduced her idea of creating a place for race unity, peace, and the study of world religions.

In 1893, Sarah traveled to the World Parliament of Religions at Chicago's World's Fair. The Parliament was initiated by the Swedenborgian Charles Caroll Bonney, and for the first time in history, religious leaders came from around the globe to learn from one another. Sarah connected with Vivekanada, a teacher of Vedanta philosophy from Calcutta, and Dharamapala, a respected Buddhist from Ceylon. Both gentlemen paid multiple visits to Green Acre where they lectured on their traditions and exposed audiences to beliefs that were considered very unusual by most Americans.

Inspired to pursue her vision, she established the Monsalvat ("Mount of Peace") School for the Study of Comparative Religion. The school served as a platform to study a variety of traditions and to debate contemporary philosophical questions.

Green Acre developed into a well-known and popular destination. The steamship *Queen City* made regular runs from Portsmouth to

The Sarah Farmer Inn at the Green Acre Bahá'í School was completed in 1890 and serves as the main residence for retreat guests.

Eliot. A tent village was set up for overflow guests. The weekly newsletter *The Green Acre Voice* was published to keep people informed of events. The adventurous flocked to Green Acre to take advantage of the lectures on religion, the environment, education, parenthood, health, and osteopathy. A health center was established that espoused new ideas about physical well-being and, in one example, a hydro-therapist had guests walk barefoot in the morning dew. People experimented with yoga and meditation, sometimes donning saffron robes. Nature was an essential ingredient in the Green Acre experience and was praised for its healing and transformative benefits. The arts flourished with theater productions, music, poetry, fine art, and crafts. In the first decade of its opening, the guest list included such notables as W. E. B. DuBois, Booker T. Washington, John Greenleaf Whittier, Sara Bull, Edwin Markham, General Neal Dow, Horatio Dresser, Mirza Abdu'l-Fadl, Edward Everett Hale, and Clarence Darrow, among others.

Even though Green Acre enjoyed popular success, it had serious financial problems. A fortunate friendship with Phoebe Apperson Hearst, the mother of William Randolph Hearst, led to an endowment that kept the doors open. Even though the financial crisis had been avoided, the strain of worry weakened Sarah's already poor health and, in 1900, she embarked on a Mediterranean cruise to regain her strength. During the cruise, a series of events led Sarah to study with 'Abdu'l-Bahá, the son of Bahá'u'lláh, who founded the Bahá'í Faith. 'Abdu'l-Bahá was bestowed with the sole permission to interpret his father's sacred writings, and to study with him was considered an immense honor. Sarah immediately felt kinship with 'Abdu'l-Bahá and found what she had long sought in her spiritual life—a religion that was socially progressive with the utopian goal of unity and equality.

She returned to Green Acre re-invigorated and excited to share the beliefs of the Bahá'ís with her comrades. Ongoing classes on the "Persian Revolution" were taught by the highly regarded Bahá'í scholars Miri Abu'l-Fadl and Ali-Kuli Khan. Other religions were still taught, but Bahá'í was given preference, causing some people to feel betrayed and uneasy in the new atmosphere. At one point, tensions ran so high that plumbing was stolen from the inn to shut down operations.

During this time, Sarah's family home burned, destroying all of her father's work. Financial problems, threatened lawsuits, internal bickering, interference from well-meaning friends, and philosophical arguments stressed Sarah's health and, in 1904, she entered a sanatorium for a time. In 1907, she suffered a serious fall and became an invalid. Green Acre was run by a fellowship and a board of trustees, and her invalid status caused some members to call for her resignation from the board. The ongoing controversy took its toll and, in 1909, friends committed her to a sanatorium in Portsmouth, New Hampshire, where she would remain for years.

The defining event for Green Acre was a weeklong visit from 'Abdu'l-Bahá in 1912. Green Acre is the only Bahá'í school in the world that can claim this distinction. 'Abdu'l-Bahá arrived on a bright day in August, greeted by five hundred people and an impressive display of Japanese lanterns decorating the road to the inn. The residents of Eliot housed guests who traveled from far and near for the visit. 'Abdu'l-Bahá spent most of his week giving public lectures and offering encouragement to followers of the faith. He held Sarah in great regard, and through the years had sent her at least twenty-eight letters. They visited twice in the sanatorium, toured Portsmouth and Kittery one afternoon, and visited Green Acre, which Sarah had not seen in three years. Together they walked to Monsalat, and it was there that 'Abdu'l-Bahá prophesied that Green Acre would be home to the first Bahá'í university and the second Bahá'í temple in the United States. The land received a blessing from 'Abdu'l-Bahá and this, combined with the prophecy, made Green Acre a sacred place to Bahá'ís who had no doubt that his vision would be reality one day.

Meanwhile, there were people on the board and in the fellowship who were adamantly against Green Acre becoming a Bahá'í institution. This conflict came to a head in July 1913, when Sarah's illness escalated. If Sarah could not continue offering the educational programs, then the property's administration would transfer to the Union Trust, as dictated by a trust prepared some years previously. A group of fellowship members avoided such a transfer by arranging the summer programs themselves, amending the by-laws, and appointing a new board of directors and a prominent Bahá'í as trustee. Some members of the fellowship reacted to these new developments by bringing a lawsuit against the new board of directors. The local community became highly involved in the issue and eventually joined the fellowship in a critical referendum in support of Sarah and the Bahá'ís. They also provided complete newspaper coverage of the debate as it continued to the Maine Supreme Court. The Court's ruling favored the new board of directors, and it became clear that Green Acre was on its way to becoming a Bahá'í institution.

Throughout this, Sarah was held in the sanatorium against her will. After a failed attempt to kidnap her, a legal warrant was issued, and she was allowed to leave in 1916. She died several months later surrounded by friends. Sarah is a revered figure in the Bahá'ís' short history and has been named a disciple of 'Abdu'l-Bahá. Her life was frequently painful, but she fulfilled her vision of creating a place where people could join together in unity and peace.

In 1925, members were elected to the first National Spiritual Assembly of the United States and Canada, and Green Acre came under its auspices. Since that time, the Green Acre Bahá'í school has continued to grow. It is now a year-round family retreat and conference center with twenty buildings on two hundred fifty acres. There are fifty-nine sites in the area that are associated with Bahá'í history.

The main campus of Green Acre maintains the charm of its Victorian heritage. The former Eliot Hotel, built in 1889 to 1890, is now the Sarah Farmer Inn. Visitors will find the accommodations very pleasing as its recent restoration has produced a retreat center that is comparable to the finest bed and breakfast inns. Upon entering the double doors, guests are greeted by a lobby and registration desk that maintain the elegance and charm of the hotel's original design over a century ago. Original woodwork has been conserved, including a fascinating mantle with a pagoda design. Most of the furnishings are period pieces, and the décor is decidedly high-end. Green Acre's captivating history is on display along the wide second- and third-floor landings, and on the third floor is the room where 'Abdu'l-Bahá slept. It is currently open to guests for prayer and meditation.

The Sarah Farmer Inn has twenty-one bed-and-breakfast-style rooms and can sleep up to forty-five people. Bathrooms are shared by no more than four rooms. There are three break-out rooms and a dining room with views of the river through its many windows.

Down the lane from the Inn, nestled behind pines, is the riverside residence Olé Bull Cottage. Newcomers to New England should not be misled by the word "cottage," which does not mean a cozy bungalow but refers to a Victorian mansion that was built along the coastline as a summer dwelling. The Olé Bull was built as a music school by one of Green Acre's first music teachers and has very interesting architecture that includes a series of porches looking out to the water. It holds the Green Acre library, an executive conference room, and seven bedrooms with private bathrooms.

Separated from the main campus, but still within walking distance, is the Fellowship House, built in 1916. This lovely shingled cottage of pleasing proportions has five bedrooms and one dormitory, sleeping up to twenty. A large living room and winterized porch serve as meeting rooms. By combining the three facilities, Green Acre can sleep one hundred twenty-five people. There are also three small buildings awaiting renovation, which will add to the total.

Back on the main campus, the Kelsey Center, built in 2002, is designed to complement the period homes that surround it. It is an impressive building; on the exterior, a wrap-around porch sweeps almost the entire circumference, and the interior is marked with rich wood trim, beams, and paneling. It houses the well-stocked bookstore, a large snack room, nursery, childcare center, five classrooms, and an auditorium that seats two hundred. The spacious snack room has the expected tables and chairs, but also couches arranged by a fireplace provide a nice touch in the winter. The auditorium has state-of-the-art technology for sound and video, some of which allows parents who are in the nursery with their children to watch and listen to the presenters in the auditorium. The nursery and classrooms have all the amenities of a top-notch facility.

There is evidence everywhere that Green Acre is lovingly and efficiently maintained. Not only are the structures well cared for, but the sweeping lawns are beautifully groomed. One of the first things visitors may notice when driving into Green Acre is the peace flag garden. In 1894, Sarah Farmer raised a peace flag, believed by Bahá'ís to be the first in the world. It still flies and is now surrounded by lovely flowers and a stone path laid in an east-west direction. The grounds also have a volleyball net, soccer field, picnic tables, and three different playgrounds, including a pint-sized one that is fenced in for the littlest visitors.

Green Acre employs a full time chef and an assistant. Bahá'ís encourage vegetarianism, so meals always include meatless options. The food is fresh, plentiful, and served buffet style. Breakfast is hearty and offerings include eggs scrambled with feta; roasted red peppers, and spinach; French toast; hotcakes with blueberry sauce; and assorted cereals and fruits. Lunch includes an extensive salad bar and sandwich fillings such as curried tofu, hummus, seafood salad, chicken salad, and assorted cold cuts. People travel to Green Acre from all over the world, and Bahá'ís promote travel to enhance cultural understanding; therefore, the menus offer ethnic dishes. Examples are salmon with mango salsa, Persian beef and celery koresh, tofu kabobs, and Thai chickpeas. People with restricted diets, including vegans, should contact the food service manager in advance.

Programs are hosted year-round with offerings scheduled from Friday through Wednesday in the summer and on weekends the rest of the year. Most of the time, classes for children ages three to fourteen are offered during adult programs. All of Green Acre's offerings are inspired by Bahá'í writings, and the various topics are of general interest to many. Previous knowledge of the religion is not required or needed, and Bahá'ís have a policy against attempting to convert the curious. A visit is an excellent way to be introduced to Bahá'í teachings, or for Bahá'ís to deepen their knowledge and reinforce their faith. Examples of general interest programs are *Love, Power, and Justice; Striving for Excellence and Balance in Your Life; Renew*

Your Divine Creation: A Retreat for Married Couples; and *The Ethics of Globalization.*

An example of a typical program is *Spiritual Intelligence: The Missing Link,* in which the instructor Keyvan Geula integrates the core teachings of Bahá'u'lláh with the latest scientific findings to explore the interactions between sense perception, thoughts, feelings, intentions, and deeds in human relationships. Like many Bahá'í intensives, the course is concerned primarily with family life, and this one focuses on raising children that are spiritually, emotionally, and socially intelligent. Geula is dedicated to this premise and established the Center for Global Integrated Education in California.

True to its goal of working towards racial unity, Green Acre has offers programs that support diversity such as *Latin American Weekend, the Persian Conference, Perspectives on Islam, Models of Multi-Racial Community Building,* and the *Annual Black Bahá'í Men Spiritual Retreat.*

Family life is a consistent emphasis in the Bahá'í faith, and children are welcome at Green Acre, through camp-style classes, to special programs developed from a sequential curriculum. Their programs might include *Creating Art for the New World; Turning 15: Beginning the Journey;* or *Badasht Academy for Youth in grades 9–12: Spiritual Descendents of the Dawn Breakers.* Periodically, programs for the Junior Youth Academy, ages 11 through 14, are scheduled concurrently with the adult programs.

Understanding the Bahá'í faith is largely dependent on study circles that are conducted by trained leaders. Training intensives on core curricula for children and teenagers and on the Ruhi Books, which are adult study guides, are frequently scheduled.

Spending a summer afternoon at Green Acre is a life-affirming experience. Parents, grandparents, and children come together for the shared experience; husbands and wives attend the same courses; teenagers study respectfully while also finding time for a soccer game; and children of all ages populate the playscapes. Young adults barely out of their teens come from as far away as Africa to commit to service on foreign soil. People of all skin colors mingle easily and without self-consciousness.

An easy way to be exposed to the Bahá'í experience is to attend the summer "Concert-Picnics on the Piscataqua" that are open to the public. Visitors may bring a picnic or purchase one on the grounds, and the concert is free of charge as Bahá'ís do not accept donations from those outside the faith.

Being able to study in a beautiful place that honors its history is a gift that Bahá'ís deeply appreciate. They are on a "mystical path with practical feet," and Green Acre Bahá'í School offers people of all ages and persuasions the opportunity to focus on the tools necessary to make the prophecy of unity and peace a working reality.

Prices: 2005

There are a number of pricing options depending on the length of stay. An assortment of discounts are available as are work-study and scholarships. Commuters pay per meal and a smaller program fee. Camping options are available.

Weekend Two-day Sessions:
Adult and Youth (ages 15 and up) $130.00
Children and Junior Youth (ages 3–14, with parent(s)) $60.00
Infants (ages 0–2) $30.00

Five-Day Sessions:
Adult and Youth (ages 15 and up) $325.00
Children (ages 3–14) $150.00
Infants (ages 0–2) $60.00

Nonprofit and faith-based organizations are welcome to host their own retreats and should contact the center for prices.

Contact Information:

Green Acre Bahá'í School
188 Main Street
Eliot, ME 03903
Telephone: (207) 439-7200
Web site: *www.greenacre.org*
E-mail: greenacre@usbnc.org

About the Area:

Eliot is a lovely country town close to the outlet malls of Kittery, local beaches, and the historic and lively city of Portsmouth, New Hampshire. The Portsmouth Naval Shipyard Museum in Kittery, Maine, shares a history with Green Acre. In 1905, Japan and Russia were negotiating a peace plan at the shipyard with Theodore Roosevelt. Sarah Farmer invited them to Green Acre and was declined by the Russian diplomat and Roosevelt, but the Japanese accepted. The national anthems of all three countries were sung and prayers for peace were offered.

Greenfire
Women's Retreat

Tenants Harbor

When Greenfire was still in the vision stage, a friend of the founders was recounting her springtime walk through the forest. When she came to a place where the sunlight shone through the canopy of newly green trees, she described the effect as "green fire." The name intuitively sounded right to the four Episcopalian priests who were planning a retreat and community where they could do their own spiritual work and welcome others to do theirs.

Greenfire has been open to guests since 1990. The idea for it began in 1987, when Judith Carpenter and Constance Chandler-Ward, who were chaplains in Wellesley, Massachusetts, and Rosanna Kazanjian, who had a parish in Jamaica Plain, Massachusetts, shared their desire to reinvent their work. They wanted to work in a non-hierarchical setting where the primary purpose would be to support women from any tradition—or none—in their connection to the Holy. Their vision moved to a reality in 1989 with the purchase of a farmhouse in Tenants Harbor, Maine. Joined by two more priests, Alison Cheek and Maria Marta Aris-Paul, they printed their first brochure in 1990. Many years later, Greenfire has maintained its nonhierarchical goal, although the staff has shifted and grown to include a large circle of volunteers. The retreat is managed by a multi-cultural board of directors comprised of sixteen women.

The Greenfire women (a reference to those directly involved in the day-to-day operations) sought to explore new and old models that specifically addressed women's experience of God, growth, and empowerment. The formula they arrived at was deceptively simple: conversations in a circle. This is how women have historically communicated and is one cornerstone of Greenfire's mission. Their other mission is simply to provide space for silence and reflection.

Greenfire offers three types of circle work: Conversations, Consultations, and Work-Visions. A Conversation is held with two Greenfire women and lasts seventy-five minutes. During the session, the individual's most pressing area of concern is discussed. Traditional therapeutic or counseling models are intentionally avoided. This eliminates people who have serious problems and also keeps the individual in the position of authority. In a typical counseling model, the patient views the therapist as a teacher, an authority, or a parental figure, and may relinquish their power too easily. In a Conversation, two Greenfire women listen deeply and offer differing perspectives and insights. Their task is to see the woman's strengths and mirror them back to her. The woman then draws her own conclusions based on self-knowledge. It has been their experience that the women who schedule Conversations are empowered by the process of being truly heard.

The Conversation is also available to couples, be they together through marriage, partnership, friendship, or work. One partner has a discussion with two listeners while the other is a silent witness, then the roles are reversed. The technique offers the couples fresh insights and a starting point for growth-oriented discussions.

A Consultation lasts for two hours, has three listeners, is more concentrated, and tends to need more than a single session. Individuals and groups pursue this form for a variety of reasons.

Work-Vision is the original model the founders created and used for Greenfire's development. It involves three two-hour sessions with three listeners. The individual is first guided through an exploration of her core self, then her work story of frustration and creativity is told, and finally a vision for manifesting fresh ideas in all areas of her life is planned. Listening and sharing is focused, yet intuitive, so that the outcome is not evident until the end.

On Wednesday evenings, a meditation, followed by a conversation, is open to all house guests, Greenfire women, and area residents. This is followed by a potluck dinner.

Dinnertime is a special event at Greenfire, with at least two Greenfire women attending. A beautifully appointed table and candlelight set the mood. A typical dinner may be tortellini soup, bread, salad, and blueberry cobbler. The food is always homemade, fresh, and when possible, organic. Meals are vegetarian or include chicken or fish. Reasonable dietary accommodations are honored.

Breaking bread is always a source of bonding, and conversations at the dinner table are lively. Dinner companions may include the Australian priest Alison Cheek, one of the founders of Greenfire. Cheek is famous for being one of the eleven Episcopalian deacons who were ordained as priests by three bishops before the ordination of women priests was accepted. At the time, this was huge news and considered very radical. It took several years for the church to affirm the validity of these ordinations in 1976. Guests at Greenfire are in the rarified company of women who have paved their own way against conventional norms and have done so by first knowing exactly who they are, and then fully accepting their findings.

Greenfire is divided into guest quarters and the home of the resident staff. The two-hundred-year-old shingled farmhouse was built from two houses that were floated over to the Saint George Peninsula in the early 1800s from two nearby islands. Later, the barn was added and is now the guest wing. The guest quarters consist of a large, comfortable living room, small kitchen, and shared bathroom on the first level, and a reading alcove with futon cots, and four tiny rooms on the second level. Each space has a skylight and holds a futon cot, small nightstand, lamp, and fan. There is just enough room for a suitcase and to change clothes without bumping into the walls. Recently, an apartment was built onto the back of the house and is often available for guests. It has a living room, bathroom, bedroom, sleeping loft, and sunroom.

There are two yurts at the edge of the woods for people who desire this type of solitude. Yurts are insulated, circular, canvas structures. Each one has a port-a-pot, lantern, bed, desk, counter, comfortable chair, and gas wall heater.

Guests fix their own breakfast and lunch according their own timetable, with food options provided by Greenfire. Dinner is a community meal.

The grounds are exactly what would be expected surrounding an antique New England farmhouse. A kitchen garden is steps away from the kitchen doorway. Off to one end of the house is a lovely perennial garden with a grape arbor that is the source of the grape juice used for Sunday services. Raspberry bushes, apple trees, lilacs, and birches dot the grounds, as do small stonewalls. A field spreads out long and low and is the source of the wildflowers that decorate the guest quarters.

The Greenfire property consists of fifty-nine acres and several trails. The trails begin close to the house and meander through fields, woods, and a wetland. Directions to other trails, beaches, and waterfront areas are furnished at the retreat. Art supplies are always available.

Greenfire's visitors span all age groups. A board member brought her girls' group from East Boston for a retreat where they met with Maine girls. Mothers have planned passage rites with their daughters. Young women visit to escape the chores of motherhood for a few days. Middle-aged and elderly guests come from near and far to enjoy the retreat's offerings. Silent retreatants of any age are welcome and honored.

Generally, visitors plan a Conversation, and many people from the surrounding community schedule Conversations or Consultations, often on a regular basis. Groups from ten to twelve are accommodated; occasionally arrangements have been made for larger groups. Conversations or Consultations can be adapted to group needs.

Greenfire women are experts at establishing circles of women. They are often consulted by women about how to create a circle or how to maintain one that is faltering. The Board of Directors works from a circle model and starts meetings by discussing personal issues before moving onto business.

Once a month throughout the year, themed one- or two-day retreats are planned. Topics include timely issues, gardening, photography, writing, bread making, exploring Islam, and Enneagrams, a system for exploring spiritual growth and transformation that has ancient roots.

On Sundays, Greenfire has an open and inclusive worship service. Readings are from different wisdom texts, a Jewish round is sung, and homemade bread and grape juice are shared. The service involves music, silence, discussion, and prayer. The following is a prayer that they have written together:

> With gratitude
> And in the presence of our ancestors, all those
> Who have gone before us in the awareness
> Of the radiance and the terror
> Of earth's life death life cycle
> We remember
> That we are fed and called to be food.

Greenfire woman say that they have been called to a ministry of hospitality. However, hospitality fails to encompass the connection they create by listening and sharing within a nonhierarchical circle. They have formed an environment for replenishment, renewal, and contemplation, and they have built a community of sisterhood for all who are touched by their authenticity and generosity.

Prices: 2005

$68.00 per night includes three meals
$100.00 per night for the apartment
Conversations are $70.00 for 75 minutes
Consultations are $150.00 for 2 hours
Work-Visions are $390.00 for three two-hour sessions
Special event weekends range in price from $150.00 to $400.00
Scholarships are available for a portion of the cost.
Donations are gratefully accepted.

Contact Information:

Greenfire
329 Wallston Road
Tenants Harbor, ME 04860
Telephone: (207) 372-6442
Web site: www.greenfireretreat.org
E-mail: greenfir@midcoast.com

About the Area:
Tenants Harbor is located on Saint George Peninsula, which is a short drive southeast from Rockland. The peninsula has fishing villages, lighthouses, beaches, and trails. Port Clyde is a scenic fishing village with ferry service to Monhegan Island.

This New England farmhouse, situated on fifty-nine acres, is home to Greenfire.

Living Water
Spiritual Center
Ecumenical Retreat Center

Winslow

Guests at the Living Water Spiritual Center will find well-landscaped grounds, groomed nature trails, cheerful accommodations, and knowledgeable, warm staff members. They also find a progressive vision of spirituality that encompasses more than just religion. Programs fall into seven broad categories: Faith Formation, Family, Global Inspiration, Healing, Nature, Nurturing Ministries, and Spirituality. One would be hard pressed to find an area of living that is not touched upon in the programs. Woven throughout it all is the theme of finding the Divine through nature and in nature.

Living Water Spiritual Center offers adults retreats and day programs that provide the opportunity for people of all ages to reflect and meditate on nature. In their grounds management, food production, and building operations, the staff at the spiritual center has made a commitment to be green. The center recycles, has an organic garden, composts, serves fair trade coffee, uses only environmentally friendly cleansers, and is outfitted with compact fluorescent bulbs. A no-spray agreement with the local utility protects the river from pesticide runoff, and trails and acreage are maintained to create habitat for area wildlife.

In 1964, the Living Water Spiritual Center was a novitiate and provincial headquarters for the Sisters of Saint Joseph. The timing was not the best; throughout the 1960s women chose religious vocations in dramatically decreased numbers. Like many Christian religious communities of the time, the Sisters were challenged by the societal demands and rapid changes of the late twentieth century. They rose to the occasion by surveying the needs in their community and responding with a succession of programs. Between 1972 and 1994, the Sisters opened a daycare center, staffed a hotline for single mothers, offered family-living workshops, ran a shelter for abused women, housed Mt. Merici students, and lastly, had an addiction rehabilitation program for women.

In 1994, the Sisters refocused their ministry to serve as a retreat center and renamed it The Saint Joseph Christian Life Center. They remodeled the center to create a homelike atmosphere and saw their new mission as one of meeting the physical, spiritual, and social

A quiet spot for reflection is found on the grounds of the Living Water Spiritual Center.

needs of Christians. With a nod to creation spirituality, they envisioned "that all may be one."

Within a few years the center had evolved again, and a new name, mission, and philosophy were established. The name Living Water Spiritual Center announces that all faiths are welcome, and the reference to living water honors the blending of spirituality and ecology, as well as gives recognition to the beautiful Sebasticook River that borders the property. Their new mission statement declares:

> With care and love
> we offer sacred space for all —
> to seek the Divine
> and to embrace the interconnectedness of all creation.

At that time, Susan MacKenzie, Ph.D., was hired as the program director. MacKenzie has a doctorate in natural sciences, has done post-doctoral work at Harvard, taught at Colby and Bates Colleges, and published an academic text. She chose to work at Living Water because of a hunger to marry her love of science and nature with her spiritual life.

At Living Water, she has designed eco-spirituality programs for all age groups including EarthWorks, an enrichment program that invites young people to connect ecological principles and spirituality. EarthWorks seeks to show how spirit, nature, and science are interrelated and interdependent. One to four sessions lasting two hours each are available for K–12 students. The program is based on the premise that people will protect what they love, and if children are shown the wonders of nature, they will naturally become good stewards of Earth. The four sessions are the Web of Creation, Sense of Place, Earth-Keeping, and Peace-Making. The two hours include instruction, a short reading, a thirty-minute nature walk, discussion, and teaching games. During the nature walk, the children remain silent, walk slowly, and are encouraged to listen and observe carefully. The response is overwhelmingly positive, as most of the children find comfort and delight in their own company. Afterwards, discussions are lively, with the children sharing stories from their experiences.

Though committed to ecology, the essence of Living Water's programming is for people to know their God more deeply in solitude or in a sharing community. Programs encompass a plethora of topics and range from full weekends to short morning or evening sessions.

Weekend retreats generally begin on a Friday night and end on Sunday after lunch. Five meals are included. Typical retreats are *Feasting on Prayer*; *Faith Scrap Booking*; *Encounters with the God of our Experience*; and *Prayer Weekend: the Psalms*. A popular repeating retreat is 11th Step weekends, based on that step from Alcoholics Anonymous. The 11th step states, "Sought through prayer and meditation to improve our conscious contact with God, as we understand Him, pray only for knowledge of His will for us and the power to carry that out." Men and women meet on separate weekends and have different themes. A sample men's program is called *The Joy of Recovery: If I Didn't Laugh I'd Drink*, while a women's is *Becoming Usefully Whole*.

Full-day programs are on Saturdays, last for six or seven hours, and include lunch and a snack. *Topics include Sounds of Glory: Encountering the Sacred Through Great Music of Faith*; *Aramaic Words: Praying in the Language of Jesus*; *Marriage Encounters*; and *Spirituality and Sustainability: Faith Communities Caring for Earth*.

Weekends are booked well in advance, so to fully utilize the facility, many one-and-a-half- to two-hour programs are scheduled during weekdays in the early morning or evening. Some of these meet for several consecutive weeks such as *The Old Testament, Women of the Bible, Spirituality in World Religions, Monday Morning Book Club*, and even *Stretches for Women*. Others meet for a single session but, due to popularity, run regularly throughout the year. In the evening, ecumenical Taize services combine chants, scripture, and silence. In the morning, *Midweek Reflection with Inspirational People* combines readings, meditation, discussion, and perhaps a creative activity. Thich Nhat Hahn, Rachel Carson, Thomas Berry, Saint Hilde, and Evelyn Underhill are some of those who have been explored.

The second Friday of every month is set aside for personal renewal. Renewal Day lasts from 8:30 a.m. to 4:00 p.m., and attendees follow a self-directed schedule where they are welcome to use the facilities and trails, attend an optional guided meditation, or schedule a session with a trained spiritual director. Massages and holistic healing are available for an additional fee. Restore/24 is a similar program in which guests stay for 24 hours, and many choose to remain in silence. This is an increasingly popular offering for people in high-stress occupations or circumstances.

It is not necessary to attend a learning retreat to enjoy Living Water. Directed eight-day retreats are silent and include a daily spiritual guidance session. During a session, the spiritual director listens, reflects back what is shared, and makes suggestions for prayer, reading, or reflection. Guided retreats include all of the above, except there is a morning group presentation and spiritual direction occurs less frequently. It should be noted that four Sisters still live on the premises in private quarters, so guests are never truly alone in the center.

Sr. Angela Fortier, executive director of the Center, oversees a staff of five, while program leaders come from a wide range of backgrounds and expertise. There are over thirty listed in the annual program booklet, offering skills in recovery, music, yoga, healing, art, spiritual direction, environment, hospice, counseling, and more.

The nondescript institutional exterior of the Living Water Spiritual Center belies the warmth and cheerfulness of its interior. Rooms are light filled and brightly painted, with comfortable, attractive furnishings. A large screened-in porch on the east side provides a place for early risers to watch the sunrise, while an indoor sunroom catches morning light. Guests have adopted individual bedrooms by supplying the bedspreads, decorations, and some of the furniture lending each bedroom a unique personality, and yes, return visitors request their favorites. Excellent upkeep and cleanliness contribute a sense of sparkle.

There are twenty-five single and three double bedrooms. Each one has a bed, bureau, desk with a reading lamp, comfortable chair, linens, closet, and sink. Bathrooms are shared, but have private showers and stalls with solid wood doors. Retreat leaders stay in a suite with a private bath and sitting room.

A large conference room accommodates up to one hundred, the lounge up to fifty, and the sunroom up to twelve. Area hotels can house overflow from large groups. The cheerful conference room is equipped with thirty very cozy platform rockers, and the lounge is furnished with couches, lounge chairs, games, and a television with video equipment. Lecterns, microphones, flip charts, and projection screens are provided for presenters. Other amenities include a well-supplied library, an exercise room, chapel, massage room, and private spaces for solitude or private conversations. The stairway is equipped with a stairlift elevator chair; a scooter is available; and the bathrooms are handicapped accessible. Food is available twenty-four hours a day in the snack room, which is stocked with beverages, cookies, crackers, and healthful snacks.

Living Water prides itself on its excellent, home-cooked, nutritious meals. Organic produce and herbs from its own garden are used whenever possible. Vegetarians are presented with food that is truly filling—not just a garden salad. All reasonable dietary limitations are accommodated. The dining room seats seventy-five and can be divided to provide privacy for silent retreatants. Thoughtful touches extend to the table decorations that have changing seasonal themes.

The grounds of Living Water complement its theme of nature and spirituality. The center sits on sixty-one acres that border the Sebasticook River. Four marked and groomed trails meander through fifty-four of those acres. The hikes range from twenty to ninety minutes, and the center provides a map of the trails that includes the location of benches. The trails cover several different landscapes, with a special highlight being the river and a lovely overlook.

When guests are not enjoying the trails, they can find outdoor comfort at the swimming pool, in the three-season gazebo, on the glider benches, by the memorial garden, walking the seven-circuit labyrinth, or in the pine grove that features the Cosmic Walk. The Sisters created the Cosmic Walk in 1998. The universe story, starting five billion years ago, is told through painted slates attached to pine trees.

Living Water Spiritual Center provides visitors with the opportunity to restore themselves through God and nature and offers a number of classes, programs, and experiences to deepen spiritual wisdom and expand faith. The cheerful warmth of the center, the beautiful grounds, and the gracious hosts make this a splendid getaway.

Prices: 2005
Program Booklets are available at no cost.
Prices range from a free will offering for evening and morning programs to $50.00 for programs with multiple sessions. One-day programs are $35.00. Weekend retreats are generally $125.00.
Prices for private retreats are based on length of stay and number of meals. Nonprofit and faith-based organizations are welcomed to host their own retreats and should contact the center for prices.
Holistic healing sessions are scheduled with professionals and are $50.00 to $70.00 depending on the service rendered.

Contact Information:

Living Water Spiritual Center
93 Halifax Street
Winslow, ME 04901
Telephone: 207-872-237
Web site: *www.e-livingwater.org*
E-mail: info@e-livingwater.org

About the Area:

Waterville is home to Colby College, which dates from 1813 and has a beautiful campus that is both scenic and historic. The Colby Museum of Art has an impressive collection of contemporary and historical works.

Marie Joseph Spiritual Center
Catholic Retreat Center

Biddeford Pool

As you round the curve on Biddeford Pool's picturesque coastal road, a grand turreted building stands in honor of another era. The former resort is perched on the coast as a beacon of serenity and a place where escape from the world is promised. It harkens back more than one hundred years when wealthy guests filled its ballrooms, dining halls, and guest rooms, basking in Maine's splendid summer weather and allowing themselves to be lulled by the sea. Now, it offers another type of respite from everyday life. The Marie Joseph Spiritual Center welcomes those who come to seek solace in religious tradition.

Before the Marie Joseph Spiritual Center was created to fulfill its spiritual mission, it was the Hotel Evans. In the 1890s, wealthy tourists, called rusticators, flocked to Maine's coastline on trains and steamships. Grand resorts were built on Maine's most gorgeous geography to accommodate the newcomers who came with their nannies and stayed for the entire season. Around the turn of the century, the hotel changed hands and became The Ocean View Hotel. The behemoths of the late 1800s had a difficult time surviving as vacation habits changed, and in 1948, the Sisters of the Presentation of Mary purchased the hotel and converted it to a girl's boarding school, called Marie Joseph Academy. Again, times changed and the demand for Catholic boarding schools declined. The Sisters of the Presentation of Mary closed the school, and after attempts to sell it failed, it was reopened in 1979 as a retreat center.

The Sisters of the Presentation of Mary was founded by Marie

Rivier, who was born in 1768 in Montpezat, France. When she was sixteen months old, she was disabled in a bad fall. Every day afterwards her mother carried her to the statue of the Pieta and prayed for her child's healing. Soon Marie came to know that she would be cured by Mary's intercession. In 1774, after four years, she began to walk. The healing led Marie to devote herself to Jesus and the Blessed Virgin Mary. Twenty-two years later, on the feast day of the Presentation of Mary, Marie and four companions dedicated themselves to God and created a new community. This occurred at a time in France when most convents were closing and all religious activity was repressed. The sisters dedicated themselves to orphans, the poor, and to educating both children and adults.

At the time of Marie's death in 1838, there were 350 sisters carrying on her ministry. The Sisters of the Presentation of Mary currently serve in eighteen countries and continue Marie's vision of passing on hope, educating young people, and alleviating the needs of the poor through their focus areas of education, retreat work, and pastoral work.

At its heart, the Marie Joseph Spiritual Center is Roman Catholic. Highly educated nuns who live on the premises shatter stereotypes about the parochial nuns of the past—these women twinkle with joy. Though it is a Catholic organization, effort has been made to welcome people of all denominations and faith traditions. Morning and evening prayer are open to all visitors, but not required. It is requested that everyone who visits, including groups and organizations, come for spiritual purposes. Their mission statement clearly defines what the visitor can expect:

"A Sacred Space for persons seeking to encounter God in solitude and in stillness, in the beauty of nature, in the healing rhythm of the ocean, in the presence of a praying Community."

There is a year-round calendar of events, excluding three weeks in late spring when the center is closed for repairs and upkeep and two weeks in late summer. From late June until late August, private or directed retreats are offered, with separate weeks for men and women. All summer retreats are silent, and priority is given to those who have chosen religious life as a vocation.

The rest of the year is dedicated to directed weekend retreats, covering topics that change according to demand. Examples of themes include: *Julian of Norwich, Living with Loss, Personality and Human Relations, Young Adult Retreat, Writing: A Healing Path, Joy in the Journey,* and *Dreams as Spiritual Practice.* They offer a workshop on Enneagrams, which is often described as the Meyer-Briggs test of spirituality. Retreats are also offered during New Year's and Holy Week.

Programs start on a Friday night and end on a Sunday after lunch. Single-day or ongoing programs are scheduled throughout the year. Individual retreats can be scheduled for people who are seeking a quiet time for reflection and prayer. Guests can request a directed retreat, which includes a daily session with a trained spiritual guide. Pastoral and grief ministry are also available.

The accommodations are simple without being monastic. Single or double rooms are comfortable, quiet, and many have ocean views. Up to seventy people can be accommodated in forty-eight guest rooms, with twenty-four hundred people passing through their doors each year. The chapel is especially attractive due to the windows that line two walls and look out to the Atlantic Ocean. There are several guest lounges, with a favorite being the large, closed, ocean-side porch. Amenities include meeting rooms, a conference room, a library, a wonderful ecumenical bookstore, and, best of all, beach access.

Two dining rooms make it possible to eat in silence or in community. The food here is strictly institutional cooking that will bring back memories of school lunches. People with dietary restrictions do not go hungry as there is variety offered at each meal.

The nostalgic character and traditional Catholicism can fool visitors into thinking that the Marie Joseph Spiritual Center is old-fashioned. The offerings here are contemporary and facilitated by experienced professionals. The ocean-front setting is stunning and conducive to reflection. Rates are very reasonable, making this an affordable retreat for most people. Another advantage is the year-round calendar. When many retreat centers are closed for the season, the Marie Joseph Spiritual Center is a wonderful place to enjoy the serenity and drama of winter along Maine's coastline.

Prices: 2005

Self-directed retreats are $50.00 per night and directed retreats that include a session with a spiritual director are $60.00 per night. Both rates include room and board. Weekend retreats begin on Fridays at 6:30 PM and end on Sundays after lunch. The rate is $125.00 for room and board, $85.00 for commuters including meals, and $75.00 without meals.

Contact information:

The Marie Joseph Spiritual Center
10 Evans Road
Biddeford, ME 04005-9561
Telephone: 207-284-5671
Telephone: *www.presmarymethuen.org/english/mariejo.htm*

About the Area:
Biddeford Pool is a small, predominately summer community named after the central rounded inlet that fills with each high tide, creating a shimmering blue mirror on clear days. The visitor will find a tiny village center, a private golf course, two miles of public and private beach, and the beautiful East Point Sanctuary that offers a 1.6-mile hike along rugged and rocky coastline.

Notre Dame
Spiritual Retreat Center
Catholic Retreat Center

Alfred

Notre Dame in Alfred is a unique place. A first-time visitor may find the buildings, businesses, and landscapes a bit baffling. The oldest building is dated 1780, the newest is from the 1960s, and there are a lot in between: an 1833 Shaker barn, an 1875 Carriage House, and a 1950 Quonset hut from Eastport, Maine, to name only a few. There are several businesses, including a bakery, an orchard, a maple sugar house, an emergency shelter, a retirement home, and a retreat center. To add more confusion, there are several vegetable and flower gardens, three tennis courts, a football field, a softball field, trails, and a street called Cemetery Lane.

The variety reflects rich history and changing times. Shaker Hill serves as the campus of Notre Dame, the American Province Headquarters for the Brothers of Christian Instruction. It is home to the Notre Dame Spiritual Center and the Brothers' retirement community. The Brothers bought this property from the Society of Shakers in 1931 and through the years have added and deleted buildings as well as businesses.

The Brothers of Christian Instruction is a teaching order with thirteen hundred members in twenty-five countries. Its motto, *Deo Soli*, means "For God Alone" or, as it is sometimes stated, "We work for God alone." The brothers serve as school administrators, teachers, counselors, campus chaplains, retreat directors, and missionaries. The order originated in 1819 in Brittany, France. Father Jean-Marie Robert de la Mennais and Father Gabriel Deshayes founded it with the mission of teaching children left uneducated by the chaos of the French Revolution. They were particularly concerned with children living in poverty, and brothers went to Africa and the West Indies as missionaries. At the time of Fr. de la Mennais' death in 1860, there were 852 brothers in the order.

In 1903, the French government shut down the institution and suppressed the brothers' activities. They fanned out of France into England, Italy, Spain, Canada, and the United States. The brothers flourished in the United States, leading to a demand for a regional formation (education) center. Brothers came from Canada and purchased three hundred sixty-four acres for $10,000 from the Shakers, who were consolidating their community by moving fifty miles north to Sabbathday Lake. (For more information on the Shakers, see page 74.)

The brothers immediately set about becoming self-sufficient. There were five houses and ten buildings on the property that were in various states of disrepair. They renovated buildings; dug wells; and installed heat, electricity, and plumbing. Before long, they had a bakery, dairy cows, gardens, five hundred hens, and a pigsty. The farm operations peaked in the 1960s with 100 head of cattle, more than 3,000 apple trees, and a fully mechanized chicken coop for 4,000 birds. In one year the orchard produced 9000 bushels of apples, the bakery baked 105,000 loaves of "Brothers' Bread," and 2,000 eggs were collected a day.

The brothers not involved in the farm operations were teachers in Catholic schools in Biddeford, Waterville, and Sanford, though many taught on their own campus as well. Their longest running school was the La Mennais Preparatory, established in 1931 and closed in 1967. La Mennais College was chartered soon after the high school, though it moved to Ohio in 1960 as recruitment proved to be difficult in the North East, and it exists today as Walsh University. In 1956, the Denis Junior High opened and had one hundred students enrolled within ten years. They were at the forefront of multiculturalism when they opened enrollment to international students in the 1970s.

Twelve countries were represented in the student body by the time of its closure in 1980. In 1981, the Notre Dame Retreat Center opened in its place.

As the brothers' numbers declined and their ages increased, they were left without replacements for retiring brothers and gradually were unable to maintain Notre Dame's many offerings. The retreat center replaced the junior high because it could be run with minimal staff. By the 1970s, the farming and chicken operations were closed, and currently, the orchard and maple syrup operations are leased by a local orchard. York County Shelters Inc. manages the bakery for vocational training of the shelter's residents. The brothers maintain the grounds, though it is a challenge due to the age and health issues of the retirees.

The Notre Dame campus experienced its "fifteen minutes of fame" when it was realized that a brother who had taught biology on campus in 1950 was Waldo Demara, the subject of the 1961 movie "The Great Imposter," starring Tony Curtis. He is most famous for his masquerade as a surgeon in the Canadian Navy during the Korean War. There is a brother at Notre Dame who remembers having Demara as an instructor and claims he was excellent. Demara also assisted a doctor in removing one of the brother's tonsils! After a year had passed, several of the brothers grew suspicious of Demara. Perhaps he sensed this when he borrowed a car that was later found at Boston's Logan Airport, and the brothers heard nothing further of him until he became the subject of media attention years later.

The legacy of the Shakers is evident throughout the campus. The Shakers settled in Alfred in 1783 but did not build their community until ten years later when it grew rapidly, peaking at two hundred members. Their numbers started to dwindle after 1850 and by 1930, there were only twenty-two members left on Shaker Hill. There are eight original Shaker buildings, though changes have been made to them over the years. The grounds contain a number of gardens that are in keeping with the Shaker tradition of growing plants that are useful for household or medicinal purposes as well as beautiful. In 1931, seven hundred fifty plants were documented on Shaker Hill. Indigo, which was used to make blue dye, still grows profusely on "Indigo Hill." Prickly-ash grows between the barn and the pond and was used for toothaches, congestion, rheumatism, and nerves. Under the trees by Brothers' Cemetery, a large-leafed groundcover called May-apple produces tiny edible apple-like fruit.

The brothers work closely with the Friends of the Alfred Shaker Museum, who are carefully restoring the carriage house, built in 1875, which will become a museum. They have been instrumental in getting the Shaker Hill campus included on the National Register of Historic Sites.

Another unusual aspect of the campus is the oak-lined dirt road, Cemetery Lane. Brothers' Cemetery was dedicated in 1944, and among the rows and rows of identical white crosses are unmarked stones that are awaiting brothers who have not yet passed. The DS on the stones signifies their motto, *Deo Soli*. Farther on is the Shaker Cemetery with its large, modern, granite monument dated "1790–1928." The only original stones are the six rectangular slates by the cemetery entrance. In the 1940s, the Shakers at Sabbath Day Lake requested that the brothers remove their stones to honor the Shaker philosophy of living anonymously.

The Stations of the Cross mark the way down Cemetery Lane to the quaint Shrine of the Sacred Heart. There is also a 1962 sculpture of the crucified Christ, which was the first piece done by an artist who now enjoys a degree of fame. The brothers prefer he remain anonymous to protect against theft.

Brother Ted Letendre and Sister Regina Darody efficiently administer the Notre Dame Spiritual Center. The center hosts an estimated four to five thousand guests a year and is booked several years in advance. Their skills are not limited to running the retreat center, but they are trained professional counselors, and Brother Ted is the campus chaplain. They are also exceedingly warm and inviting individuals. Though they occasionally direct retreats, it is very rare. Almost all of the retreats are self-directed, independent groups that bring their own leaders. To honor the privacy of the visiting groups, usually only one retreat is on campus at a time. The center offers individual silent or directed retreats, but it is booked so far in advance that individuals can usually be accommodated only Monday through Friday, and in mid-summer or mid-winter.

Approximately half of the retreats scheduled are for spiritual groups, such as Crossroads Emmaus, a United Methodist group that schedules seventy-two-hour retreats named the "Walk to Emmaus." The Catholic Cursillo movement schedules retreats for providing laity with a model for evangelization through daily activities performed in a Christ-like manner. Through the years, the center has hosted Buddhist, Baptist, and Anglican organizations.

Regular secular groups include teachers, state employees, professional and fraternal organizations, and various treatment/recovery groups. Fire marshals and police officers who train dogs for specialized tasks have been guests here for many years. The facility is especially appreciated by large Alcoholic Anonymous and Narcotics Anonymous groups. Up to one hundred fifty people attend these functions and, because the center can house only one hundred ten, the remaining retreatants camp on the grounds.

Guests are housed in Eugene Hall, an 1825 Shaker building with fifteen rooms and thirty-seven beds, or in Denis Hall, with fifty beds and nineteen rooms. When the number of guests exceeds the number of beds in these two halls, other facilities are offered. Each room has a window, washstand, sink, desk, lamp, and fan. The rooms are arranged around a large central hall, containing a table and chairs that offer reprieve from the bedrooms. Bathrooms are shared, and males and females are housed in separate wings. The rooms are clean, with attractive matching quilts, and because there are two or three beds per room, the space is a bit cramped, but not unusually so for a retreat center.

Denis Hall has a large conference room that holds up to eighty people and, because this was formerly a school, it has a very inviting wall-to-wall blackboard. There are several small rooms used for group activity or discussion. A pleasing feature

Guests at Notre Dame Spiritual Center enjoy picnics, boating, and swimming at Shaker Pond.

throughout the center is the number of windows in most rooms. The Denis Hall chapel has eight windows, allowing light to flood the room. The first floor also has a library and a coffee room. In the basement there is an entertainment room with two pool tables, two ping-pong tables, and a fooz ball table. There is also a living room with a refrigerator, toaster oven, and microwave.

Next door is Henry Hall and the chapel, built in 1966 after a fire destroyed the original buildings. The dining facilities are in Henry Hall, and it is obvious that this is a frequently used facility by the ready availability of condiments, cereals, and toasters. It, too, is well lighted by expansive windows. The kitchen is large, professional, and clean. Beyond the kitchen is the "plant hospital" where a retired brother with a green thumb rejuvenates failing plants.

The chapel seats one hundred eighty and was built in classic 1960s style with curved, exposed wood beams and hanging lamps. Enough time has passed that the architecture has become appealing again. Services are held on Saturdays at 4:00 p.m. and Sundays at 9:00 a.m. Special services are performed for groups upon request.

When guests have free time, the grounds offer miles of trails, with one leading to Bunganut Pond. In the warmer months, guests have access to boating and picnic equipment at Shaker Pond, across Route 202, less than a mile from the main campus. Other activities include football, softball, tennis, and Saturday night barn dances.

Brother Ted claims that guests always rate the food as one of the highlights of their stay. They accommodate special requests for celebration cakes and certain dietary restrictions, though it is advised to call first to confirm that meal requirements can be addressed. Vegans and others who have very specific needs are asked to bring their own food and are given access to the kitchen for storage and preparation. Cooking separate meals for individuals with a large group is too time consuming and costly for most retreat centers.

Disabled people will find ramps into buildings, and there are two first-floor bedrooms. Being listed with the National Registry of Historic Sites makes changes restrictive and cost prohibitive, so the facility is not considered "handicapped accessible" in the legal sense of the term. All possible measures, however, are taken to insure the mobility and comfort of those with special needs.

Notre Dame has played a significant role in the community of southern Maine. People visit to attend Sunday mass, buy Brothers' Bread, participate in spaghetti suppers, buy apples in the fall, and indulge in maple syrup in the late winter. The Brothers had an estimated thirteen hundred people for Maine Maple Sunday in 2004. For years, hundreds of people took advantage of ice-skating in the Shaker barn—$1.00 for three hours! Unfortunately, insurance premiums recently forced the closure of the unique rink. The Brothers opened their community to the homeless and offered their facilities for vocational training. This hospitality and flexibility keep people returning to the Notre Dame Spiritual Retreat Center year after year.

Prices: 2005
$40.00 per night includes three meals and unlimited use of the facilities.

Contact Information:

Notre Dame Spiritual Center
133 Shaker Hill Road
P.O. Box 159
Alfred, ME 04002-0159
Telephone: (888)306-2271 Toll-free (Maine only)
　　　　　(207) 324-6160
　　　　　(207) 324-1017

About the Area:
Alfred is a charming country village with a small center. Nearby Sanford has shopping, movies, and restaurants.

Sewall House Retreat
Yoga Retreat

Island Falls

Sewall House Retreat's unique offering is two yoga classes per one night stay. The proprietor, Donna Davidge, teaches yoga October through May in New York City, and from June through Columbus Day, opens the Sewall House to visitors. How did a big city yoga instructor find her way to this rural community that is approximately 270 miles from Maine's southern-most border? Her story is rich with history, family, and healing.

Davidge's ancestors were the original settlers of Island Falls, and her family's roots still run deep here. The Sewall House dates back to 1865 and was built by her great-grandfather, William Sewall. The home had never been out of the Sewall hands, but due to unfortunate circumstances, the house and all of its belongings were in danger of going to auction. Davidge was not willing to let that happen. Feeling trepidation but propelled by events, she purchased her ancestral home and set about transforming it into a restful and healing yoga retreat. In 1997, her dream came true and Sewall House opened its doors to guests.

This is not a slickly renovated bed and breakfast. It is a cozy and comfortable home—the quintessential grandma and grandpa's house. The three-story house has a wraparound porch and a series of additions growing off it as is often seen on old houses. The rooms come in a variety of sizes from large to small. There are special touches such as pond lilies floating in a bowl on the nightstand or an antique quilt bedspread hand-sewn by one of Davidge's relatives.

The furnishings and accessories chronicle the family's history including lots of Teddy Roosevelt memorabilia. Interestingly, Sewall was Teddy Roosevelt's nature guide and lifelong friend. They corresponded regularly, and Sewall built Roosevelt's house in North Dakota.

166

The Sewalls visited the White House after Roosevelt became president in 1901. Their third-floor history room could be a Teddy Roosevelt museum, and the family is making plans to catalog and protect the artifacts and letters.

Roosevelt's first visit to Island Falls occurred when he was a sickly nineteen-year-old student at Harvard. One of his college professors was acquainted with Sewall and brought Roosevelt to Island Falls for a hunting expedition. Roosevelt returned for the next two years and for many visits afterwards. Sewall believed deeply in the healing power of nature, and the time they spent together was credited with curing Roosevelt's asthma, improving his general health, and giving him a deep appreciation of nature and of Maine.

The belief that healing may be found in nature is kept alive at Sewall House. Davidge and her husband, Kent Bonham, act as guides for guests who are interested in boating and hiking. A boat ride across Mattawamkeag Lake reveals a shoreline dotted with camps (a Maine term for seasonal cottages) that can be reached only by water or by dirt trails through acres of woods—a sure indication of rural living. For those who choose, the lake tour stops at a trail head that leads approximately one mile through the woods to Bible Point, so-called because Teddy Roosevelt came here to read his Bible. There is a guest book to sign and a plaque outlining Roosevelt's history in the area. Three thousand acres have been secured and protected by the state as a preserve. In woods this deep, wildlife is a common sight, and bald eagles are frequently spotted overhead.

The main attraction at Sewall House is the two yoga sessions that are

The Sewall House Retreat was built by the owner's great-grandfather in 1865.

included with each night's stay. The afternoon session is Kundalini yoga, which originated in India. In 1969, Yogi Bhajan challenged the traditional secrecy surrounding the practice by teaching it to Westerners. He created 3HO—Healthy, Happy, Holy Organization—and taught students through yoga centers. Davidge is trained and certified through this organization.

Kundalini yoga is not considered a religion by its practitioners, but a sacred science. It is sacred because it deals with spirituality, and it is science because it utilizes developed and proven technology to enhance health. It works by integrating the seven chakras. Chakras are energy centers located along the spine and brain. Kundalini energy is said to be the serpent or spiral energy that is located at the base of the spine and travels upward through the chakras. Much has been written about the effects of kundalini rising and its relationship to awakening the body and spirit.

The chakras are said to be driven through prana, or life force, which the body takes in through breath. The mind follows the breath, and the body follows the mind. Breathing techniques are essential to kundalini yoga. The postures, or asaunas, create angles within the body that balance the glandular system. The third primary tool used is the repetition of sound, the mantra. The mantra works by focusing the mind and stimulating a heightened state of consciousness. Breath, postures, and sound combine to strengthen the nervous system and harness energy while increasing strength, endurance, and focus.

The yoga/meditation sanctuary is separated from the inn by French doors and is outfitted with a soft green carpet. It is of a comfortable size with music equipment, a Jacuzzi, and a sauna. Bonham plays music at the beginning and end of many sessions, creating a personal ambience.

Yoga sessions last one hour and fifteen minutes and are offered in late afternoon and mid-morning. As stated earlier, kundalini yoga takes place in the afternoon and hatha/astranga yoga is taught in the morning. Hatha/astranga focuses on specifics of poses with some breath work. Sessions begin with chanting and then move through a series of postures that are doable at any level of experience. A variety of breathing techniques is employed. Davidge is an experienced teacher who expertly rearranges limbs into the most beneficial postures, insuring no one will be injured or overly sore the next day. Closure includes a song led by Bonham and with the chanting of Om, the sacred Hindu mantra representing the beginning, continuation, and end.

A large breakfast, "mid-day munch", and dinner are included in the price, and the food is vegetarian, mostly organic, and impressive. Davidge recruits vegetarian chefs from different parts of the country, making for fare that is sophisticated and gourmet. The Amish farm stand fifteen minutes away supplies fresh vegetables. (For more on the Amish, see page 71.) A typical dinner is spinach salad with a warm vinaigrette dressing, followed by an entrée that is a beautifully presented tower of brown rice mixed with corn and currants, topped with caramelized onions, and flavored with the warm spices of cinnamon and clove. Homemade bread, zucchini blossoms, and freshly sautéed zucchini accompany the meal. Dessert is delicious pudding with fresh fruit and sweet Indian spiced tea. Dietary limitations are accommodated.

Sewall House is open from June 4 through early October, and during the Christmas holiday. Guests arrive from all over the country. Visitors who are not interested in yoga are discouraged as it is an integral part of the retreat. It is also an alcohol-, nicotine-, and drug-free establishment. The television is for viewing videos and DVDs from the inn's library only. There is no radio, and cell phone users are asked to be out of the hearing range of the other guests. Guests may participate in seva, selfless service, if they wish. The recommended length of stay is four to seven days, with most guests staying four.

There are five bedrooms that share two full baths, a first floor suite with a private bath, and a studio in the barn for work-study guests. Amenities include breakfast, lunchtime snacks, dinner, a Jacuzzi, and a sauna. The library contains numerous self-growth videos, books, and cassettes. Sewall House sells their signature tank tops, Kent's music CDs, books, and Donna's instructional videos. Yoga Journal chose her video "The Challenge" as one of their top ten videos for enhancing practice. Lake tours, bicycle rentals, private yoga classes, and massages are available at additional cost.

Deep relaxation is a real possibility at Sewall House. There are no shops, no cultural events, no must-see museums—just nature, yoga, good food, and good company. It does not feel like a retreat or a bed and breakfast; it feels like being a houseguest without having to worry about overextending your visit. Donna's relatives drop by for chats, the cat looks for attention, the screen door swings open and shut, and the sounds of the household hum through the air.

Uniting a bed and breakfast with a retreat is an inspired idea. Many retreat centers are large, have limited room options, and keep participants on a busy schedule. Sewall House offers the opportunity to practice yoga and to have unfilled time in a remote environment with a minimum of distractions. Donna and Kent are warm, inviting, and enthusiastic, and Sewall House is an apt reflection of them.

Prices: 2005

Single occupancy is $145.00 per day
Double occupancy is $125.00 per person
Suite with private bath is $20.00 additional
All rates include two yoga sessions, breakfast, dinner, and snacks.
Lake Tours are $25.00
Bicycle rental is $5.00
Private yoga class is $75.00
Massage is $70.00 for an hour or $95.00 for an hour and a half

Contact Information:

Sewall House Retreat
P.O. Box 254
1027 Crystal Road
Island Falls, ME 04747
Telephone: (207) 463-3428 or (888) 235-2395
Web site: *www.sewallhouse.com*
E-mail: info@sewallhouse.com

About the Area:

Northern Maine offers nearly endless expanses of woods for hiking. The territory north of Bangor is home to Baxter State Park, Mount Katahdin, and the Appalachian Trail. They are within one hour of the Sewall House. For those who do not wish to travel as far, directions are provided to a number of trails that are closer. Mattawamkeag Lake offers swimming, fishing, and canoeing. The chances of spotting eagles, moose, loons, or even a bear are excellent.

Temple Heights Spiritual Camp
Spiritualism

Northport

A visitor to Temple Heights can expect to meet very interesting people, though not all of them will be living on the physical plane. In the religion of Spiritualism, contact with deceased family and friends is made through mediums, thereby proving the afterlife. Temple Heights has been a gathering place for Spiritualists since its founding in 1882, and offers the public many opportunities to work with mediums through private readings, message circles, gallery readings, workshops, and church services. (For more on Spiritualism, see page 16.)

Temple Heights is in Northport, nestled between Belfast and Camden, on Shore Road, a street easily missed but well worth the detour off Route 1. The road follows the shoreline and passes a charming neighborhood of Victorian cottages trimmed with gingerbread. Proceeding along the street, one encounters houses that range from traditional Maine camps to new, huge, shingle homes. When the houses and trees clear, the views of Penobscot Bay are stunning. Mounding islands rise out of endless ocean, making for picture postcard scenes. Temple Heights is perched on a sharp rise across the street from the water, affording it great views of the bay. At one time, it owned much of the surrounding property and still owns the point on the water across the street.

Temple Heights is open for eleven weeks from June to September. It hosts a different medium from around the country each week, with Maine mediums assisting in message circles. The weekly residing medium, who is frequently a reverend in the Spiritualist church, holds three church services, a workshop, two message circles, and a gallery reading. Some examples of workshops include *The Book of Revelation According to Edgar Cayce*, *Mechanics of Mediumship*, *Understanding Your Dreams*, and *Sharpen Your Intuition*. In a message circle, the medium sits with up to fifteen people, and everyone gets a message from the beyond. In gallery readings, not everyone is guaranteed a reading depending on how many people attend. Between these events and personal readings, Temple Heights counted over six hundred participants in one week in July.

Reverend Steve Hermann was the visiting medium on that particular week in July, and he visits each year. He is a member of several professional organizations, has traveled throughout the world as a professional medium, and has appeared on radio and television. He views his abilities as a medium to be a serious spiritual calling that demands discipline. To keep himself finely tuned, he has never indulged in caffeine, nicotine, alcohol, or drugs and is a vegetarian who meditates daily.

According to Reverend Hermann, there are rules that people need to follow during a reading. A person should never "feed the medium" by giving him or her information about the person that is coming through the medium. A simple yes or no is all that is required to let the medium know if the spirit is recognizable. If the spirit is not recognizable, more evidence is offered, and then the medium suggests you ask family members. One cannot expect to have all questions answered or to have a particular person's spirit appear. Though predictions about the future may be offered by the spirit world, mediumship is not fortune-telling. People who are open to the experience have better readings than those who are skeptical or closed-minded. A good reading is when a lot of solid evidence is given about the spirits.

Spiritualists believe that many people who pass over continue to be around those they knew in physical life. The personality stays the same, although some may evolve quickly in the afterlife. The spirit has greater access to information but is not all knowing. Spiritualists stress that the readings are for the "highest good", with prayers and faith keeping negative energies at bay.

Reverend Hermann teaches that spirits evolve with us, and when people heal on the physical plane, they assist in healing their ancestors as well. The belief that evolution in the spirit world occurs when living individuals grow emotionally, psychologically, and spiritually runs through many teachings, including those of Carl Jung and Rudolf Steiner. If this thinking is to be accepted, then each person has a responsibility to develop to the best of their ability.

In Reverend Hermann's workshop "Mechanics of Mediumship"

he defines mediumship as a process whereby spirit personalities use an individual to present information. The spirit may also cause paranormal activity and may be capable of manifesting physically or causing sounds, smells, and the movement of objects.

A spirit must learn to connect with the medium just as the medium must learn to work with spirits. The medium must raise his or her vibration, and the spirit must lower his in order for the two to meet. Information comes to mediums in a variety of ways: vision, sensation, and/or sound. The medium must acquire discipline and recognize the difference between his or her consciousness and that of the spirit's message. Reverend Hermann joked that there is a fine line between psychic and psychotic. He advised that learning to distinguish between imagination and spirit is a skill that takes practice.

Spiritualists believe that life after death has been proven, and they have faith in the accuracy of the mediums that are certified through the National Spiritualist Association of Churches. They are quick to caution people about the pitfalls of working with mediums. If mediums are not disciplined or experienced, they may confuse their own information with the client's. When they are not ethical, they will use negative information to convince clients to schedule more sessions. To decipher the quality of the reading a person should look for specifics such as names, descriptions, personalities, and relationships. In addition, a medium is always psychic, but a psychic is not always a medium.

A message circle, gallery reading, or church service is a good way to be introduced to readings, as they are given to an assortment of people and generally last no longer than five minutes each. This offers the opportunity to hear other people's readings and observe reactions to the messages. At Temple Heights, there are church services on Sunday afternoons and Wednesday nights. All Spiritualist services end with approximately twenty minutes of readings for parishioners. The Sunday service is followed by a potluck dinner open to all comers and offers a table groaning with food and very interesting conversations.

There is another adventure available to the open-minded. When Pam Strickland, former President of the Board of Directors for Temple Heights, and Janice Nelson are available, they might be convinced to do a table-tipping session. In table-tipping, mediums channel the energy of spirits, who move the table to answer questions. A standard is one tip for yes and two tips for no. This is the format used during the séances of the nineteenth century, many of which were fraudulent. Keeping that in mind, the women allow newcomers to thoroughly investigate the table and the room for any signs of trickery. To begin, everyone's fingertips lightly touch the table and thumbs are visible. Within minutes, the table will start to vibrate, then to move, and then dance quite energetically. Each person asks a question either silently or aloud and receives a yes or no answer. It is a good idea to watch out for crushed toes—the table can get wild!

Perhaps the table dances so energetically because there is over one hundred twenty years of history at Temple Heights. Dating back to an even earlier time is the remarkable story of its founder, Doctor Ben Colson. According to Temple Heights' history and Colson family genealogy, Benjamin Colson went into a coma as a young man. While in the coma, he was visited by a Native American spirit guide named Nickawa. He taught Colson his native language and healing remedies, which Colson retained after he emerged from the coma.

Colson became famous throughout Maine for his healing abilities and came to be known as Dr. Ben. It was said that he cured the wife of a governor, who gave him a reward of $5,000. Colson used the money to buy a huge tract of land along Shore Road and built a healing center on the water, just below Temple Heights. The healing center burned to the ground in 1882 and, with that, the Temple Heights Spiritual Camp was born.

Hanging in the lodge is the portrait of Nickawa that Dr. Ben commissioned. He is portrayed as he appeared to Colson, and people have speculated that he is South American because of his headdress. A photograph of Dr. Ben is next to Nickawa's portrait, paying homage to the Spiritualist tradition of partnership between guides and people for the purpose of healing.

Temple Heights has been a gathering place for Spiritualists since its founding in 1882.

Originally the camp was open for one week in the summer and had more than a hundred 40' by 40' tent lots. Over time, there were several lodges, cabins, and a central meeting hall. The Nickawa Lodge was built in two parts: half in 1927 and half in 1956.

Presently, the camp consists of two buildings: the Nickawa Lodge and the chapel. Upkeep is good but depends on the kindness of volunteers, so there is an ongoing list of things that need to be done. The Nickawa Lodge houses guests and has a library, two meeting rooms, a kitchen, and reception area. A large porch spans the front, with plenty of room for tables and chairs.

The chapel is quite large and traditional. The chairs appear to be old theater seats, and the furnishings and decorations can probably be traced back to every decade of the twentieth century.

The camp is self-supporting and is kept running by volunteers who appear to enjoy the work and the sense of community it provides. The sole paid employee is the housekeeper, whose wage barely covers her expenses. The sheets smell fresh because she hangs them out to dry at her home. It is those touches that make the people who run Temple Heights so special.

The amazing price of a single waterfront room is $35.00 per night. This is prime vacationland where room rates do not dip below $60.00 and may easily go over $300.00 per night. Rooms are pleasantly comfortable and homey. They are furnished with a bed, bureau, nightstand and two chairs. Extra touches include a fan, an alarm clock, hooks for hanging clothes, and even sample soaps and shampoos. The bedding and towels are more than adequate, and the mattresses were all recently replaced. Three bathrooms accommodated nine rooms. Be cautioned that the walls are paper thin.

The Temple Heights Spiritual Camp is a down-to-earth retreat that will leave you flying high. There is nothing sanctimonious about Temple Heights even though spirituality is the theme. People feel comfortable smoking on the porch, drinking coffee at 10:00 p.m., staying up late, and eating rich comfort foods. You will not be judged for those pesky indulgences that have not been conquered yet on the path to making the body a temple.

Novices to Spiritualism should be prepared to have their presumptions about the afterlife either redefined or validated, depending on their beliefs. Those who are sensitive to energy should be warned, this place is buzzing!

Prices: 2005
Single room: $35.00
Double room: $45.00
Private reading: $40.00 for 30 minutes

Message Circle: $10.00
Gallery Reading: $10.00
Workshops: $20.00

Contact Information:

Temple Heights Spiritual Camp
P.O. Box 311
Lincolnville, ME 04849
Telephone: (207) 338-3029
Web site: *members.tripod.com/templeheights/grid2heal.html*

About the Area:

Northport is a small coastal town between two major attractions:
Belfast and Camden. Both of them are scenic port towns, offering
shops, restaurants, art galleries, and historical points of interest.
Belfast is less congested and has beautiful architecture downtown.

Two Roads
Healing in Nature

Pownal

When people enter a life crisis, be it through illness, loss, or trauma, their lives are never the same again. Those who experience these trials are sent reeling into a world where decisions are of staggering difficulty and enormous importance. The unfolding is inevitably accompanied by confusion, anger, fear, grief, and regret. A question arises from the turmoil: "How do I want to live the rest of my life?" David Hyde, the founder of Two Roads, refers to this as the "critical crossroads." People at that juncture make crucial decisions regarding their healing, and Two Roads, through its nature retreats, aims to support that process.

Two Roads grew out of David's personal experience with illness and job loss. In 1999, at the age of 49, a routine medical exam led to a diagnosis of prostate cancer. Two days later, his management position with L. L. Bean was eliminated after seventeen years with the corporation. His family and friends rallied around him to support him through the critical decisions and difficult choices that lay ahead. He sought solace in nature and recognized that the natural world was in a continuous process of self-healing. His woodland treks and kayaking excursions opened him to a new understanding of healing. Six months after his diagnosis, while kayaking on Muscongus Bay, David had an intense experience that changed the course of his healing and the course of his life. This was accompanied by a desire to offer others the opportunity to heal in nature and in community. He envisioned an organization that would bring people on wilderness retreats to free them from life's distractions while allowing them to directly experience the healing power of nature and their own power to heal themselves in community. For David, the epiphany was an invitation to transform his life.

The vision became a reality as David put his corporate skills to the task. He understood how to make a business plan and act on it. The first step was to enlist the support of the Chewonki Foundation to provide wilderness expertise, leadership, and enthusiasm for the natural world.

Since 1970, the Chewonki Foundation has been guiding people of all ages into the wilderness. From their base in Wiscasset, they host wilderness trips in Maine, Canada, Florida, and Georgia. The trip leaders are Registered Maine Guides and/or Maine State Trip Leaders. They are certified in Wilderness First Responder First Aid, CPR, and water safety. They are knowledgeable about Maine's natural history and have years of experience leading trips.

David knew that Chewonki was an organization with integrity and wanted nothing less for Two Roads. Discussions with Chewonki's President Don Hudson and Director of Wilderness Trips Greg Shute led to an enthusiastic agreement that the two organizations were a good match. Chewonki was looking to expand their excursions but, until meeting with Two Roads, had not found a group that fit with its mission, which states in part, "... is dedicated to helping people grow individually and in community with others by providing educational experiences that foster an understanding of the natural world and that emphasize the power of focused collective effort." The fit was perfect.

David's wife Sarah fully supported his dream and took on the tasks of marketing and writing grants. An English teacher and writer, she became a hospice worker in the 1980s when her father died from cancer. David's brother Steve, an ordained Zen priest, brought his talent in writing, philosophy, and meditation. Together with Chewonki staff, they designed a series of four-day retreats and workshops.

In August 2000, after one year of planning, Two Roads hosted its first retreat. Each year since, it has hosted seven to nine wilderness trips that are scheduled throughout the year. The lineup includes *Snowshoeing on Big Wood Pond near Jackman, Exploring Cumberland Island off the Coast of Georgia, Lake Memphremagog in Canada, Canoeing on Lake Umbagog on the Maine and New Hampshire border, Coastal Kayaking in Maine,* and *Fall Canoeing on Big Wood Pond.* In addition, a program is scheduled at least three times yearly for those who are unable to travel. *Contemplative Practice in Nature: Illness and Initiation* is a four-day program that meets from 9:00 a.m. to 4:00 p.m. in Pownal. Most participants live within driving distance, but arrangements for overnight accommodations can be made.

The Two Roads' trips are designed to appeal to all levels of comfort with the outdoors. For example, the Harbor Island trip follows "leave no trace" camping guidelines. In Canada, participants stay in a fully furnished private home, complete with flush toilets and electric lights. The intent is not to create an endurance test but to provide the best possible experience in nature and in community. There are no bosses, and everyone shares in chores and cooking. No experience is needed, and no one grumbles when accommodations are made for people with physical limitations such as surgical issues, multiple sclerosis, cerebral palsy, or any number of other conditions.

The maximum number of guests per trip is six, plus David, Steve, and two Chewonki guides. The brothers are committed to the integrity of small groups and believe intimacy is sacrificed when the number of guests gets too large. Small groups quickly progress to a level of mutual trust and comfort, leading to friendship and community.

No one under eighteen or over seventy has ever joined a Two Roads excursion, but those who are younger or older are welcome. Initially, David thought he would host only people who were diagnosed with life-altering illnesses. That was short-lived as people approached him who had experienced the loss of loved ones, had a family member with illness, or struggled with divorce. The resulting diversity of mixed experiences and ages enriches the retreats.

The retreat schedule is simple, to allow people time for exploration and reflection. Each day there is time set aside to be alone, to explore the outdoors, and for sharing stories. Group sharing is referred to as council and is intentionally not spelled "counsel," as there is no professional therapy involved. No one on the staff is trained in counseling or group facilitation, and they like it that way. Everyone, including David, Steve, and the Chewonki guides, participates in the councils as a learner, not a leader. Discussion protocol is set to ensure that communication is shared equally.

The council recreates an ancient practice from tribal communities in which each person, if he or she so chooses, has the opportunity to speak without interruption or discussion. This context is native to everyone; people innately know how to share, support, listen, empathize, and nurture one another. Healing is an aspect of human experience and not separate from it; therefore, councils reinforce that healing occurs in community. Everyone in attendance can be a resource for healing. Therapeutic work happens in council when people leave behind roles, labels, and expectations, and are open to their most heartfelt emotions. It is a time of laughter, tears, and deep insights.

Councils are just one example of how Two Roads' philosophy manifests in healing. David and Steve do not consider themselves teachers, though between them they certainly have a wide range of life experiences that provide insights and empathy. They are not healers, nor do they have a prescription for healing. Their task is to provide the container to support self-healing that comes from within. Contemporary people tend to experience physical and mental health as outwardly determined by the medical establishment, while Two Roads asks people to see healing as an inward journey as well.

The brothers believe that the quiet of the natural world guides people as they look inward and serves as an example of healing. Nature heals in community—nothing stands alone. In nature, there is a continuous process of recreating, reestablishing, and rebuilding. It is always in the process of destruction and creation as it finds and keeps balance. When people can learn from nature's pattern of disintegration followed by renewal, it allows them to let go of the old that is dissolving and to give birth to what is new and fresh. There is a complete field of possibilities and, by releasing old ideas and fears, people mimic nature's actions and open themselves up to limitless options.

Two Roads brings people to the experiential classroom of the natural world. They ask participants to turn off their analytical minds, move beyond thinking, and open themselves to a direct experience with nature. Immersed in creation, people may arrive at an inexplicable place where the self slides away with all of its fears, despairs, hopes, and desires. What enters in its place is mysterious and beyond words— a profound connection to all of existence and to being alive. Few people remain the same after experiencing such moments.

Two Roads makes no claims about spirituality, but nature is imbued with it for those who are seeking. Whatever people's beliefs are, they will find healing through the inherent health and wisdom of the natural world.

Part of the journey with Two Roads is to move from the "left brain," the overly busy side, to the heart. The mind creates endless obstacles to healing. Two Roads removes as many barriers as possible, recognizing that people will forcefully resist change even to their own detriment. Some barriers are easier to deal with than others. The easy ones involve physical needs. Chewonki supplies all of the camping and boating equipment, and for those who lack appropriate clothing, it is supplied from their lost and found or from David's family and friends. If money is an issue, partial or full scholarships are available. Meals are vegetarian, food is abundant, and restricted diets are accommodated. Adjustments are made for physical limitations.

Societal barriers are trickier, as they involve recognizing and letting go of other people's expectations. People must fight against the huge cultural message that taking time off from work for self-healing is weak, selfish, unprofessional, or any number of other projections. Concerns about money and wasting time add to the load.

The hardest barriers to overcome are those from within.

Perhaps it is fear of roughing it, being uncomfortable, not liking the other participants, taking risks, being vulnerable, change, letting go, or showing up for life. Anger, feelings of betrayal, and sadness block the road to healing. David and Steve put great effort into removing obstacles and will listen with deep ears to all concerns people have about participating.

The brothers have a passion and an intuitive knowing that inspires hope and confidence. Two Roads is an original model for healing. It is not based on textbooks, another person's idea, or a corporate model; it is born from experience and wisdom.

Healing comes in many guises, and four days in nature is not going to miraculously cure disease or heartbreak. Healing also comes in the forms of optimism, hope, insight, friendship, love, and joy.

Daring to take the risk is liberating; nature and community will do the rest.

Prices: 2005
All retreats in Maine and Canada: $675.00
Exploring Cumberland Island, Georgia: $800.00
Contemplation in Pownal: by donation
Two Roads is a nonprofit organization. Donations are appreciated and used for scholarships.

Contact Information

Two Roads Maine
P.O. Box 415
Freeport, ME 04032
David and Sarah Hyde
Telephone: 207-865-4517
Web site: *www.tworoadsmaine.org*
E-mail: tworoads@maine.rr.com

Chautauqua-by-the-Sea
Ocean Park

Ocean Park is a neighborhood in Old Orchard Beach that is populated mostly by summer residents who enjoy old-fashioned summer fun due to the unique efforts of the Ocean Park Association. The association has been offering religious, educational, cultural, and recreational opportunities since its founding in 1881 by Free Will Baptists, whose intent was to establish an interdenominational summer assembly. Referred to as Chautauqua-by-the-Sea, it is part of a network of summer communities related to Chautauqua Institute in Chautauqua, New York.

From Memorial Day to Labor Day, the weeks are packed with activities planned to have broad appeal. Every Sunday night, Ocean Park Music Festival features different professional musicians whose performances include ragtime, big band, opera, concert piano, and vocal. Monday Evening Picnics offer a chance for socializing while indulging in a barbeque dinner. Book groups, Ocean Park Forum, and Morning Watch appeal to those who enjoy discussions and the study of timely topics concerning faith. There are opportunities to cruise the Saco Bay, explore area trails, square dance, partake in sing-a-longs, and join the choir or band. There is a strong emphasis on family, and children are kept busy with camp activities, Bible study, family game night, and weekly story time.

Annual events include the Independence Day Parade and Band Concert, Sand Castle Competition, and 5K Road Race. Illumination Night celebrates lights, music, food, and community. The evening begins with the Strawberry Shortcake Festival, followed by a concert and then a "walk about" from street to street viewing cottages aglow with light, while enjoying the company of fellow strollers.

Each week a different visiting preacher, often of national

renown, is invited to give an interdenominational sermon. The service is a lively affair with the Temple Choir, Temple Bell Choir, and Ocean Park Brass Band providing rousing music.

The Temple is the centerpiece of Ocean Park and where most of the cultural activities are held. Built in 1881, it is an extraordinary building that was, and still is, one of the largest octagonal buildings in the United States. The appealing architecture has an extended post and beam superstructure and a seating capacity of approximately eight hundred people. Nearly 25,000 visitors attend services and events at the temple each year. The temple and several other Ocean Park Association buildings have been named to the National Register of Historic Places.

For more information:

Ocean Park Association
P.O. Box 7296
Ocean Park, ME 04063-7296
Telephone: (207) 934-9068
Web site: *www.oceanpark.org*
E-mail: opa@oceanpark.org

Transforming Vision to Action: Organizations and Councils

Feminist Spiritual Community

Interfaith Maine

Kairos Outside

Maine Council of Churches

Maine Gnosis Center

Spiral Arts

Feminist Spiritual Community

Portland

The Feminist Spiritual Community (FSC) offers exactly what its name implies—the opportunity for women to explore their spirituality from a feminist perspective within a community of mutual support. The ever-evolving organization has provided empowerment, healing, and education in Portland since its inception in 1980.

The Feminist Spiritual Community did not begin as one person's vision but was the initiative of an enthusiastic class of college students. They were the students of Eleanor Haney, an ethics professor who taught their class in feminist theology. The class chose to study ritual as their final group project. The results were so electrifying that the students wanted to continue their explorations of women's spirituality and maintain their bonds of friendship.

While the women were establishing the foundation for their gatherings, Haney pursued funding for a meeting space and a coordinator. With her encouragement, the United Church of Christ agreed to underwrite the fledgling feminist theology organization through its outreach division that provided money to marginalized spiritual groups. The church generously donated funding for the first three years. In response to the gift, Haney traveled throughout Maine speaking to United Church of Christ groups about feminist theology, Native American spirituality, goddess traditions, and the need to understand women's historic role in religion.

It sounds mild to 21st-century sensibilities, but at the time it was radical. Feminist theology surfaced in the 1960s and steadily progressed through the 1970s hand-in-hand with the women's movement. Well-informed women appraised religion through new eyes and made their first attempts to articulate what they found. By the 1980s, women in greater numbers were recognizing that men defined mainstream religions and had created a structure and language that was alienating to many women. Across the country, women began to live out what they had awakened to by experimenting with spiritual communities and gatherings.

These occurrences were largely under the radar of the general public, therefore FSC and Haney's activities appeared provocative and controversial to many people. Some of the participants in Maine's first feminist spiritual group were lesbians, which increased negativity directed at the group. Though they were stung by the criticisms, they recognized the valuable education and exposure they were bringing to those who were ready to listen.

In the first decade of its existence, social activism was a significant arm of the FSC. They organized the Women in Power Conference that was attended by nearly five hundred people. The Feminist Speakers Series hosted an array of well-known feminists. When community members traveled to Guatemala and connected with women villagers, FSC sent money and prayers of support to the woman. Funds were raised for the Hopi and Navajo at Big Mountain, Arizona, when government manipulations began plans to resettle the Navajo in order obtain mining rights.

FSC had a role in the creation of the Displaced Homemakers program, now known as Women, Work & Community. The group co-sponsored the 1988 Conference for Incest Survivors and Their Allies. In 1989, a publications committee branched out to form Astarte Shell Press, a small women's press which, in its nine-year existence, published fifteen books focusing on women's spirituality and social justice.

The social reform activities have dropped away, but ad hoc committees are formed as issues arise. The group is still concerned with social and political justice, but a specific agenda is not part of Monday gatherings, and women of all political leanings are welcome. The same holds true for spiritual beliefs—all are welcome. Women arrive at FSC from different religious traditions or none at all. Some women are affiliated with a religion outside of the group, while others fulfill all of their spiritual needs at FSC.

Women attend the gatherings to share their stories and feel the welcoming spirit of the group. Usually there are between twelve and twenty people in attendance, with more for holidays or special events. Some have been participating since the 1980s, while others are newcomers. Women sit in a circle on chairs or cushions around a center altar that reflects both FSC tradition and the evening's theme. Participation in activities is voluntary, and all names and situations are confidential.

Discussion and planning by the original group of university

students produced a framework for FSC that remains intact today. The group is open to all women, meets weekly, conducts activities in a circle, and encompasses ritual. Entering the meeting is called being enfolded. As each woman enters the room, she can choose to receive a hug that serves to celebrate her arrival and to share energy and connection.

Enfolding is followed by announcements, which may be personal or related to community events. Each week, five candles are lighted in the opening ritual. Each of the first three are respectively for those present, those not present but there in spirit, and those who are first time visitors. Next, a candle is lighted for a social justice cause, and the last candle is lighted to share joys and concerns. Then, in the naming circle, each woman names herself as she wishes to be called in the circle that night, and she can choose to state what she needs, offer what she has in abundance, bring in the spirit of a woman who would like to be there, and/or send helpful energy to someone. She then takes hold of the next woman's hand. When the circle is complete, there is silence for several moments to circulate the energy and send helpful energy to those who requested it. The comments during the candle lighting and naming are brief in order to allow adequate time for the ritual.

The focus of the gathering is the ritual. Each week a different volunteer plans and leads the ritual. Rituals vary widely and reflect the planners' interests and talents. They may involve art, personal reflection, education, meditation, hands-on healing, drumming, story telling, or sharing. Often rituals mark life passages such as pregnancy, birth, death, rites of passage, personal milestones, croning, or naming. Individualized rituals are designed to fit a personal path, to bless someone who is moving, or encourage someone who is in a difficult period. Due to the variety, newcomers are encouraged to try at least three gatherings before making a decision about their participation in the group.

Family gatherings that include children and men are scheduled several times a year. Special rituals are held to celebrate the seasonal holidays of the solstices and equinoxes, Imbolc (winter's end), Beltane (May Day), Lammas (harvest), and Samain (autumn and pagan New Year). At times, a "listening" is requested, which provides a structured environment for communication about personal or FSC issues.

A collection of FSC's past rituals, *Keep Simple Ceremonies: the Feminist Spiritual Community of Portland*, was published in 1993 by Astarte Shell Press. The collection presents rituals for a myriad of occasions, plus guidance for creating them and encouragement to adapt them to individual use. Newcomers may find the book helpful when it is time to present their first ritual, and even those not involved with FSC will find the book to be a treasure trove of celebrations that range from sacred to silly. Copies of *Keep Simple Ceremonies* are available through FSC.

The intention of all of their rituals is to offer the opportunity to open to love, power, and justice. When performed in a safe place within a supportive community, rituals are powerful tools for healing, self-development, and transformation. Participants find their gifts through learning from others and witnessing others learning from them. Throughout, their spiritual identity is honored by the use of poetry, writing, and art by women and with female images and icons.

FSC is a volunteer organization that is orchestrated by two committees and a treasurer. One committee organizes the ritual schedule and the other deals with business issues. Business meetings are open to all and occur on the fourth Monday of each month. All decisions, including the meeting agendas, are made by consensus.

It is estimated that more than five hundred women have been involved in FSC since 1980. Their history is rich with experimentation, education, activism, and healing. Each woman who has grown through participation with FSC has influenced and educated others, making it impossible to estimate their impact. The group has been larger, and it has been smaller, but always their message remains the same: "We meet each Monday evening to celebrate, support, and heal one another and to explore areas of spirituality, theology, personal and social transformation and empowerment."

The evenings end with a circle of women holding hands and singing joyfully.

Cost

A Prosperity Basket is passed at each meeting to pay for rent and expenses.

Contact Information:

Meetings are held on Monday evenings from 7:00 to 9:00 p.m. Call or write for more information.

Feminist Spiritual Community
P.O. Box 3771
Portland, Maine 04104
Telephone: (207) 774-2830
E-mail: terra@maine.rr.com

Interfaith Maine

Portland

Interfaith Maine is an apt reflection of Maine's changing religious landscape. The discussion groups and events that they organize are attended by people from a range of faiths: Bahá'í, Buddhism, Christianity, Christian Science, Muslim, Judaism, Mormon, Pagan, and Quaker. They regularly schedule gatherings to exchange ideas around set themes, and when political, cultural, and religious events occur that prompt fear and resentment in the community, they respond quickly with activities that promote dialogue and support. All of their activities are informed by their mission that states, "Interfaith Maine seeks peace and justice through deepening interfaith understanding and relationships."

Interfaith Maine incorporated as a nonprofit organization in 2003. Its history dates back to the spring of 2001 when a coalition from Bangor Theological Seminary, St. Joseph College, and the University of Southern Maine came together to discuss religious pluralism in Maine. Called the Portland Interfaith Seminar, they organized discussion groups in the Portland area. They recognized how dialogue could bridge differences, heal historical injuries, and remove the walls of separation between religions. After September 11, 2001, those elements were needed in large doses to heal individual and national grief. Their response was to offer the opportunity for dialogue, to educate the public about Islam, and to provide support and protection to Maine's Muslim community.

During this same period, the Academic Council for Post-Holocaust Christian, Jewish, and Islamic Studies developed and had many of the same people involved as the Portland Interfaith Seminar. It is housed at the University of Southern Maine in cooperation with Bangor Theological Seminary and St. Joseph's College. The Academic Council works to improve relationships between the three religions through academic and public activities.

In the spring of 2002, they held a conference titled "The Children of Abraham Downeast: Judaism, Christianity, and Islam for a New Religious Pluralism." The highly successful conference drew the interest of those who did not practice the Abraham religions but wanted to participate in an interfaith organization. From that point forward, Portland Interfaith Seminar became less focused on academia and more pluralistic. Shortly thereafter, the organization was renamed Interfaith Maine.

Interfaith Maine's most visible activity after its incorporation was its quick response to religious and racial controversy in Lewiston involving a large influx of Somali Muslims. In 2003, the mayor wrote a letter to leaders within the Somali community requesting they not bring anymore of their relatives to Lewiston as the population was straining the city's resources. The national press covered the story extensively, often in an incendiary manner. A national racist hate group held a rally in Lewiston, further increasing tensions. Interfaith Maine, Bangor Theological Seminary, and the United States Conference for Religions for Peace organized a conference, bringing together leaders from the religious, business, social services, and ethnic communities. A coalition formed to develop strategies and set goals that addressed the Muslim community's issues.

When Mel Gibson released his film *The Passion of the Chris,* controversy quickly followed. Was it anti-Semitic? Was it an accurate interpretation of the Bible? Was it overly violent? Interfaith Maine arranged a special screening that drew approximately one hundred twenty clergy and lay leaders. Opinions varied so widely, and community interest was so great that a second discussion was scheduled, which was open to the public.

Building community takes ongoing effort, and toward that end, Interfaith Maine and the University of Southern Maine's Office of the Chaplaincy co-sponsor the monthly interfaith program "The Spirit of Maine." The program was developed to offer students and local community members a forum for interfaith dialogue. The programs occur once a month during the school year and last for an hour and a half. A theme is chosen for each year's programs. Examples are world religions, aspects and obligations of religions, and religious community resources. A spokesperson speaks on a predetermined topic, and a group discussion follows. Past topics have included "Prayer," "The Nature of God/Divine," "Rituals and Rites of Passage," "Learning in the Light of Faith," "Spirituality and Expressive Arts," and "Women's Spirituality." The meetings are interfaith, intergenerational, interethnic, and interracial dialogues of sharing.

"Dinner Discussions" are planned four times a year when those from faith communities join to break bread together and discuss pertinent issues. The evenings begin at 6:00 p.m. with a potluck dinner, followed by brief presentations and a round table discussion. This group does not avoid difficult issues; topics include the role faith plays in education, economics, the environment, and elections.

Maine's religious diversity comes as a surprise to many people and, in 2004, it was documented through Harvard University's Pluralism Project. The Pluralism Project engages researchers across the country to study America's changing religious landscape with a particular emphasis on communities from the Middle East and Asia. The research results are posted on their website (*www.pluralism.org*), which is a guide to centers, temples, and organizations. The Pluralism Project research in Maine, done by Colleen Rost-Banik, shows a plethora of diverse religious activity. According to her research, Maine's growing racial and religious diversity is due in part to Catholic Charities Maine, which is a major organization involved in refugee resettlement. Rost-Banik found that since 1975, Catholic Charities Maine has resettled in Maine five thousand refugees from twenty-five countries. Buddhists and Muslims make up the majority of this new population. Anyone needing further proof of the importance of Interfaith Maine need look no further than the research completed by Rost-Banik.

The goals of Interfaith Maine provide a framework that builds a spiritual community that does not shy away from difficult issues or social activism. They are:

> To find ways to remove suspicion, fear, resentment
> of the other
> To fully respect others' freedom and dignity
> To give and to receive truth and convictions
> To celebrate common traditions and values
> To engage in joint witness and social action
> To recognize the gifts and the blessings of each other
> To be open to growth and understanding
> To engage in public activities to heal historical and
> present-day wounds
> To promote the path of pluralism through public
> educational efforts

Under Interfaith Maine's leadership, Maine is growing into a state that honors diversity through unity.

191

Contact Information

Interfaith Maine

The following board members may be contacted for more information:

Cynthia Jane Collins, M.Div., M.S.
86 High Street
Saco, ME 04072
Telephone: (207) 282-1491
E-mail: oldelucy@maine.rr.com

Douglas Cruger
E-mail: dcruger@mainecouncilofchurches.org.

Andrea Thompson McCall
Assistant Dean & Interfaith Chaplain
University of Southern Maine
Telephone: (207) 228-8284
Web site: *www.interfaithmaine.org*
E-mail: atmccall@usm.maine.edu

Kairos

Kairos is an ecumenical, lay-led, volunteer, international prison ministry. Its interesting name is Greek for "God's appointed time." Time is hugely significant to inmates and "karios" holds special meaning for those who are served by this program.

Kairos has grown rapidly since its inception in 1976. It is active in 270 penitentiaries in 33 states and the countries of Australia, Canada, England, Costa Rica, and South Africa. Kairos consists of three programs: Kairos Prison Ministry serves incarcerated men and women; Kairos Outside began in 1989 to support the spouses, parents, and relatives of inmates; and the most recent addition in 1997, Kairos Torch, which serves and mentors imprisoned youths aged 13 to 19. In Maine, Kairos Prison Ministry does not visit the women's prison, and Kairos Torch began its first weekend at Long Creek Youth Development Center in the summer of 2005.

Kairos Prison Ministry arose from Cursillo programs that were offered in a small number of prisons. Cursillo began as a religious movement in the 1930s in the Church of Spain. It evolved into a program that encourages self-transformation through Jesus Christ with the goal of living each day as an apostle of Christ, thereby positively transforming the world. The Cursillo method entails retreats where discussion, prayer, meditation, and individual and group activities provide the framework for spiritual transformation. Kairos is an ecumenical Cursillo program that uses the same method but is tailored to the unique needs of inmates.

Kairos Prison Ministry has been serving men at the Maine State Prison since the mid-1990s. By 2005, over three hundred inmates joined Kairos team members behind prison walls for biannual weekends that begin on Thursday nights with an introduction and proceed for the next three days meeting from 8 a.m. to 8 p.m. The men are informed of the program through the chaplain's office and are made aware that it is a Christian gathering, though they do not have to be Christian to attend.

Participants are cleared by the prison administration, have a background check, and take a short training course required by the prison. There is usually a waiting of list of eight to ten men.

Kairos team members spend the weekend with twenty-four inmates. The group is divided into four communities consisting of six inmates and three team members seated at four round tables. The team goes through over forty hours of training and most have had attended Cursillo retreats. A three-hundred-page manual from Kairos International is closely followed and insures that each Kairos weekend is the same no matter where it is held in the world, barring minor differences due to institutional rules.

The team members give talks on topics that range from goal setting and choices to forgiveness and the church within. Many of the men have a need to forgive themselves and others, and team members serve them best by listening deeply and sharing Christ's love and forgiveness with them. There are no denominational rituals, sacraments, or services, as they could be construed as a bias towards a particular tradition.

Weekends used to entail homemade meals and snacks until prison officials discontinued the practice in 2004. The team was initially disappointed because the food drew men into the program and the alternative of eating prison food was unappealing, but dining with the inmates in their cafeteria proved to be a valuable bonding experience.

Several months after the biannual weekends, two-day follow-up programs are offered for all former participants. Follow-up also occurs on the second Saturday of each month when twelve to fifteen team members hold an open meeting for several hours. The inmates who have attended Kairos weekends form a loose community in the prison, but regular meetings are impossible due to the hostile atmosphere and prison regulations.

Kairos Outside was inspired by a chaplain at San Quentin State Correctional Facility in California who observed that men who participated in Kairos became more concerned with family unity. Because family support is known to reduce recidivism, Kairos Outside was begun to support the loved ones of the incarcerated.

Kairos Outside's first weekend in Maine took place in 2004. The program serves adult women impacted by the sentencing of loved ones, with no restrictions on the duration of the sentence or the nature of the crime. All group leaders and team members are women as well, with the exception of volunteers from the Kairos Prison Ministry, who prepare and serve food. The guests are recruited through churches, word of mouth, personal contact, or recommended by inmates who have experienced Kairos Prison Ministry.

The approach taken by Kairos Outside is significantly different from the prison ministry. The weekends, which are held at retreat centers, begin on Friday night and end on Sunday night. Before the weekend occurs, each team member is matched to a guest and establishes a relationship with her through telephone calls and visits. On Friday evening, the guest is greeted at the door by her team member, assuring that she will feel comfortable upon arrival. The emphasis for the women's weekends is to pamper them and shower them with attention. Weekends have themes to create a celebratory atmosphere. The first Kairos Outside weekend followed a holiday theme with each of the six home cooked meals representing a different holiday. One of the meals was a happy birthday lunch in which each woman received a birthday cake and present. Other meals included a Valentine's Day breakfast, Easter breakfast, St. Patrick's Day lunch, Fourth of July lunch, and Thanksgiving dinner. Behind the scenes, four men cook and serve, while four "angels" do whatever needs to be done to ensure the weekend proceeds smoothly.

The guests, whose identity is strictly confidential, are often isolated by the community, shunned at church, and harshly judged by others. Some of them have lost their jobs and their connections with their birth families. Spouses of the incarcerated frequently have problems with money, transportation, and childcare. It is a difficult position that can lead to a lack of confidence, along with feelings of shame, guilt, and embarrassment. These feelings are addressed during the weekends through sharing, prayer, and activities designed to promote spiritual growth. Team members spend much of their time listening, encouraging, and assuring the women that they are not alone. As with the prison's program, one does not have to be of any religious persuasion to attend, but the discussions are from a Christian perspective.

During the weekends, guests are encouraged to become friendly with one another and to stay in touch afterwards. Reunions are held three months after the weekend, and team members continue to support their guests with regular contact.

Kairos offers valuable ministry to inmates and their families, and maintaining and funding a viable program takes ongoing effort. Kairos Outside is the most challenging of the Kairos programs. First, Maine's geography makes it necessary to hold weekends in southern, mid-state, and northern locations. Second, it is very expensive to provide the facility, meals, gifts, and, when needed, transportation and childcare. Kairos programs are dependent on volunteers, who must make a substantial commitment of forty-three hours of training, advanced training for leaders, and the sacrifice of many weekends throughout the year. Kairos Prison Ministry has found that it takes a special man who is willing to volunteer in a penitentiary. (In Maine, there has never been an incidence where the team was concerned for their safety; in fact, the inmates are very protective of the team.)

Clint Daggett, who began Kairos in Maine, stated four needs of the program in the following order:

1. Prayers for the incarcerated, their families, and for Kairos volunteers.

2. Letters to the prisoners. During prison weekends, packets of letters are given to the inmates expressing concern and prayers.

3. Financial support. Fund raising is an ongoing challenge.

4. Volunteers.

Kairos' mission statement best expresses its ministry:

"The mission of Kairos ministries is to bring Christ's love and forgiveness to all incarcerated individuals, their families, and those who work with them, and to assist in the transition of becoming productive citizens."

Contact Information:

Kairos of Maine
Clint Daggett
137 Hooper Road
Shapleigh, ME 04076
Web site: *www.kairosofmaine.org*
         www.kairosprisonministry.org

Kairos Outside
Phyllis Curtis
42 Provencher Driver
Limerick, ME 04048

Maine Council of Churches

Portland

Maine Council of Churches (MCC) has a prophetic vision of a culture of peace built through its commitment to environmental, economic, and criminal justice. The interfaith organization has a membership of eight denominations that encompass roughly six hundred churches, a majority of which are Christian. With roots that date back to 1938, MCC has evolved into an influential source of advocacy and education on social issues that are of concern to Maine's congregations and communities. It encourages social action by recruiting congregations through grass roots programs; by tracking, monitoring, and addressing state and federal legislation; and by working within a coalition of dozens of organizations.

The vision for a culture of peace is grounded in shalom, the Biblical principle of right relationship, harmony, and peace. The three-pronged approach to shalom focuses on building sustainable communities through environmental stewardship, caring for the economically disadvantaged, and approaching conflict with the process of restorative justice, which restores right relationships with meaningful accountability and reconciliation. Three programs fulfill these goals: the Environmental Justice Program, the Economic Justice Program, and the Restorative Justice Program.

The mission of the Environmental Justice Program is to awaken faith communities to their connection with creation and to build bridges between congregations, the public, environmental organizations, businesses, and state governments, thereby forming a coalition that unites in one voice to address global warming, clean energy, sustainable agriculture, and pollution. To that end, it has developed a number of successful initiatives.

One of the Environmental Justice Program's most remarkable initiatives is the co-founding of Maine Interfaith Power and Light

Inc., a nonprofit organization that provides green electricity to Maine businesses and individuals. In an incredible achievement, the Environmental Justice Program not only brought clean electricity to the state, but it also created a market for it. As of 2005, Maine Interfaith Power and Light had three thousand accounts.

The Environmental Justice Program and Maine Interfaith Power and Light joined forces to create the EarthCare Team Initiative, which brings practical information to congregations. EarthCare teams consist of one to eight members and are formed within congregations, by combining congregations, or across denominations. The teams work to help congregations change their daily habits that have negative effects on the environment. As part of the program, free energy audits that include a plan of action are offered to houses of worship. Through activities, projects, workshops, and celebrations, EarthCare teams ask participants to examine their religious values in connection to creation and then give them practical suggestions on how to live out these values by reducing waste and improving energy efficiency.

While the EarthCare teams work at the grassroots level, the Environmental Justice Program reaches out to businesses and government agencies to promote clean and renewable energy. The State of Maine, which has taken a leadership role in energy efficiency, represents a quarter of the Maine Interfaith Power and Light accounts for its buildings that have been retrofitted for energy efficiency.

Environmental Justice Program initiatives often dovetail with state programs. When the Environmental Protection Agency asked states to develop a plan to reduce greenhouse gases, Maine became the first state to sign into law specific goals based on the Maine Climate Control Action Plan that was developed at the Environmental Protection Agency's direction. Doing their part, the Environmental Justice Program sponsored the Maine Interfaith Climate Change and Energy Initiative to rally Maine's religious leaders to organize study groups around the devastating effects of global warming. Congregations are asked to act individually and collectively to reduce energy usage and to encourage their congressional representatives to promote laws that will lessen global warming.

Many of the Environmental Justice Program's projects are not designed for years of longevity but to raise awareness for a time; as a given project's effectiveness wanes, it is retired, and a new initiative is found to capture people's attention. Along with the Sierra Club and the American Lung Association, it implemented the "No Idling Clean Air Campaign," which places "No Idling" signs at schools and in select parking lots. Leaflets are left on windshields to educate drivers about the negative impact idling has on their cars and the air, and "I Don't

Idle" windshield decals are given to the newly converted. The consumption and production of food is essential to environmental issues. In the "Soul Food Project," presentations on the political, social, economic, and environmental impact of industrial agriculture follow potluck dinners made from local ingredients. Another campaign asks people to pledge to spend $10 a week on locally produced food. An example of a short-term issue is the tireless work done to get electric cars legalized on Maine roads with speed limits of 35 mph or lower. Once the law was passed, the Environmental Justice Program was free to focus its efforts in another direction.

Developed in 2002, the Economic Justice Program is the youngest of MCC's three-pronged approach to a culture of peace. The Economic Justice Program stays abreast with national and state laws directly affecting the poor, ill, and disabled. It works in concert with other social advocacy groups by testifying at the statehouse and contacting policy makers, and it designs initiatives to address concerns as they arise.

The Economic Justice Program spearheaded the General Assistance Project after hearing reports from several congregations that general assistance was not being dispersed fairly to people in need. (General assistance is welfare programs governed by the state and run by the municipalities.) The Economic Justice Program found that in some towns the employees administering aid were not adequately trained as to the availability of funds. Together with religious communities it evaluated various general assistance programs while also supporting administrators and accompanying recipients through the process.

To build public awareness of homelessness, the Economic Justice Program organized, co-sponsored, and presented "Hear Our Stories, Know Our Names," a drama based on the experiences of the homeless. It was written and acted by people who were homeless at least once in their lives. The drama presents the challenges of poverty, using poetry, story telling, and vignettes and is performed at congregations to remind them of their religious obligation to the poor and downtrodden.

Restorative Justice is the oldest of MCC's three programs, and its Restorative Justice Center in Hallowell is the first in the country founded by a council of churches and not housed by a university. The center works with national and state organizations to promote and implement restorative justice models for criminal offenses. By introducing various agencies, schools, prisons, and policy makers to the concepts of restorative justice, it hopes to change the cultural bias toward punitive "eye for an eye" retribution to one of shalom and mercy for all parties impacted by crime. Restorative justice offers an alternative framework that is a true crime deterrent as it recognizes justice for the victim by holding the offender accountable in a meaningful way.

In this model, the victim and offender meet face to face along with family, community members, and facilitators. The victim explains his or her experience and feelings. The community supports the victim, holds the offender responsible, and explores contributing factors that are the community's responsibility. The offender must be an active participant in making restitution to the victim. When a Cape Elizabeth church was horrendously vandalized, the church chose the restorative justice process to deal with the crime. The vandals, their families, the church pastor, some congregation members, and facilitators met in a circle to discuss the impact the violence had upon the church community and an appropriate payment for the vandalism. It was agreed that the offenders would work at the church and during church suppers. Because of the congregation's acceptance of their sincere efforts towards reparations, the offenders eventually became members of the church—something that likely would not have occurred if traditional punitive action had been taken.

Maine Council of Churches is living its religious values and recruiting others to join it as it strives for social justice. It is a credible and influential force in Maine that is shaping the state for the better.

Contact Information:

Maine Council of Churches
19 Pleasant Avenue
Portland, Maine 04103
Telephone: 207-772-1918
Web site: *www.mainecouncilofchurches.org*
E-mail: info@mainecouncilofchurches.org

Environmental Justice Program
Director Anne Burt
E-mail: adburt@gwi.net
Economic Justice Program
Director Dolores Vail
E-mail: dvail@mainecouncilofchurches.org

Restorative Justice Center of Maine
40 Water Street
Hallowell, Maine 04037
Telephone: 207-623-0516 or 207-623-0500
E-mail: info@rjcmaine.org
Director Suzanne Rudalevige
E-mail: srudalevige@mainecouncilofchurches.org

Maine Gnosis Center
Gnostic Institute of Anthropology

Portland

The Four Pillars of Gnosis—science, art, philosophy, and religion—are the topics discussed at weekly classes offered by the Maine Gnosis Center, an affiliate of the Gnostic Institute of Anthropology. Founded in 1950 by Master Samael Aun Weor, the Gnostic Institute of Anthropology is a worldwide, nonprofit organization that advances the study and practice of Gnostic teachings. Centers are in North and South America, Europe, Japan, Australia, and Africa, with approximately forty centers in the United States.

Venerable Master Samael Aun Weor (1917–1977) was an anthropologist and physician born in Colombia, South America. He is considered to be a bodhisattva, meaning an enlightened master whose role is to assist humanity with timely and relevant wisdom. Master Samael wrote nearly seventy books, lectured widely, and spoke at countless seminars on gnosis and the esoteric path. After his death, and in accordance with his will, his wife became President-Director of the Gnostic Institute. For more than twenty years, Venerable Mistress Litelantes guided the expansion of the organization throughout the world. Before her death in 1998, she chose her son Osiris Gomez Garro to carry on the mission of Master Samael.

Gnosis is derived from the Greek word for knowledge and is variously defined as "intuitive knowledge," "knowledge of spiritual truth," or "deep wisdom." Gnosticism is characterized by the belief that knowledge and direct mystical experience is the path to salvation. Interest in and understanding of ancient Gnostics increased dramatically after the 1945 discovery of the *Nag Hammadi Library*, a collection of fourth-century manuscripts. The collection allowed many scholars, who tended to see Gnosticism as having obscure pagan beginnings and dying out by the fifth century, to determine that it shares commonalities with major religions found throughout the ages.

Through years of investigative study and intense mystical meditation, Master Samael synthesized the Gnostic wisdom and esoteric mysteries of the world's mystical traditions into teachings referred to as the Universal Doctrine of Gnosis. The Gnostic Institute explains the Doctrine as follows:

> Gnosis is a Greek word that means "esoteric wisdom." It is wisdom that is apprehended by direct inner experience. Gnosis is the perennial philosophy that illuminated Sakyamuni Buddha, Hermes, Jesus the Christ, Pythagoras, Moses, Socrates, Plato, Mohammed, Orpheus, Quetzalcoatl, Krishna, etc. While Gnosis has been expressed in many different forms in many cultures and civilizations, by means of different symbols and structures, nevertheless, beyond this illusionary veil of differences exists the *Golden Thread* that unites them all, which is Gnosis—the pure and universal expression of Love and Wisdom. Gnosis is the path of self-realization through direct inner experience. With the awakening of our consciousness and the realization of all the possibilities that lie dormant within man, we can achieve a direct experience of the *Truth* that exists within us all.

The goal of the Gnostic Institute of Anthropology is to provide, through classes taught in its centers, the spiritual, psychological, and scientific keys for the awakening of consciousness. Self-remembering is stressed throughout Gnosticism as a way to reach an awakened state, which occurs naturally as the individual learns to recognize the tricks of the ego and cultivate the divine light within. This is achieved through meditation, study, dream yoga, and a concentrated effort to "know thyself." Science, religion/mysticism, art, and philosophy are integrated throughout the teachings and are taught without separation, as each on its own is incomplete. Classes entail PowerPoint presentations using timeless artwork that reinforces the topics, often through symbols. Science is woven throughout the lectures, as are the philosophies of various religions and cultures. Most classes begin or end with a meditation that includes relaxation, breathing, mantras, and concentration.

An important key to gnosis is relentless self-observation in order to eliminate and weaken the countless "I's" that make up the ego. One exercise is to observe how internal states are matched with external events. For example, an individual's feelings of jealousy at a friend's wedding have nothing to do with the actual event and everything to do with his recent divorce. The displaced emotion creates inappropriate negativity that prevents him from enjoying the wedding. Self-remembering and self-observation are put into practice by dividing one's attention into three parts using the S.O.L. Key: subject, object, and location. The 'subject' requires moment to moment self-remembering; the 'object' asks that the circumstance be observed without emotional identification; and the 'location' is analyzed in detail for insights. The exercise's goal is to catch the ego in action and to recognize how it determines emotional and intellectual reactions to events.

Learning is divided into levels, entailing approximately fifteen classes that build on previous knowledge. Level A classes are preceded by four public lectures designed to demystify Gnosticism and introduce some of its basic tenets. Examples of Level A classes are "The Ego, the Essence, and the Personality," "Internal States and External Events," "Introduction to the Science of Meditation," "Introduction to the Science of Mantrams," "Interior Chatter," and "The Wheel of Samsara."

Levels B and C follow a less structured time frame, enabling students to move at their own pace. Examples of Level B classes are "Dream Yoga," "Occult Anatomy and Physiology," "Kabbalah," and "Gnostic Psychology." Level C classes include "Alchemy and the Perfect Matrimony," "The Science of Tarot," and "Gnostic Psychology."

Samuel and Sophie Rodriguez are the directors and certified instructors at the Maine Gnosis Center. Instructors must exhibit a true and sincere yearning to disseminate the teachings of Universal Gnosis and complete an eleven-week training course. They teach on a voluntary basis, and no fee is charged for classes, though donations are gratefully accepted.

The Rodriguez's have created a décor at the center that is a warm and serene invitation to both study and meditation. They are extremely knowledgeable about all aspects of Gnosis, and their enthusiasm is contagious. The center sells Master Samael's books, Gnostic Calendars, Synthesis magazine (the institute's quarterly publication), and tools to enhance meditation such as candles and high quality incense. Through the Maine Gnosis Center, students keep informed of the activities offered through the parent organization, which includes national conventions, congresses, workshops, seminars, and excursions to cultural events and places of anthropological interest.

The teachings of Master Samael Aun Weor weave together ancient beliefs and mystical practices from the world's religious traditions into a fascinating study for contemporary students. The Maine Gnosis Center provides an environment that enhances the teachings through the sincerity and "gnosis" of the Rodriguezes.

Contact Information:

Samuel and Sophie Rodriguez
Telephone: (207) 828-1949
E-mail: gnosisme@maine.rr.com

Gnostic Institute of Anthropology
Web site: *www.gnosisny.org*

Spiral Arts
Gnostic Institute of Anthropology

Portland

Spiral Arts is a blessing to Portland and anywhere else in Maine that it sets its sights. Evidence in found in the ever-increasing number of people and agencies who benefit from collaboration with this creative and idealistic organization. Spiral Arts explores creativity and spirituality in a fashion that brings people of all ages, incomes, faiths, ethnicities, races, and backgrounds together through art projects, festivals, classes, and retreats. The spiral is an ancient symbol for life's journey, and in this case an acronym for spirituality, art, and learning. Its vision follows:

"Spiral Arts affirms: that art is a doorway to the soul; that we all embody the divine creative spirit; that we are all companions on the journey of creativity. Through creating art together in community, Spiral Arts celebrates the diversity of spiritual and cultural traditions of the people of our neighborhood, our city, and beyond."

The founder and executive director, Priscilla Dreyman, had the seeds of Spiral Arts percolating within her since she was a ministry student at Union Theological Seminary in New York City. In 1970, while doing fieldwork in a Brooklyn neighborhood, Dreyman dreamed of establishing a neighborhood ministry involving creative expression. The goal proved to be elusive, and she now recognizes that not all of the pieces were then in place. After school, she became an ordained United Methodist minister, worked as a hospital chaplain, and later served three churches in Down East Maine simultaneously.

As the years passed, Dreyman became aware of a small voice from within—the third-grade child who wanted to grow up to be an artist. In 1985, she planned to attend art school for one year, expecting it to be a creative and monastic experience. Her bucolic image of art school was torn apart as she found that accessing her creativity was one of the most challenging and rewarding experiences of her life. Four years later, she graduated as a sculptor.

The time had come for Dreyman to revisit her dream of an urban ministry of creative expression aimed at a community not normally found within the walls of a church. As an artist and a minister, she had the credentials and the vision to establish a nonprofit organization that would assist people of all ages and backgrounds in finding the spirituality, empowerment, and gifts that are inherent in creating art.

Spiral Arts came into being in 1992, when a group of co-visionaries brainstormed around Dreyman's kitchen table. The United Methodist Church supplied seed money, and the following year the National Division of the General Board of Global Ministries awarded a large grant.

Spiral Arts programs are acts of collaboration with participating parties. Ideas are developed through discussion, and goals are set through consensus. No single art method is given preference. Workshops can involve anywhere from ten to eighty people depending on the activity. Spiral Arts provides the materials, opportunities, and guidance with the goal of allowing participants to be transformed by the experience of making art within community. For many people, creating art is a risk they never knew they could take, and the reward of seeing themselves in a new light is a delightful surprise. It is impossible to narrowly define program participants. One of its missions is to make art available in diverse workshops that allow for unity, and with that promise in mind, it reaches out to those who are disenfranchised, poor, isolated, ill, or lonely. Spiral Arts also works with professionals for community building, which makes for projects that are incredibly varied.

In 2003, the Augusta Mental Health Institute was preparing to move to the Riverview Psychiatric Institute, a new facility next door. Spiral Arts was contracted to develop a plan that would build community between staff and patients, and ease the transition to the new building. It was collaboratively decided that painted quilt squares would be used to create quilts for wall hangings in the new facility. Prior to beginning the quilt squares, Spiral Arts's teachers planned four visits with art activities designed to build confidence and excitement. By the third visit, ninety staff and patients were painting squares with confidence and, more importantly, with a sense of unity. The two hundred five squares were sewn into forty-one quilts that currently line the "treatment mall," humanizing the space and reminding everyone of the way art can build community when people abandon their roles.

At the Maine Department of Human Services, the staff brainstormed with Spiral Arts to develop a project that would allow employees to overcome the "silo effect" of working on different floors and not knowing co-workers. The group decided upon quilt squares and named the project, "Art of the State." One hundred fifty employees painted squares depicting their work or interests, with many showing their love and concern for children and families. Several staff members volunteered to spend countless hours sewing the squares into thirty-five quilts that now adorn the building's walls.

In a particularly heartwarming project, Spiral Arts was commissioned to fill a fourteen- by five-foot wall in the Barbara Bush Children's Hospital, in Portland. Over a three-month period, twelve artists visited the hospital with unfired tiles and guided young patients in expressing themselves. While the children were compiling two hundred tiles, the enthusiasm became contagious, and doctors, nurses, staff members, and parents expressed their desire to participate. The result was five hundred tiles and three murals. These walls of healing are not only beautiful but act as a memorial to those children who created tiles and have since passed away.

As can be witnessed through Spiral Arts projects, creating sacred space is an integral part of their work. Dreyman defines sacred space as surroundings that are beautiful, stimulating, thought provoking, and at times, challenging. The best places have a magical quality and act to unify people. Her favorite example is the Village of Arts and Humanity Sculpture Park in Philadelphia. The park replaced an ugly abandoned lot in the inner city of North Philadelphia with mosaic and mirror sculptures, benches, and murals. All of the artwork was completed in intergenerational neighborhood workshops. The Village of Arts and Humanity has expanded to an internationally recognized organization offering community-based art education and neighborhood development.

Dreyman was so inspired by its work that she pursued a grant to allow Spiral Arts, People's Regional Opportunity Program, and eight children and adults from the Parkside neighborhood in Portland to travel to the Village of Arts and Humanity where they learned to make the mosaics. Parkside is one of Maine's highest risk neighborhoods and is benefiting from the lessons learned in North Philadelphia. The Parkside project is titled "Mosaics for Hope," and as of 2004, neighborhood residents and all who chose to participate are designing a three hundred fifty foot mural.

Not all Spiral Arts projects are as involved. Occasionally it proclaims an art day or festival. Its home base, the Immanuel Baptist Church on High Street in Portland, is turned into a wonderland of art studios where from 10:00 a.m. to 5:00 p.m. the public is welcome to make cards, origami, prints, menorahs, Navaho spindles, and more. As always, the intent is to bring together people of all ages, incomes, and backgrounds.

Often Spiral Arts works with churches by organizing activities with the congregation that pertains to the Sunday service. The Gorham United Methodist Church explored the theme of mystery. Church members of all ages discussed what the theme meant to them and then broke into activity groups that worked with collage, song, prayer, sacred dance, clay, sermon, and music. The Sunday service followed a loose order of worship with the art created the day before playing an active role.

In addition to one-time and ongoing projects, Spiral Arts offers neighborhood classes that meet for six to eight sessions, three times a year. Topics may include song circles, drawing, painting, mask making, carving, urban gardening, art and prayer, journaling, travel writing, clay, and culinary arts. Summer programs generally meet four times and, whenever possible, they meet in Deering Oaks Park to enjoy the fleeting summer weather. Offerings change frequently depending on interest and teacher availability. Though the classes are held in Portland, Dreyman stresses that all people are welcome and invites those from the suburbs to join their urban neighbors. Many classes are open to all ages, some are limited to over age seven or eleven, and free childcare is available for those who need it. Nominal donations are requested but not required. Classes are an important aspect of Spiral Arts, and Dreyman has consistently witnessed the power of making art within community to build lasting connections.

A full one-third of Spiral Arts's work is done with the elderly. Seniors at the Barron Center in Portland enjoy a weekly open studio to explore their creativity. The activities are not craft projects, but are open-ended processes, intended to explore personal expression. The goal is not to conduct art therapy but to deliver the joy of creativity. Each week up to thirty-five participants experiment with clay, writing, painting, story telling, and music. The benefits cross over to the physical as the elderly artists enjoy better sleep, and are more alert and social.

Spiral Arts is certified as a Community School of the Arts by the National Guild of Community Schools of the Arts (NGCSA). The NGCSA offers grants, certification, and intensive training for art directors and managers of non-degree-conferring art schools that are accessible to the public and welcome people from all walks of life. The organization originated in the settlement houses of the late 19th and early 20th century. The settlement houses sought social reform for the diverse urban populations that struggled with the effects of industrialization. They offered lifestyle classes in cooking, homemaking, and art, while organizing clubs, exhibitions, and lectures. For most of the 20th century, the NGCSA focused solely on music education but by the century's end had expanded to include the visual and performing arts as well. Spiral Arts is an active member and in 2004 was chosen for a three-year pilot program in Portland's Kennedy Park, where they have space in the community center for regular art activities.

A multitude of people behind the scenes contributes to Spiral Arts' many successes. Teachers, artists, board members, and volunteers give their time and talents. Maine College of Art provides interns from their "Art and Service" class. Participants in projects assist each other and volunteer for upcoming events. Each year, Spiral Arts serves three hundred people in its classes and more than two thousand through its other programs. It has a mailing list of twenty-four hundred and continues to "spiral" outward as word about the organization's integrity spreads.

The effort put into Spiral Arts achievements should not be underestimated. Working with diverse populations whether they be agencies or individuals takes flexibility, skill, and patience. Organizing events, coordinating staff and volunteers, securing space, finding materials, and maintaining momentum are Herculean tasks. Funding is a constant concern and dependent on donations and grants that do not offer long-term security. Of course, the rewards are also great: an elderly person expresses artistic creativity for the first time in his life; a family forgets their problems during an art class; residents in a mixed-race, low-income neighborhood come together in the spirit of community; a young person is empowered by the budding artist within; and those committed to their roles and labels shed them while engaged in artistic endeavors.

In 1986, Dreyman traveled with a group from the United Methodist Church to Kenya. While in the world's largest shantytown, they visited a huge center that provided humanitarian services. "Harambee" was painted on the side of the building—"Let us all pull together." Harambee is Spiral Arts inspiration and anchor.

Contact Information:

Spiral Arts Inc.
156 High Street
Portland, Maine 04101
Priscilla Dreyman
Telephone: (207) 775-1474
Web site: *www.spiralarts.org*
E-Mail: community@spiralarts.org

The Institute of Noetic Sciences

In 1971, Edgar Mitchell manned Apollo 14, the United States' third manned lunar landing mission. On the return trip, Mitchell experienced a profound epiphany of universal connectedness while viewing Earth from space. He described it in these words: "The presence of divinity became almost palpable, and I knew that life in the universe was not just an accident based on random processes . . . The knowledge came to me directly."

Mitchell's experience compelled him to seek out other scientists who felt the need to explore an expanded view of reality using scientifically rigorous methods. In 1973, Mitchell and a small group of scientists founded the Institute of Noetic Sciences (IONS) with the purpose of investigating aspects of the mind's influence on reality, consciousness, and spirituality in order to increase understanding of human potential. The word "noetic" was chosen because it is from the Greek word "nous" meaning "mind" or "consciousness". Noetic scientists are those who research intuition, spiritual knowing, psychic phenomena, and inner states such as compassion, wisdom, forgiveness, empathy, and altruism.

Using the world's wisdom traditions as a guiding vision, IONS bases research projects, learning programs, and community-building initiatives on three assumptions:

1. Reality is more than merely physical.
2. Everything and everyone are interconnected.
3. We can consciously participate in our own evolution.

Since its founding, IONS has sponsored hundreds of research projects using in-house scientists and an extended faculty. Innovative research includes how mind and matter interact, distance healing, the efficacy of compassionate intention on healing AIDS patients, a com-

210

prehensive bibliography on the physical and psychological effects of meditation, and an extensive bibliography on spontaneous remission. Their website has online tests and games developed by IONS that measure intuition and psychic ability. Current programs are focused on "Extended Human Capacities", "Integral Health and Healing", and "Emerging World Views".

IONS members and the public are kept informed of their research findings through their newsletter, online programs and conversations, educational events, international and regional conferences, retreats, local self-organizing groups, and their publication *Shift: At the Frontiers of Consciousness.*

IONS has more than thirty thousand members that hail from all fifty states and forty-seven countries. There are two hundred fifty local groups led by volunteers. The institute is located in Petaluma, California, where, along with offices and a scientific laboratory, it houses a retreat center, which hosts educational activities and workshops.

Southern Maine's IONS members host monthly meetings that are free of charge and open to the public. Guest speakers often present material or the group leaders conduct workshops that usually focus on expanded consciousness, healing, and spirituality.

For more information:

IONS
101 San Antonio Road
Petaluma, CA 94952
Telephone: (707) 775-3500
Web site: *www.noetic.org*

For Maine programs contact:

Kathy Izzo
E-mail: heartmore@gwi.net

Sacred Architecture: Churches

Cathedral of the Immaculate Conception

Cathedral Church of St. Luke

St. Ann Indian Island Church

Ss. Peter and Paul Basilica

St. Saviour's Church

Cathedral of the Immaculate Conception
Roman Catholic

Portland

The Cathedral of the Immaculate Conception, standing at the corner of Congress Street and Franklin Arterial, was designated a Greater Portland Landmark in 1984 for its historic significance and architectural appeal. It is hard to imagine Portland's skyline without the cathedral's 204-foot-high steeple, which makes it the city's highest structure.

The cathedral was designed by the famed Brooklyn architect Patrick Keely, whose cathedral designs can be found in Boston, Buffalo, Chicago, Cleveland, Hartford, Newark, and Providence. Construction of the cathedral began in 1866, but it had to be restarted after the infamous Great Fire of 1866 burned it and most of the surrounding neighborhood to the ground. Misfortune struck again when on the day of the cathedral's consecration in 1869, the steeple was blown off by a severe storm. Within a month it was replaced and has stayed firmly in place ever since.

The Neo-Gothic architecture features three steeples, interior Gothic arches, and ceilings that are 70 feet high. The nave is 186 feet long and 70 feet wide and seats 900. The cathedral's interior, with its impressive proportions and light-filled nave, is an excellent example of the way Gothic cathedrals use their grand scale to emphasize the soaring glory of God and the insignificance of humans.

There are several exceptionally striking features in the cathedral. The Immaculate Conception stained glass window behind the main altar and above the Sacred Heart Altar is a masterpiece of grace and artistry. It is dated 1902, while the other stained glass windows are mostly from 1909. The rose window above the entrance and the windows lining the nave, depicting Our Lady Mary's Presentation in the Temple through her crowning as the Queen of Heaven, are richly colored and elegant. The Cathedral of the Immaculate Conception is one of the few churches in the world where all of its windows are from the highly respected Royal Bavarian Glass Company in Munich, Germany.

The cathedral is in beautiful condition and has undergone renovations in 1921, 1969 (after Vatican II called for the altar to face the congregation), and in 2000. Everything in the cathedral seems to glow. The baptismal font was added during the 1921 restoration and was recently moved to the main part of the cathedral for easy viewing. It is 13 feet high and 5 feet in diameter. It is modeled after a baptismal font in the Cathedral of Pietrasanta in Italy but modified to complement the Neo-Gothic architecture of the cathedral. The front panel of the font is a bronze bas-relief door depicting Jesus being baptized by John the Baptist. During baptisms, water flows from under the bronze door into the marble receptacle below. There are four niches that circle the font, each holding a statue of one of the prophets from the Old Testament who foretold the Messiah's coming: Jeremiah, Ezekiel, Daniel, and Zechariah.

Many other beautiful features enrich the interior. The fourteen stations of the cross, which depict the passion of Christ, are each composed of six thousand quarter-inch Venetian glass tiles. The Henry Erban organ from 1869 has 3,336 pipes, all of which are still in use. During the 2000 restoration, a French Gothic paschal candle stand was recovered from the basement. There are silver urns, glass cabinets, marble chip floor designs, and beautiful altars and niches.

The crypt beneath the main Cathedral was renovated and is open for tours. The crypt has hosted members of the Dead Theologians Society, an organization where college- and high-school-aged young people learn about the lives of saints in the recesses of crypts while chant music is played, incense is burned, and candles complete the atmosphere.

The cathedral hosts a very informative website that includes photographs of all of the windows, the stations of the cross, the baptismal font, and other works of art. There is information on the history of stained glass, how it is made, and a glossary of religious symbols. Bible passages, meditations, and prayers complement the information.

A cathedral is always a grand church, but more important, it is the seat of the bishop. The Cathedral of the Immaculate Conception is the mother church of the Diocese of Portland, and there can only be one cathedral per diocese. With this special designation comes the responsibility of taking a leadership position in timely issues, education, and liturgy. For well over one hundred years, the Cathedral of the Immaculate Conception has played an important role in urban ministry as well as welcomed immigrants and refugees from around the world. Presently, their membership is comprised of twenty-one nationalities from Africa, Asia, Latin America, and Europe, with sixteen languages spoken. They offer extensive religious education, music ministry, and opportunities for involvement. The Cathedral of the Immaculate Conception is a spiritual, as well as a physical, landmark.

Contact Information:

The Cathedral of the Immaculate Conception
307 Congress Street
Portland, Maine 04101
Telephone: (207) 773-7746
Web site: *www.portlandcathedral.org*
E-mail: rectory@portlandcathedral.org

The Baptismal font at the Cathedral of the Immaculate Conception is over thirteen feet high and is five feet in diameter.

The Cathedral Church
of St. Luke
Episcopalian

Portland

    For people who are accustomed to rural or suburban Episcopalian services, a visit to St. Luke's Cathedral is a big city experience. The Neo-Gothic interior is rich, warm, and impressively appointed. Gothic arches, brilliant stained glass windows, a dramatic altar, and huge nave lend it a sense of grandeur. The large congregation enables the cathedral to maintain pageantry, splendid music, and formal traditions during the high holidays.

    St. Luke's Cathedral is the first Episcopalian church in the United States built specifically to be a cathedral. The designation of cathedral is used by Episcopalians and Catholics to specify the seat of the diocesan bishop. St Luke's is the mother church of the Diocese of Maine, and the 'seat of the bishop' can literally be found to the left of the high altar.

    Construction of the cathedral began after the Great Fire of 1866 destroyed one of the two parish churches in Portland. Services were held Christmas Day in 1868, but the cathedral was not consecrated until nine years later when the debt was paid in full. The exterior is English Neo-Gothic style and built from stone quarried in Cape Elizabeth. The bell tower from the original design was not added until 1958, at which time it was specifically angled so that the pitches of the bells would harmonize with the area churches. Through the years, St. Luke's has regularly added features and embellishments: the rose window was added in 1900, the Emmanuel Chapel in 1905, the reredos (decorative panel behind the altar) in 1925, the Spinner organ in 1928, and the Arts-and-Crafts-style lanterns in 2000.

216

The front of the church presents a resplendent scene. The rose window, which measures seventeen feet in diameter, crowns the apse with a depiction of the ascension of Christ. The circular window is designed with twelve rosettes picturing the apostles encircling Christ. The reredos below the window portrays the incarnation of Christ on intricately carved oak. A nearly life-sized Holy Mother with the infant Jesus dominates the central part of the design. On either side is the Crucifixion and Resurrection of Christ. The elaborate piece includes four scenes leading up to the birth of Jesus, plus St. Luke, St. John, four bishops of Maine, twelve saints, and Christian scholars. Small niches hold forty-eight angels singing or with musical instruments.

The Emmanuel Chapel is a darkened Neo-Gothic octagon-shaped room with a mysterious personality. The brick walls are adorned with elegant gilded mahogany carvings. Mosaic inlay decorates the marble altar, which is trimmed with mahogany and gold inlay. The altarpiece is a striking painting by John LaFarge called *American*

St. Lukes!!

Madonna. Lafarge (1835–1910) was a versatile painter, illustrator, decorator, and author. He is noted for his stained glass windows, murals, and eclectic choice of subject matter. The untraditional painting shows Jesus as a young child stepping away from the protective arms of his mother, signifying her releasing him for humanity. The model used for the painting was Jeanie Frost, sister of the poet Robert Frost.

St. Luke's Cathedral has gained a considerable reputation in Portland for exceptional musical events presented by its choirs and by noted musicians in the Greater Portland community and beyond. In 2003, a $1.2 million renovation was completed that included the restoration of the Skinner organ, installation of a new sound system, and other features that improved the acoustics.

Evensong, an evening prayer service featuring music, is scheduled weekly. Once a month, Taize is held in the Emmanuel Chapel, which is a wonderfully intimate space for the traditional service of prayer, chant, and meditation. Musical events of the past have included *Sacred Jazz, Early English and American Carols,* and *Bell' Italia.*

The Cathedral Church of St. Luke is noteworthy due to its beautiful design, glorious music, and exceptional liturgy. It is also an important part of Portland's community through its service to the poor and fellowship opportunities.

Contact Information:

St. Luke's Cathedral
143 State Street
Portland, Maine 04101
Telephone: (207) 772-5434
Web site: *www.cathedralofstluke.org*
E-Mail: stlukes@gwi.net

St. Ann
Indian Island Church
Roman Catholic

Indian Island

Located on the Penobscot Nation's reservation, St. Ann Indian Island Church is the oldest continuous site of Catholic worship in New England, and the present church building is the third oldest church in Maine. The first church was constructed in 1688 and presided over by Father Louis Thury. It is believed that the Baron de St. Castine financed the construction. Baron Castine married a Penobscot chief's daughter and played a significant role in the 18th-century French and Indian Wars.

In 1723, the British burned the Indian Island village and church. The following year, they raided Norridgewock, massacring the inhabitants and scalping Father Sebastian Rasle. Father Rasle was living in the Penobscot village and attempting to create a boundary over which the British could not pass. The British blamed him for inciting the Penobscot Nation and accused him of being involved in several raids in southern Maine. (Maine was part of Massachusetts until 1820.) In American history Rasle is demonized, but to the Penobscot people he is remembered in a positive light and for an Abenaki-French language dictionary he wrote that is now housed at Harvard University. Father Thury and Father Rasle were associated, so after the battle, surviving Native Americans joined the tribe at Indian Island and, to this day, there are people who can trace their ancestors back to Norridgewock. In an act of loyalty and remembrance, the Penobscot Nicolar, who had one arm, carried the iron cross from the Norridgewock church to Indian Island. The 18th-century cross was attached to the exterior of the present church, but due to its historic significance is now housed in the Bishop's office.

Shortly thereafter, French Catholic priests were banned from the territory, making only sporadic visits from Canada to the island until 1798, when the second church was built at the request of Penobscot representatives who had visited the Bishop. This church was poorly built and quickly fell into disrepair. The third (and present) church was built in 1828–1830, but did not have a priest in residence until 1928.

Historically, Native Americans felt more kinship with the French Catholics than with the British Protestants. The Protestants viewed the native people as uncivilized and wanted to convert them not only to Protestantism but also to the English way of life. The French sent priests to live among the tribal villages. Catholicism and traditional Penobscot spirituality had similarities: a reverence for the ancestors/saints, water as a sacred element, ritualized ceremonies, and the use of icons.

From the outside, St. Ann's is a pretty but undistinguished church with only one hint at its heritage among the Penobscot Nation: the crosses that adorn the steeples are pounded wrought iron, and each tip is shaped into an arrowhead. Crosses have a dual meaning for Native-Catholics because of their observance of the four directions in their spiritual beliefs.

Tribal art and stained glass windows decorate the interior and speak to the blending of two spiritual traditions. The centerpiece of the church is the magnificent painting behind the altar. The piece depicts the crucifixion with Mary Magdalene at Christ's feet and both of them having Native American features. It was painted at the close of the 18th century by a reclusive Penobscot named Joseph Paul Orson, who was nearly blind at the time and had never had art lessons. There were no art supplies available, so Orson pieced together two altar cloths for canvas, used berries for paint, and an animal tail for a brush. Despite his lack of training, poor eyesight, and limited supplies, Orson created a powerful work with impressive form, proportion, and color.

At some point in its history, the painting was framed and varnished. In time, the varnish turned black and the painting was rolled up and put in a storage closet. During a major cleanup in the 1980s, the painting was nearly thrown away. Fortunately, it was saved and restored by the University of Maine.

The walls and arches of the church are stenciled with lovely, graceful tribal symbols. The symbolic meanings of the designs have been largely lost, though it is known that many speak of the balance of energy created by giving and receiving. The vinelike curves and flower imagery are indicative of the art of the northeast woodland Native Americans. It expresses an environment that is flowing, as opposed to the straight lines and angles of southwestern native art.

The pulpit is supported by legs carved with Native American symbols: a chalice, hand, and eagle feather, representing the Father, Son, and Holy Spirit respectively. The glass base protects an expertly carved eagle, symbolic of the spirit to the Penobscot people and of St. John to the Catholics.

The eight stained glass windows are memorials to those who served St. Ann and to important figures in Maine's Catholic history. One window is dedicated to Father Rasle and another to Mother Xavier Ward, who sent the Sisters of Mercy to Indian Island in 1878. The most famous man memorialized is Bishop James Augustine Healy, an African-American and Irish man who was consecrated in 1875 and made many trips to Indian Island.

The oldest Catholic cemetery in northern New England was consecrated in 1688 and is a short walk from St. Ann. There are a few old markers, but most were probably wooden crosses that have long since deteriorated. Non-Catholic Native Americans are buried inside a fenced area, and sightseers are asked to remain outside of the fenced area.

Over three hundred years of Penobscot Nation and Catholic history blend at St. Ann. The church has lost membership through the years, even though many Penobscots practice elements of both Catholicism and their traditional religion. There are still occasional Sundays when there is standing room only, and the church is filled with people from tour busses who are saying their prayers before they head to high stakes bingo down the road.

Contact Information:

St. Ann Catholic Church
P.O. Box 560
Indian Island
Old Town, ME 04468
Telephone: (207) 827-2172

At St. Ann's Church, Catholic and Wabanaki spirituality are blended. The eagle is sacred to the Wabanaki people.

Saints Peter and Paul Basilica
Roman Catholic

Lewiston

The towers of the Ss. Peter and Paul Basilica rise 163 feet into the Lewiston skyline. Inside, it is 286 feet long, 79 feet wide, and 64 feet high at the transept. The Basilica, built by French-Canadian immigrants, is the largest church in Maine and the second largest Catholic church in New England.

In 2004, the Vatican honored Ss. Peter and Paul as a Minor Basilica. There are six Major Basilicas, all of which are in Rome, and fifty-four Minor Basilicas in the United States. It is a high honor awarded to churches and entails ceremonial privileges and responsibilities. A church receives the designation based in part on its physical attributes. It must have a cross-shaped design, with a tall main nave that has two or more side aisles, and a high transept. (The transept crosses the nave at right angles.) Other determining factors are its historical significance, the number of baptisms and weddings performed, the quality of the liturgy, educational initiatives, and service to the needy.

From the 1850s until the 1890s, New England's industrial centers experienced a huge influx of French-Canadians, who arrived to work in the factories and mills. In the mid-1860s, hundreds arrived daily at Lewiston's train station. The new immigrants were mostly poor farmers from Quebec who felt isolated in their new communities by their Roman Catholic religion and their French language. Maine was then largely Protestant, and though Lewiston had Catholic masses for the Irish who arrived in the 1840s, few of the French attended the English-speaking-only churches.

St. Peter's Church, the original Ss. Peter and Paul, was founded in 1870 as the first parish in Maine established for French-speaking Canadians. The congregation's numbers grew quickly and by 1894, masses were often held to standing room only crowds. By the turn of the century, there were over ten thousand parishioners and dire need for a larger church.

In 1904, the plans for a Neo-Gothic replacement were drawn. A wooden shed that held twelve hundred people was built for masses until the lower part of the new church was completed. The old church was dismantled in 1905, and on December 25, 1906, Midnight Mass was held in the lower church. Little did the parish suspect that they would wait until 1938 for the rest of the church to be finished.

The original estimate for the cost of the church was $250,000, but the actual cost was approximately $625,000, not including the $40,000 stained glass windows that were added in 1948. It is a testament to the faith and fortitude of the parish that they raised the money for such a grand edifice by donations from their meager wages and fundraisers. Collecting money for the construction went on during the worst years of the Depression, at a time when churches were the only social safety nets.

The Basilica is glorious. Throughout the 1990s, more than two million dollars was spent on renovations, and it shows. The Norman-Gothic exterior, constructed with granite from Jay, Maine, is exquisitely carved. The entrance is marked by grand oak doors with carved panels. The granite blocks used in the interior are buttery hues of cream, sand, and gray. The impressive organ claims the distinction of being the largest Casavant organ in Maine with its 4,500 golden pipes over the main portico and 500 more on either side of the chancel. The altar depicts a mosaic of a pelican with a stain of blood on her chest, feeding her young. It was believed that the stain of

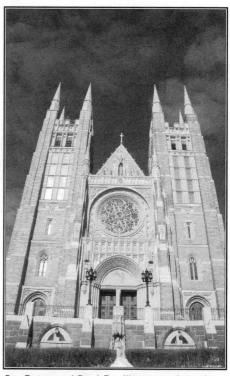

Ss. Peter and Paul Basilica was given the designation of basilica in 2004. It is one of the highest honors given to a church by the Vatican.

223

blood was the pelican feeding her young the flesh and blood of her heart, and it became a symbol for Christ offering his body and blood in the Eucharist.

The stained glass windows are modeled after the Cathedral of Chartes in France and are visually striking. The ten windows, which look like jeweled mosaics, depict the holy mysteries of the rosary. The rose window above the narthex at the church's entrance is also based on the French Gothic architecture of the 13th century, where the finest examples of rose windows are found. Rose windows are circular with stained glass petal-shaped designs radiating from a small center circle.

The Dominican friars of Lille, France, arrived at St. Peter's in 1881 and stayed for 105 years. The friars have departed, but their influence is found throughout the basilica. On the floor at the entrance is their black and white crest, and the former Dominican chapel is now open to parishioners. The Dominican crest bearing the motto "To Praise, To Bless, and To Preach" is above the choir.

The church's membership peaked in 1950 with approximately 15,000 parishioners and has since declined to 1,200. Possible reasons are stagnant economic growth in Lewiston, the assimilation of the French-Canadians, and an aging congregation with many housebound members. Throughout Maine, Catholic churches are consolidating, but Ss. Peter and Paul Basilica has a guaranteed future and will play an important role for Maine's Roman Catholics.

Contact Information:

Ss. Peter and Paul Basilica
27 Bartlett Street
Lewiston, Maine 04240
Telephone: (207) 777-1200

The granite used to build the Basilica was quarried in Jay, Maine.

Saint Savior's Church
Episcopal

Bar Harbor

Saint Savior's Church is Bar Harbor's most visited church and is the oldest, largest, and tallest public building on Mount Desert Island. Its fame is attributed not to its size, but to its forty-two stained glass windows dating from 1886 to 1992. Ten of the windows were designed by the studios of Louis Comfort Tiffany, and the thirty-two others are by various American and English artists.

The Tiffany windows demonstrate the realism for which he was known. His experimental techniques were aimed at reproducing the glass used in medieval windows, and he developed "fabrille" or "art" glass to create his signature iridescent effect. A memorial window to a man lost with his friend in a canoeing accident is titled, "The Sea Shall Give Up Its Dead." Other windows by Tiffany include, "The Savior," "Guiding Angel," "Angel of Praise," "The Last Supper," and "Flight from Egypt."

The name Saint Savior is taken from the French Jesuit 17th-century colony on Somes Sound, Saint Sauveur. At the time of the church's founding in the 1870s, romanticized stories about the Jesuit colony were circulating in the area. People were also feeling enthusiastic about the emerging restoration of the French Republic.

Visitors will find numerous historic memorial plaques lining the walls. The brass plaque in the center aisle marks the burial place of "Governeur Morris Ogden," one of the founding members of Saint Savior's. It was a common practice in Europe for those with prestige to be buried under the church, with the grave's proximity to the altar traditionally determined by the importance of the deceased.

The Old Town Cemetery lays at the entrance to Saint Savior's. The small graveyard is dominated by a large memorial dedicated to Bar Harbor's fallen Civil War soldiers. The gravestones are predominately from the 19th century with several impressive sea captain memorials and many touching epitaphs.

The church was completed in 1878 with a seating capacity of 325. It was quickly outgrown as Bar Harbor became the preferred vacation destination of the wealthy, swelling the summer congregation to over one thousand. Prominent families from Boston, New York, and Philadelphia funded the expansion of the church in 1885–86. In the following years, improvements continued with the ninety foot bell tower, Italian marble high altar, the first stained glass windows, and the Chapel of the Virgin Mary. The church and the rectory are listed in the National Register of Historic Places.

In 1947, Mount Desert Island suffered a disastrous fire that burnt nearly one third of the island's eastern side. The fire skirted Bar Harbor's business district but destroyed sixty-seven seasonal estates and five large hotels. One hundred seventy local families were left homeless, with forty-two from Saint Savior's. The fire changed forever the summer culture of Bar Harbor where the wealthy had summered for fifty years. Likewise, Saint Savior's dealt with the challenges brought on by the loss of a large summer congregation.

Today, Saint Savior's is a thriving and active congregation especially known for their wonderful choir. Their newest challenge is to raise funds to repair memorial windows that are in dire need. The Window Restoration and Preservation Fund has been established and donations are gratefully appreciated.

Ten of St. Saviour's forty-two stained glass windows are original Tiffany's.

Contact Information:

Saint Savior's Episcopal Church
41 Mount Desert Street
Bar Harbor, ME 04609
Telephone: (207) 288-4215
Web site: *www.ellsworthme.org/ssaviour/*
E-mail: stsaviour@adelphia.net

Saint Savior's offers free guided tours in July and August.

Donations made to the Window Restoration and Preservation Fund
are tax deductible.

Inspirational Teachers:
Recommended Reading

The following is a list of book recommendations made by the people interviewed for this book.

Inspired Alternatives: Religions

Bahá'í
God Speaks Again: An Introduction to the Bahá'í Faith
by Kenneth Bowers

The Bahá'í Faith: The Emerging Global Religion
by William Hatcher and J. Douglas Martin

Bahá'u'lláh and the New Era: An Introduction to the Bahá'í Faith
by J. E. Esslemont

The Secret of Divine Civilization
Some Answered Questions
by 'Abdu'l-Bahá

Paganism
Building a Magickal Relationship: The Five Points of Love
by Cynthia Jane Collins and Jane Raeburn (Maine Authors)

Celtic Wisdom: Anicient Wisdom for the 21st Century
by Jane Raeburn

The Recovery Spiral: A Pagan Path to Healing
by Cynthia Jane Collins

The Spiral Dance: A Rebirth of the Ancient Religions
of the Great Goddess
by Starhawk

Drawing Down the Moon: Witches, Druids, Goddess-Worshippers,
and Other Pagans in America Today
by Margot Adler

Wicca: A Guide for the Solitary Practitioner
by Scott Cunningham

Spiritualism
The Eagle and the Rose: A Remarkable True Story
by Rosemary Altea

Betty Book
The Unobstructed Universe
Across The Unknown
by Stewart Edward White

A Guide for the Development of Mediumship
by Harry Edwards

Swedenborgian Church
Heaven and Hell
by Emanuel Swedenborg,
translated by George Dole (Maine Author)

Divine Love and Wisdom
Awaken from Death
by Emanuel Swedenborg

Wings and Roots: The New Age and Emanuel Swedenborg
in Dialog
by Wilma Wake (Maine Author)

The Country of Spirit: Selected Writings
by Wilson Van Dusen

Unity Church of Greater Portland

The Story of Unity
by James Dillet Freeman

Discover the Power Within You: A Guide to the
Unexplored Depths Within
  by Eric Butterworth

How, Then, Shall We Live?: Four Simple Questions
That Reveal the Beauty and Meaning of Our Lives
  by Wayne Muller

Spirits in Rebellion: The Rise and Development of New Thought
  by Charles Braden

Practicing Mindfulness: East Meets West

Hridaya Hermitage
  Ayurveda: A Life of Balance
    by Maya Tiwari

  Ayurvedic Healing: A Comprehensive Guide
    by David Frawley

  The Hidden Secret of Ayurveda
    by Robert E. Svoboda

Meetingbrook Dogen and Francis Hermitage
  Living Buddha, Living Christ
    by Thich Nhat Hanh

  Contemplative Prayer
    by Thomas Merton
      (Anything by Thomas Merton is recommended.)

Morgan Bay Zendo
  The Empty Mirror: Experiences in a Japanese Zen Monastery
    by Janwillem Van De Wetering

  Loving-Kindness: The Revolutionary Art of Happiness
    by Sharon Salzberg

  Insight Mediation: The Practice of Freedom
    by Joseph Goldstein

  The Heart of The Buddha's Teaching:
    Transforming Suffering and Peace, Joy, and Liberation
      by Thich Nhat Hanh

Shambhala Center

Cutting Through Spiritual Materialism
The Myth of Freedom and the Way of Meditation
 by Chögyam Trungpa

Turning the Mind into an Ally
 by Sakyong Mipham

*Zen Mind, Beginner's Mind: Informal Talks on Zen Meditation
 and Practice*
 by Shunryu Suzuki

Start Where You Are: A Guide to Compassionate Living
 by Pema Chödrön

Sufi Order International
The Call of the Dervish
Awakening: A Sufi experience
 by Pir Vilayat Inayat Khan

Inner Life
 by Hazrat Inayat Khan

*Tying Rocks to Clouds: Meetings and Conversations with
 Wise and Spiritual People*
 by William Elliott

Pursuing Higher Wisdom: Degrees, Certificates, and Programs

Bangor Theological Seminary
Body and Soul: Rethinking Sexuality as Justice-Love
 by Marvin Ellison and Sylvia Thorson-Smith (BTS Faculty)

The First Edition of the New Testament
 by David Trobisch (BTS Faculty)

Celtic Prayers from Iona
 by J. Philip Newell

Making All Things New: An Invitation to the Spiritual Life
 by Henri I. M. Nouwen

Chaplaincy Institute of Maine

Roadsigns: Navigating Your Path to Spiritual Happiness
by Philip Goldberg

Callings: Finding and Following an Authentic Life
by Gregg Levoy

*The Direct Path: Creating a Personal Journey to the
Divine Using the World's Spiritual Traditons*
by Andrew Harvey

The Universe is a Green Dragon: A Cosmic Creation Story
by Brian Swimme

Rudolf Steiner Institute

Rudolf Steiner and Anthroposophy for Beginners
by Lia Tummer

Anthroposophy in Everyday Life
How to Know Higher Worlds: A Modern Path of Initiation
Education of the Child and Early Lectures on Education
Agriculture: An Introductory Reader
by Rudolf Steiner
Available at *www.steinerbooks.org*

Spirit Passages

Modern Shamanic Living: New Explorations of an Ancient Path
by Evelyn C. Rysdyk (Maine Author)

The Way of the Shaman
by Michael Harner

Soul Retrieval: Mending the Fragmented Self
by Sandra Ingerman

The Standing Bear Center for Shamanic Studies

The Spirit of Shamanism
by Roger N. Walsh

The Soul of Shamanism: Western Fantasies, Imaginal Realities
by Daniel Noel

Reflection and Renewal: Retreats and Camps

Greenfire

Soulcraft: Crossing into the Mysteries of Nature and Psyche
by Bill Plotkin

Blue Iris
by Mary Oliver (poetry)

Listening for the Heartbeat of God: A Celtic Spirituality
by J. Philip Newell

Coming to Our Senses: Body and Spirit in the
Hidden History of the West
by Morris Berman

Four Spiritualities: Expressions of Self, Expressions of Spirit:
A Psychology of Contemporary Spiritual Choice
by Peter Tufts Richardson

Living Water Spiritual Center

The Cosmic Dance: An Invitation to Experience Our Oneness
Inviting God In: Scriptural Reflections and
Prayers Throughout the Year
by Joyce Rupp

Bread for the Journey: A Daybook of Wisdom and Faith
The Wounded Healer
by Henri I. M. Nouwen

The Universe Story: From the Primordial Flaring Forth to the
Ecozoic Era: A Celebration of the Unfolding of the Cosmos
by Brian Swimme and Thomas Berry

Coming Back to Life: Practices to Reconnect Our Lives, Our World
by Joanna Macy and Molly Young Brown

Marie Joseph Spiritual Center

The Holy Longing: The Search for a Christian Spirituality
The Shattered Lantern: Rediscovering a Felt Presence of God
by Ronald Rolheiser

Everything Belongs: The Gift of Contemplative Prayer
by Richard Rohr

Sewall House Retreat
Kundalini Yoga: The Flow of Eternal Power
by Shakti Para Khalsa

Kundalini Yoga
by Shakti Kaur Khalsa

*Kundalini Awakening: A Gentle Guide to
Chakra Activation and Spiritual Growth*
by John Selby